New Hope

FOR PEOPLE WITH

Borderline Personality Disorder

Other Books in the NEW HOPE Series

New Hope

FOR PEOPLE WITH

Borderline Personality Disorder

Neil R. Bockian, Ph.D., with Valerie Porr, M.A.,
and Nora Elizabeth Villagran, M.A.

Foreword by Theodore Millon, Ph.D.

THREE RIVERS PRESS
NEW YORK

Published by Three Rivers Press, New York, New York.
Member of the Crown Publishing Group, a division of Random House, Inc.
www.crownpublishing.com

THREE RIVERS PRESS and the Tugboat design are registered trademarks of Random House, Inc.

Originally published by Prima Publishing, Roseville, California, in 2002.

In order to protect their privacy, the names of some individuals cited in this book have been changed.

Warning—Disclaimer

Interior design by Peri Poloni, Knockout Design
Illustrations by Laurie Baker-McNeile

Printed in the United States of America

Library of Congress Cataloging-in-Publication Data
Bockian, Neil R.
   New hope for people with borderline personality disorder : your friendly, authoritative guide to the latest in traditional and complementary solutions / Neil R. Bockian, Nora Elizabeth Villagran, Valerie Porr.
      p.   cm.—(New hope)
   Includes bibliographical references and index.
      1. Borderline personality disorder—Popular works. I. Villagran, Nora Elizabeth. II. Porr, Valerie.
III. Title. IV. New hope series.
RC569.5B67 B63 2001
616.85'852—dc21   2001036979

ISBN 0-7615-2572-6

10 9 8 7 6 5 4

First Edition

To my parents, Fred and Sandra Bockian . . .
for everything you have done and
for everything you are.

Contents

Foreword

FEW THINGS ARE more satisfying to an "old professor" than to see one of his most promising pupils prove that his estimation of the student's high potential has achieved fruition. So it is with this book's author; the "young professor," Dr. Neil Bockian, has undertaken scholarly professional work and highly useful writings such as this superb volume in the NEW HOPE series for people who are seeking an authoritative guide to understanding and resolving one of society's most distressing of disorders, the borderline personality. My favorite piece of advice to brilliant students is that they "do well by doing good," that is, utilize their exceptional skills and knowledge for the benefit of others. And so it is again with Dr. Bockian; he has drawn upon his unusual talents to provide a book intended explicitly to help others deal with their own emotional difficulties or to help those with the disorder in their families.

And what a fine and useful book it is, a highly informed and sensitive portrayal of the borderline disorder, its origins and its understanding, as well as the practical steps that may be undertaken to ameliorate its expression and its consequences.

The conception of books for the intelligent and concerned layman written by professionals is a beautiful idea. We have all heard the complaint by the lay public that they are not privy to the thinking and research of the scientific community, that those who are most affected by emotional disorders are not able to share in the controversies and subtleties of the ailments they themselves must live with. So much of what is known professionally has limited utility by virtue of not being made available to those who could benefit most directly from this knowledge. Professionals should not disparage the efforts of the public to learn about their disparate and often divergent views. How different are we from shamans and quacks of yesteryear who cloaked their "mysterious potions" behind a veil of verbal mumbo-jumbo and esoteric secrecy?

Dr. Bockian has drawn on the thoughtful work of numerous theorists and clinicians to help the lay reader understand the typical features of this problematic disorder. Written with a grace and simplicity that any caring person can follow and appreciate, this book will serve as a source of comfort and guidance to all involved with borderline personality disorder.

Each chapter of the book focuses on one of several major areas of useful information, from answers to questions posed by the novice, matters of diagnostic accuracy, psychotherapeutic procedures, and alternative medicines to numerous methods that can be undertaken by instituting wise lifestyle changes (for example, nutrition and exercise), as well as steps that families can employ fruitfully. Especially fascinating is the chapter contributed by coauthor Valerie Porr, which recounts the experiences of the families of borderline patients. In short, Professor Bockian has organized and highlighted this impressive guidebook in an intriguing manner, including numerous fascinating case materials throughout. I am especially pleased by the balance and open-mindedness he has shown among diverse treatment viewpoints. It is assuredly a landmark work that will prove of inestimable value to patients, families, and their therapists.

To say that I am proud of this book is an understatement. More important, those who read it will be pleased by how helpful a guide it is in their struggle to overcome the borderline syndrome.

Theodore Millon, Ph.D., D.Sc.,
dean and scientific director, Institute for Advanced
Studies in Personology and Psychopathology

Acknowledgments

IN MANY WAYS, the writing of this book parallels the process of coming to terms with borderline personality disorder. There came a point when I realized that I could not do it alone. I needed to write about medication, as well as numerous alternative therapies, much of which fell outside my formal training. For years, I had been trained as a scientific writer, a style inappropriate for the people we are hoping to reach with this book. By reaching out and connecting with others, I gained strength, wisdom, and clarity.

My two coauthors added to this book in immeasurable ways. Valerie Porr is the most passionate person regarding borderline personality disorder that I have ever met. Her energy, enthusiasm, and perspective added to this book in ways that go far beyond chapter 9, which she wrote; Valerie and I discussed the majority of this book and her insights were invaluable. Gifted writing expert Nora Villagran helped to bring my ideas to life. I am accustomed to dry, technical writing; I needed Nora's input to turn this into a living, breathing text.

I am deeply indebted to the editors at Prima/Random House who made this work possible. I worked most closely with Marjorie Lery, whose positive attitude and deep understanding of the process authors undergo helped me to feel understood and supported throughout the process. Susan Silva, the acquisition editor, was my first contact with Prima and was very helpful in the early stages of the project. Jamie Miller was extremely effective and efficient in her oversight of this project, and she found numerous ways to make this a better book. I am also indebted to my colleague Bernie Golden, Ph.D., who facilitated my involvement with Prima and this project.

My mentor, Theodore Millon, has influenced my thinking in countless ways. The foundation of my knowledge in personality disorders was fostered by him during my graduate training and nurtured in the intervening years. The integration of numerous approaches to the psychotherapy of a person undergirds my approach to clients, a theme that recurs throughout this book. I would like to thank him for all he has done, as well as for writing the foreword to this book.

I would especially like to thank those dedicated professionals who took time from their busy schedules to grant me an interview. Speaking with them gave me better insight and understanding than I could have achieved from reading alone. Included are psychologists John Allen, Ph.D., Cindy Sanderson, Ph.D., Dan Santisteban, Ph.D., Margaret Warner, Ph.D., and Jeffrey Young, Ph.D.; doctoral candidate Mark Johns, M.A.; psychiatrists John Gunderson, M.D., Otto Kernberg, M.D., and Ken Silk, M.D.; homeopathy expert Todd Rowe, M.D.; Vedic medicine specialist Robert Schneider, M.D.; dance/movement therapists Danielle Fraenkel, Ph.D., A.D.T.R., Penny Lewis, Ph.D., A.D.T.R., and Linda Pilus, M.A., A.D.T.R.; and traditional Chinese medicine experts Dave Malony, M.A., and Lorene Wu, M.D.

Psychiatrist Paul Soloff, M.D., read and provided comments on the initial draft of chapter 4; his input was invaluable and my gratitude to him immeasurable. I am also indebted to Eliezar Schwartz, Ph.D., neuropsychologist, who was my biopsychology "translator."

My assistant and student, doctoral candidate Heidi Baird Martin, was also invaluable in countless ways. She helped me to gather and organize materials, and, perhaps most important, she helped me to stay grounded during what was at times a daunting task. I would also like to thank my former teaching assistant and student, doctoral candidate Patricia Graham, M.A., for her help in obtaining materials.

I would like to thank the Illinois School of Professional Psychology/ Argosy University and the dean, Marc Lubin, Ph.D., for providing me with release from one of my courses, as well as providing me with Heidi as an assistant. The library staff also consistently went above and beyond the call of duty. I often needed materials in a hurry, and Fay Kallista and Qi Chen were consistently supportive, calm, and cheerful. They are dedicated professionals and, like the therapists we train, they are people who love to help. I am most grateful for their assistance.

I would like to thank my family and friends for their patient forbearance when writing took me away from them. The brunt fell on my wife, Martha, who picked up the slack at home and who supported me emotionally during times of stress. I would like to thank my parents, Fred and Sandra Bockian, my brother, Jeffrey Bockian, and my uncle and aunt, Alan and Barbara Brodsky, for their undying support.

Lastly, I would like to thank my clients, who have shared their lives with me. I have learned as much as they have from the experiences we have had together.

Introduction

BORDERLINE PERSONALITY DISORDER (BPD) is a potentially devastating condition that affects at least 6 million individuals in the United States, with tens of millions having borderline symptoms or closely related disorders. Despite its prevalence, we are still learning about BPD. The disorder, defined in 1980, is a relatively new diagnosis that has, nonetheless, led to vital research exploring its causes and possible treatments.

Most people have never heard of borderline personality disorder, even when they may be dealing with it themselves or with a loved one who has it. Some practitioners hesitate to tell clients that they are being treated for BPD for fear of stigmatizing them, or because some insurance companies do not cover treatment for BPD, or because they fear making a misdiagnosis. In addition, BPD itself is shrouded in the darkness of misinformation and myth. The primary purpose of this book is to bring borderline personality disorder into the light, for the benefit of those with BPD, for their loved ones, and for society.

In general, people with this disorder can be functioning, educated, and employed individuals who can also be highly unstable at times. Their impulsive behaviors, erratic moods, and unpredictable whims often pull them in seemingly random directions. The daily life of a person with BPD can take on all the precariousness of an emotional rollercoaster, fueled in part by inaccurate perceptions, misguided thoughts, and shortsighted assumptions about others in their environment.

Relationships with friends and lovers are often intense and short-lived for the person with BPD. Even when things are going well, the person with BPD may accuse the other person of manipulation, deceit, or disloyalty. These interactions are characterized by angry outbursts alternating with imploring apologies, overwhelming insecurity, and emotional dependency. They blame others for their pain and chaos. Often distraught, lonely, and depressed, many become suicidal. In fact, people with borderline personality disorder comprise one of the highest risks of all mental health conditions, with a 3 to 9 percent death rate from suicide.[1]

I have written this book primarily from my perspective as a therapist and an educator, with the intention of providing information on BPD that will give you or a loved one new hope for recovery.

Chapter 1 defines borderline personality and presents people's experiences with the disorder in the hope that the detailed descriptions of symptoms and indications will help readers recognize themselves or loved ones with BPD. Chapter 2 will guide you on how to get a proper diagnosis. Chapter 3 reviews psychotherapy approaches, while chapter 4 describes the various medications used to treat aspects of BPD. In chapter 5, you'll be introduced to mind-body approaches to treating borderline personality disorder, including yoga, relaxation training, and expressive arts such as dance, movement, and music therapies. These are less-known methods for treatment of BPD but offer great promise. Chapter 6 looks at alternative approaches, such as traditional Chinese medicine, Vedic medicine, and herbal remedies. In chapter 7, you'll read about exercise and nutrition-based approaches. Chapter 8 will provide you with an extended section on self-help—the many different techniques you can use to take care of yourself better, such as meditation, humor, and relaxation training.

Chapter 9, on the experiences of families of individuals with BPD, is a special chapter written by Valerie Porr, a leading advocate for people with BPD. Dr. Ken Silk recommended Valerie based on her extensive experience with people with BPD and their families, along with her unique perspective as an advocate, rather than as a therapist or researcher. I have admired Valerie—her passion, spirit, and dedication—from the moment we met. I wanted her voice in this book because we offer differing points of view on various issues and because she speaks for those with BPD and for their loved ones, who often feel that their needs go unheeded. Thus, the perspective she brings is essential.

Through my work with individuals with borderline personality disorder, I've learned about their lives through their eyes. However, when seen from the perspective of their loved ones, a very different picture often emerges. While the individual may perceive family members as having been hurtful or neglectful, family members frequently see themselves as victims of their loved one's erratic moods and unpredictable behavior. Who is right?

Some practitioners argue that trauma causes BPD. In this view, the families are hurtful, and the person with BPD is a victim. Research has shown that this point of view is not necessarily accurate, nor is it completely definitive. In addition, this view may potentially alienate the very people most likely to be the individual's greatest support system. An emerging point of view is that the families' perspective has been neglected for too long. John Gunderson, M.D., among the world's leaders in the field of BPD, puts it this way:

> I was a contributor to the literature that led to the unfair vilification of the families and the largely unfortunate efforts at either excluding or inappropriately involving them in treatment. So it is with some embarrassment that I now find myself presenting a treatment that begins with the expectation that families of borderline individuals are important allies of the treaters and that largely finesses the whole issue of whether they had anything to do with the origins of psychopathology. . . . The parents generally saw the families as much healthier than did the borderline offspring. Much of the preceding literature about the families of borderline patients derived solely from reports provided by the borderline patients, and rarely included the families' perspective.[2]

Once again, who is right? In my clinical work, I have found the answer is almost always: "all of the above." In some cases, families are neglectful, abusive, or harmful. In other cases, they are loving and supportive, even as the disorder devastates the entire family. Other families fall somewhere between. A consideration is whether the family's problems differ from those of the general population. Estimates point to the unfortunate occurrence of high rates of physical and sexual abuse in the general population, not just in families of individuals with borderline personality disorder. Perhaps individuals with emotional resilience and validating, supportive environments are less likely to develop borderline personality disorder. At this point, we are still discovering the roots of this disorder. More research is needed in this area.

As an advocate, Valerie Porr wants people with BPD to get well. She deals with families and empathizes with family members; she walks in their shoes, feels their pain, and champions their cause. She wants our society to devote the resources necessary to improve our treatments of BPD and to provide these treatments to those who need them. She challenges the status quo. She sees things from the perspective of the family and makes no bones about it. I am delighted with her contribution to the book.

Finally, chapter 10 looks to the future, exploring new directions in current, upcoming, and still-needed research focusing on the causes and treatment of borderline personality disorder. In addition to reading about ongoing research projects, you'll be exposed to efforts at advocacy and support groups and encouraged to get involved.

I hope you will find your tour through the complexities of this compelling disorder informative and enriching.

What Is Borderline Personality Disorder?

BORDERLINE PERSONALITY DISORDER (BPD) is a way of being in the world that involves massive mood fluctuations, intense relationships, desperation, and insecurity. Let's begin with a story of what the disorder looks like in one individual who exemplifies elements commonly found in the BPD case profile. Here is the story of "Carol."

Not long ago, Carol felt on top of the world. She loved being a nurse on an adolescent substance-abuse unit in a large metropolitan hospital. A petite, freckle-faced brunette, she could be wisecracking and funny and, at other times, moody and hot-tempered. Yet, Carol had a good rapport with the kids in the unit. She could relate. At 32, she still felt like a teenager.

Carol's personal life was troubled, however. Her new romance seemed destined to dissolve into disappointment, just like all the others. She had met Bill at a party. They'd flirted over the hors d'oeuvres before making their getaway together. Then, they'd spent the rest of the evening at an after-hours club, talking and gazing into each other's eyes. Over the next few days, they shared all their free time, making love passionately and frequently. After dating only a couple of weeks, they spent a romantic weekend at a mountain resort. A short time later, they moved in together.

This is when the problems started. Carol began to feel trapped and confined. She found herself irritated and angry with Bill over the littlest things. Bill, too, seemed uncomfortable. He hadn't realized Carol was so sensitive and easily annoyed. In self-defense, he began distancing himself from her to avoid triggering one of her unpredictable outbursts.

But this only made Carol upset and moody. She worried that their relationship would end. Even when she yelled at him over some imagined slight, she felt frightened inside. Meanwhile, they had sex less and less. Then one night, Bill came home late from work without calling. As soon as he walked in the door, Carol flew into a rage, hurling insults. Her temper tantrum—that's how he saw it—lasted an hour. In a verbal tirade punctuated by sarcasm and tears, she pointed her finger at him repeatedly and accused him of cheating on her. Then, to his astonishment, she threw him out of the apartment.

Once Bill left, Carol calmed down. But without Bill's presence, the silence made her heart pound. The apartment seemed cold and empty. She felt anxious being alone. How could he leave like that? Didn't he love her? Carol had a sinking feeling she'd made a terrible mistake. Bill was a great guy. He wouldn't cheat on her—they were great together!

Panic rose in her throat. What if she had blown it with him? Her anger was gone. In its place was a gnawing loneliness and despair. She flung herself on the sofa and cried with self-loathing. Then, with tears streaming down her cheeks, she grabbed her car keys and ran out to find Bill and beg him to come back. Driving through the neighborhood, the world seemed like such an uncaring place. Filled with desperation, Carol drove recklessly, barely missing an elderly man walking his dog across an intersection. She honked at the startled man, furious with him for impeding her way—as if he were an obstacle to her elusive happiness.

After driving all over town, Carol gave up trying to find Bill and headed home. She glanced at herself in the rearview mirror and saw an anxious young woman with bloodshot eyes and smeared mascara. Without Bill, she felt like a hollow container, empty and useless. Life seemed meaningless. She felt she had nothing to live for.

Turning onto her street, she saw Bill's car in the driveway. He had come back! She felt thrilled to see him. All her despair vanished. She felt euphoric. Carol burst into the apartment. She wouldn't let Bill say a word. She begged him for forgiveness, promising to never mistrust him or lose her temper again. Bill decided to forget the nasty, even vicious, things she'd said to him earlier, when she'd screamed at him to get out. He was just relieved the whole blowup was over. The night ended with lovemaking that was more passionate than ever. But, even as Carol fell asleep, she felt a prickle of anxiety and a sense of looming abandonment.

For most of her life, Carol hasn't known quite who she is. She often looks at her reflection in the mirror, as if hoping to find herself there. In her adolescence and twenties, what began as experimental sex and drug use, which often left her empty and depressed, escalated into frequent one-night stands, impulsive behavior, and drug abuse. In college, she'd drifted from one area of study to another, never settling on a specific career goal. She showed promise in art, then in writing, then in science. But she shouldered her talents as if they were burdens, rather than gifts. Later, she flitted from one job to another, afraid of feeling stuck and unable to commit herself to any one path of endeavor.

Finally, when a national nursing shortage opened up plenty of well-paying jobs, she decided to become a nurse. After nursing school, she found a position working in a drug rehabilitation unit. Given her history with substance abuse, Carol thought she could really help others with this problem. After several months, she still liked her job, but some of the staff found her too contentious and there had been conflicts.

These days, she needed Bill more than ever to make her feel loved and secure at home. After their latest fight, things went well for a

> For most of her life, Carol hasn't known quite who she is. She often looks at her reflection in the mirror, as if hoping to find herself there.

while. Carol still had her moods, of course, which often rocked out of control, resulting in her yelling at him and accusing him of being insensitive to her. He regretted calling her a "drama queen" during their latest fight. That had really set her off.

Mostly now, Bill felt anxious. He navigated his way through their days and nights, careful to avoid triggering her rage. He felt genuinely confused by her shifting moods and beliefs. No matter how careful he was, she swung from feeling totally smitten with him to feeling enraged toward him. She saw things in black or white: He was either the best thing that had ever happened to her or he was the worst thing in her life and personally to blame for all her feelings of worthlessness and insecurity.

Finally, Bill couldn't take it anymore and left for good. Engulfed by a sense of overwhelming loneliness, Carol felt empty and suicidal. Now, in utter desperation, she reached for her phone and called Alexis, the best friend she had neglected for far too long. The two women had shared troubled times as teenagers and, though they hadn't gotten together lately, they knew they could depend on each other in a pinch. Right now, for Carol, was definitely a pinch.

> *He was either the best thing that had ever happened to her or he was the worst thing in her life and personally to blame for all her feelings of worthlessness and insecurity.*

"I can't deal with it!" Carol sobbed. "I just can't seem to pull myself together, Alexis. I feel hopeless. Life has no meaning for me."

Carol sat huddled on the floor in a corner of her bedroom. Crying, she cradled the phone in her lap and held the receiver tightly. Her phone was a lifeline that had more than once helped her feel connected to someone—someone who could serve, even temporarily, as a haven or at least a distraction from the emotional storms clouding her existence.

"Honey, it's going to be okay," Alexis soothed, in her cozy Southern drawl. "Listen, you want to come over? I'll make us hot chocolate."

It was just what Carol needed to hear.

Driving to her friend's house, Carol ached with unbearable sadness. She felt as though she was careening down a dark, gloomy tunnel with no light in sight.

Knocking on the door at Alexis's house, Carol suddenly remembered how uptight, moody, and argumentative Alexis could be. Maybe this wasn't such a good idea; the last thing she needed was more tension in her life. But when the door opened, Alexis smiled warmly and hugged her, saying reassuringly, "Carol, come in. Make yourself at home." Alexis seemed different, more at ease with herself and more calmly confident than Carol had ever seen her.

"Oh, Alexis, thank you for having me over," cried Carol, before launching into the whole story of her stormy relationship with Bill. Alexis listened sympathetically—after all, she had as many "Bill" stories as Carol did.

Later, when Carol's tearful gasps eased to hiccup-like shudders and finally to sniffles, she noticed a book lying face-up on the end table. The book's title was certainly intriguing. Carol picked it up, reading the title aloud: "*I Hate You—Don't Leave Me.* Sounds like the story of my life," said Carol, with a bitter laugh.

"I *know* it was the story of mine," Alexis responded. "Reading it, and a few others like it, got me into therapy and treatment. I think what I've learned and the positives changes I've made saved my marriage— and my life."

"Alexis, I didn't know," said Carol. "And here I've spent the last hour talking about myself. Tell me, what's all this about?"

"It's about borderline personality disorder," replied Alexis. "It's about me. And I think you'll find it's about you, too."

WHAT IS BORDERLINE PERSONALITY DISORDER?

Borderline personality disorder is a condition that has its origins in both biology and the environment. The symptoms of BPD include depression, moodiness, anger, disorganization, anxiety, low self-esteem, rage, feeling that life is meaningless, and feeling that one is unworthy or unlovable. The person with BPD may live life without a clear sense of identity. Other symptoms range from feelings of inadequacy and impulsiveness to self-destructive behavior and thoughts of suicide.

"People with borderline personality disorder are sometimes overly dependent," said Alexis. "Without realizing it, we often expect others to take care of us. And when they resist or demand we take responsibility for ourselves, we feel abandoned and unloved. Carol, I can see that look on your face, saying, 'Well, what's all this got to do with me?' Honey, we've known each other forever. What do *you* think?"

Carol was sitting on the sofa with her back very straight and a surprised look on her face.

"Look, I'm sorry, Carol, I didn't mean to bombard you with all of this. You came here for a shoulder to cry on, not a lecture."

But Carol wasn't offended; she was relieved. "I haven't really felt happy in a very long time," she murmured, looking down. "I guess I've blamed others for my unhappiness. I feel like I'm still trying to find myself." Glancing up at her friend, she asked, "How do I get off this emotional roller-coaster? I'm not saying I have this problem. But . . . well, is there anything that I can do about it?"

The symptoms of BPD include depression, moodiness, anger, disorganization, anxiety, low self-esteem, rage, feeling that life is meaningless, and feeling that one is unworthy or unlovable.

"Of course there is," said Alexis, squeezing Carol's hand. "It'll help you to learn as much as you can about it. But first, let's finish our hot chocolate, okay?"

Carol smiled, taking a sip of the sweet, comforting brew. "Right. Chocolate first. Then I want to hear more about this. I've struggled along with so many questions, like why am I so lost, so angry, so depressed? I'd really like to find the answers. And do something with them."

The Symptoms of Borderline Personality Disorder

According to the *Diagnostic and Statistical Manual of Mental Disorders, Fourth Edition (DSM-IV)*, a diagnosis of borderline personality disorder requires the presence in the individual of five or more of the following nine criteria:

1. Makes desperate attempts to avoid abandonment.

2. Has unstable and intense relationships, usually involving alternately idealizing then devaluing the other person.

3. Sense of self or self-image is chronically unstable.

4. Acts on impulse in ways that can be self-damaging (for example, overspending, overeating, acting out sexually, abusing drugs).

5. Makes frequent suicidal gestures or threats, or injures himself/herself.

6. Has a highly unstable mood (for example, gets depressed, irritable, or anxious for brief periods).

7. Chronically experiences feelings of emptiness.

8. Is easily provoked to anger or rage.

9. Under stress, can become paranoid or experience dissociative symptoms.

The manual suggests that a person presenting five or more of these features may qualify for a diagnosis of borderline personality disorder. After reading the descriptions of the criteria, you might consider which features describe Carol, or yourself, your loved one, or a friend.

Carol and Alexis are composites of clients who have come to me for help in coping with borderline personality disorder. Yet both are very real in that they represent the often-valiant individuals struggling with the emotional and behavioral symptoms of this disorder. Throughout this book, they will serve as helpful guides in exploring the rocky terrain traveled by those with BPD, many of whom have learned to live happier, more successful lives.

To more completely understand this disorder, it is helpful to examine each of the nine defining criteria of borderline personality disorder, as listed in the *Diagnostic and Statistical Manual of Mental Disorders, Fourth Edition (DSM-IV)*, the mental health industry's standard psychiatric reference text (see sidebar, "The Symptoms of Borderline Personality Disorder"). An examination of these nine criteria follows.

Criterion 1: Desperate Attempts to Avoid Abandonment

Nobody likes to feel abandoned or to see a relationship end. Most of us, however, accept that there are people who will come and go in our lives. After a breakup or separation, there's a period of grieving, followed by acceptance and moving on. For the person with borderline personality disorder, the reaction can be much more extreme. Often, there's a cycle comprised of impulsively breaking up with someone, subsequent extreme regret and remorse, then desperate attempts to win the person back. After Carol screamed at Bill to get out of her life, she felt great despair and regret; she felt she'd do anything to get him back.

> *Often, there's a cycle comprised of impulsively breaking up with someone, subsequent extreme regret and remorse, then desperate attempts to win the person back.*

The person with this disorder might threaten to kill herself to prove how deeply she loves her boyfriend, or to prove to herself how much he loves her. She mistakenly thinks that putting herself at risk will provoke feelings of love and protection for her. Desperate to relieve her pain, she may try to kill herself. But a crucial goal of her suicide attempt, conscious or unconscious, is to convince him to return. The boyfriend may temporarily stay involved in order to get her through the crisis. In the back of his mind, however, the suicidal behavior just solidifies his conviction that leaving is the right decision. As soon as the situation is stable, the boyfriend leaves, while the individual with BPD provokes another crisis in order to try to keep him involved.

From a distance, these behaviors make no sense. How could a suicide attempt really convince someone to love you? Even if it could work, is it really worth risking death in order to try to get someone to stay? A closer look, however, reveals a coherent pattern.

Why do individuals with borderline personality disorder have such difficulty with separation? It often has to do with the other symptoms of the disorder. Someone who has a poor sense of identity (criterion 3) will often identify with, become one with, or merge with a partner. When the relationship ends, they experience not just a part of themselves dying, but their entire identity disappearing. The challenge, of course, is to rediscover oneself, apart from the other person. But for those with BPD, the internal turmoil is so painful that *any* way to end that feeling seems justified.

> *Someone who has a poor sense of identity will often identify with, become one with, or merge with a partner. When the relationship ends, they experience not just a part of themselves dying, but their entire identity disappearing.*

Paul Mason and Randi Kreger, in their book, *Stop Walking on Eggshells*, eloquently describe the fear of abandonment experienced by individuals with BPD: "Imagine the terror that you would feel if you were a 7-year-old, lost and alone in the middle of Times Square in New York City. Your mom was there a second ago, holding your hand. Suddenly the crowd swept her away and you can't see her anymore.

You look around frantically, trying to find her. Menacing strangers glare back at you. . . . This is how people with BPD feel nearly all the time."[1]

Such feelings, in some cases, have their roots in actual experiences with unreliable figures in their lives. Many people with this disorder were raised by parents who were emotionally or physically unavailable. Some had parents who were alcoholics or drug abusers. Others had one or both parents who had borderline personality disorder, who were emotionally erratic and placed difficult or impossible conditions on the child to prove their devotion. Still others came from single-parent homes and blame themselves for their parents' divorce. On the other hand, some people who have BPD were raised in environments that were perfectly average, but their natural hypersensitivities made it feel like a living hell. The ordinary (though I would say unfortunate) teasing that most children experience as pinpricks feel like deep stab wounds to the hypersensitive child. Ordinary inattention by typically distracted parents is experienced as eternities of abandonment. Whether the individual was "really" abandoned (exposed to an unusually neglectful upbringing) or "just felt that way" (had an average environment that was experienced as neglectful), the psychological outcome is the same: The individual experiences terror of abandonment and develops coping strategies to try to deal with those feelings. These coping strategies—"desperate attempts to avoid abandonment"—may induce others to withdraw, eliciting further desperate attempts to avoid abandonment. These cycles can be very painful and difficult for both the individuals and their loved ones.

Without perceived adequate and nurturing role models, developing children are unable to internalize a sufficiently stable image of how to nurture, including how to nurture themselves. The results are

> People with BPD go to desperate lengths to avoid the chronic feelings of emptiness they have. Drug use, sex, overspending, overeating, and other impulsive behaviors are all ways to fill the void.

adults who may find it hard to know how to soothe themselves. Early childhood separations from even an inadequate parent only serve to further increase feelings of hopelessness because of the normal human need for deep, loving relationships.

People with BPD go to desperate lengths to avoid the chronic feelings of emptiness they have (criterion 7). Drug use, sex, over-spending, overeating, and other impulsive behaviors are all ways to fill the void. Feelings of emptiness rarely emerge when they are in the company of another person. Whether they feel love or hate for the other person, whether they feel blame or guilt towards the other person, at least they are distracted from their own negative feelings. For the moment, they are not alone.

Criterion 2: Unstable and Intense Relationships

A pattern I see in my clinical practice is that individuals with BPD often meet someone, fall in love, and move in together after only a few weeks of dating, as Carol did with Bill. A couple of months later, the relationship is over, and the individual feels depressed, stupid, angry, or guilty. "How could I have fallen for him? He's horrible! I always pick the wrong type of person!" is the recurring theme.

Underlying feelings of self-hatred, ambivalence, or low self-esteem can lead to cycles of abandonment and fragile relationships. Woody Allen once joked, "I would never join a club that would have *me* as a member." For the person with BPD, the corresponding saying would be—"If you're in a relationship with me, you must be a loser—and I'd better get out before you hurt me."

Once the relationship is over, that flawed logic sometimes floats to the surface, as in "Bill didn't do anything wrong—why did I dump him? Now I'm alone. I'll never find anyone. I shouldn't have done that! I'd better try to get him back, before it's too late."

Similarly, fear of abandonment (criterion 1) and suspiciously looking for signs of impending abandonment can actually lead to abandonment—an irony often referred to as a "self-fulfilling prophecy" or "vicious circle." For example, a man with BPD fears rejection, so he demands constant assurances of love, devotion, and loyalty from his girlfriend. Eventually, she gets worn out, seeing him as insecure, overly needy, and mistrustful. His terror of abandonment elicits the consequences he fears most. Ironically, the individual with BPD rarely sees this cycle for what it is. Rather than attributing the abandonment to his own behavior, he will usually attribute the breakup to faults in the other person ("She was afraid of commitment.") or sometimes to flaws in himself ("I need to work out more and get a better body."). But if his girlfriend had responded to his possessiveness with offers of greater intimacy, it's likely he would have felt extremely ambivalent about such intimacy. His resulting stress would perhaps then trigger a greater sense of ambivalence, even terror, leading to his leaving or acting out (drugs, self-injurious behavior, or having an affair). Of course, these behaviors further destabilize his emotional life.

Other borderline symptoms contribute to the intensity and instability of relationships. Being impulsive (criterion 4), a person with the disorder may do something without thinking or planning (including things that damage or end relationships), and later regret her actions. Feelings of rage (criterion 8) can intensify a relationship. In some cases, intense rages are followed by passionate lovemaking, which often creates ambivalent feelings in both partners. Having a chronically unstable sense of self (criterion 3) makes it difficult for the person with BPD to provide the kind of consistency most people desire in a relationship.

The process of idealizing then devaluing others and dividing people into separate "black-and-white" categories is called, appropriately enough, "splitting." People are seen as either good or evil, for me or against me, and so on. Situations are seen as completely hopeless or certain to succeed, perfect or horrible. There are no shades of gray. It's difficult or impossible for many individuals with borderline personality disorder to hold contradictory information simultaneously, such as "Jack's a nice guy, but I don't like when he's late." To the mind of someone whose thinking is based on splitting, when Jack is on time he's a great guy; when he's late he's a jerk.

Splitting seems to be, at least in part, associated with impossible binds a person experiences early in life. A child, like a person with BPD, also sees things in black and white, hence the popularity of cartoons and fairy tales with evil witches, goblins, and giants, contrasted with flawless, noble heroes. Imagine, however, the situation of a young child who is being sexually abused by an adult, a caretaker, or a parental figure. Survival itself depends on the adult's beneficence. The child, however, also feels dirty, ashamed, and betrayed. Unable developmentally to hold the image of the adult who both cares for and abuses him in his mind all at once, he splits the image into alternating all-good, all-bad images, a Dr. Jekyll–and–Mr. Hyde view of the

> *P*eople are seen as either good or evil, either for me or against me. Situations are seen as completely hopeless or certain to succeed, perfect or horrible. There are no shades of gray.

abusive adult. This black-and-white way of looking at things may then generalize to other relationships and situations. For most children, this ultimately resolves. However, the person who develops borderline personality disorder continues to have this "black-and-white" cognitive style. This is due to a combination of biological predisposition (covered later in this chapter) and childhood experiences (such as invalidation or trauma).

Some individuals are born with cognitive differences that make it difficult for them to integrate disparate pieces of information; research has shown that these problems are more prevalent in people with BPD than in others. This process may interfere with their perceiving "shades of gray" in relationships. This could take on the appearance of splitting, but is in fact better viewed as a neuropsychological deficit. Ideally, this possibility would be routinely taken into account in clinical care. However, since it is based on rather recent research, this does not always occur. Other neuropsychological findings are discussed

Famous People with Borderline Personality Disorder

• **Marilyn Monroe.** According to Jerome Kreisman, M.D., and Hal Straus, in their book, *I Hate You—Don't Leave Me,* Marilyn Monroe had numerous symptoms of borderline personality disorder. She hated being alone and would fall into a "void" unless surrounded by others. She lacked a stable sense of identity, for which she compensated by becoming consumed with her roles. She had a variety of difficulties with drugs, and Monroe attempted suicide at least three times before she was finally successful. Raised in an orphanage during her early childhood, she craved affection and needed enormous amounts of support and nurturance.[2] In spite of her difficulties—or perhaps, in part, because of them—Marilyn Monroe was one of the biggest movie stars of all time, whose name evokes a sense of wonder even to this day.

• **Princess Diana.** According to Sally Bedell Smith, Diana suffered from depression, fear of abandonment, mood swings, bulimia, binge eating, self-injury, suicide attempts, feelings of loneliness, boredom, emptiness, and, most of all, unstable identity.[3] Despite her private pain, Princess Diana was beloved by millions for her charm, grace, and commitment to charitable causes.

later in this chapter, under "The Biology of Borderline Personality Disorder."

Criterion 3: Chronically Unstable Self-Image

Individuals with this characteristic literally don't know who they are. The person may flit from one occupational idea to the next, never finding anything that fits. Two months of law school are followed by a year of drifting, only to be followed by decisions to become a dance therapist or an accountant. Neither of these work out, and it's back to more searching.

- **Doug Ferrari.** Ferrari was a rising star in the late 1970s and early 80s. His friend Trent Hayward writes: "At six-foot-five, Ferrari is an imposing monolith of mirth with a track record in the volatile comedy industry that reads like the guestbook at Spago. He has performed with the best—from Robin Williams and Rodney Dangerfield to Elvis Costello and Sun Ra. He has trashed microphone stands in at least four time zones and headlined over 150 venues internationally."[4] In 1984 he won the prestigious San Francisco Comedy Competition, and seemed destined for celebrity. Instead, he became addicted to cocaine and alcohol and wound up unemployed and homeless. Ferrari had problems with anger, intense and unstable relationships, and depression. Hayward helped him to get into recovery, and Ferrari has been turning his life around. On stage at a charity function, he quipped, "In the last 6 years, I married the love of my life, I got into recovery and AA, halfway houses and hospital outpatient treatment. . . . I got into psychological therapy and anger management. I got on psych medications, so if you don't like my speech tonight, I don't give a damn. I'm on Prozac."[5] To my knowledge, Doug Ferrari is the first well-known person to publicly state that he has borderline personality disorder.

Socially, the pattern is the same. When socializing with different friends, he tries to alter himself to fit in with the mores of the group. Elements of these behaviors are frequently seen among normal adolescents. Most of us can remember the "Who am I?" experiences of our teenage years. After this "trying on" of various personas in adolescence and the early twenties, the mature individual eventually settles on a general identity and life plan. But the individual with BPD may still "personality surf" far into the adult years. This endless quest for identity can be like the search for the Holy Grail—fruitless and frustrating.

Additionally, we all share a search for significance. But the person with borderline personality disorder struggles with this search for meaning as if it were a reason to be depressed or a heavy burden, rather than one of life's most intriguing adventures.

Criterion 4: Impulsive Acts

Individuals with borderline personality disorder live under the tyranny of their impulses. Carol's years of substance abuse were largely attempts to feel good, to feel alive, and to feel less pain. Rather than dealing with her negative thoughts and emotions, she would impulsively grab a quick fix. Similarly, her sexual escapades were spur-of-the-moment choices. Many individuals use sex to feel temporary relief from distressing feelings. They will have unprotected sex with virtual strangers on the spur of the moment, risking pregnancy and sexually transmitted diseases such as AIDS. Food is another well-known means of self-soothing. Borderline personality disorder is associated with several eating disorders: binge eating (to self-soothe); bulimia (bingeing to self-soothe, followed by guilt, self-hate, and purging); and anorexia (starving to meet someone else's expectations, to self-punish, or to gain a sense of self-control).

> *Individuals with borderline personality disorder live under the tyranny of their impulses. Carol's years of substance abuse were largely attempts to feel good, to feel alive, and to feel less pain.*

World-renowned personality disorders expert Dr. Theodore Millon and his associates describe the case of "Jane," a 25-year-old woman with borderline personality disorder, who often acted on impulse: "She has just been released from the hospital, where she was recovering from minor internal injuries sustained after jumping out of her boyfriend's Jeep, while on the way to a concert, something she has done before. She insists she did it because they were arguing and she was high and just wanted to get away, describing him as 'evil.'"[6]

Once again, these impulsive behaviors are related to other symptoms of the disorder. Rapid changes in Jane's view of another person (criterion 2) left her feeling she was in a desperate situation that called for drastic action. From Jane's standpoint, her extreme actions were justified. If you were in a car with an evil monster—say someone who had kidnapped you and was planning to hurt you—wouldn't jumping from the Jeep, even sustaining minor injuries, be the right thing to do? Wouldn't the right time to act be *now*, or the first possible moment?

These interpretations of the world, these patterns of thinking often underlie the perplexing, impulsive behaviors seen among people with BPD. People can normally overrule the tyranny of their emotions. For those with borderline personality disorder, emotions are in the driver's seat—steering their thinking, making behavioral decisions, and sometimes crashing. For the person with a biologically based difficulty with impulse control, attempts at exercising self-restraint often fail. It is like a person with congenitally weak arms trying to do pull-ups: Without a great deal of training, practice, and effort, the attempts will be unsuccessful.

> *People can normally overrule the tyranny of their emotions. For those with borderline personality disorder, emotions are in the driver's seat—steering their thinking, making behavioral decisions, and sometimes crashing.*

Other emotions can also have an important impact. Feelings of emptiness (criterion 7) are so distressing to many people that they will do anything to avoid them. Substance abuse decreases the individual's already limited emotional control. The emotional lability that is the hallmark of borderline personality disorder (criterion 6) means that people with the disorder will sometimes feel an enormous depth of despair; "desperate times" then call for desperate measures.

Criterion 5: Suicidal Gestures or Self-Injury

Suicidal behavior is always born of suffering and hopelessness. Even if much of the pain is clearly a function of choices the person has made and behaviors apparently under their control, it's a safe bet the person was trying to make the best of the situation as they saw it. Life circumstances that are extreme and overwhelming can make nearly anyone feel little hope of a meaningful, productive life. Leading suicidologist Marsha M. Linehan writes:

> The desire to be dead among borderline individuals is often reasonable, in that it is based on lives that are currently unbearable . . . the problem is usually that the patient simply has too many life crises, environmental stressors, problematic interpersonal relationships, difficult employment situations, and/or physical problems to enjoy life or find meaning in it. In addition, the patient's habitual dysfunctional behavior patterns both create their own stress and interfere with any chance of improving the quality of life. In sum, borderline individuals usually have good reasons for wanting to be dead."[7]

In addition, individuals who are told or led to believe by people close to them that they are bad, no good, terrible, or inadequate internalize these criticisms. Severe peer rejection can be just as devastating and is more likely to be overlooked as a source of the problem. The clearest example of the impact of physical and emotional abuse by peers (that is, "bullying") is seen in the high rate of suicidal ideation and behavior in gay male teens. It is very likely that individuals who are vulnerable to borderline personality disorder are made much worse by peer rejection and bullying.

It is very likely that individuals who are vulnerable to borderline personality disorder are made much worse by peer rejection and bullying.

A key insight of Dr. Linehan is that suicidal behavior is often inadvertently rewarded by others. She writes: "DBT [dialectical behavior therapy] likewise targets patients' expectations about the value of suicidal behavior as a problem-solving alternative. Unfortunately, many of these expectations may be quite accurate. If a patient wants to seek revenge, make others sorry for what they did or did not do, escape an intolerable life situation, or even save others pain, suffering, and money, suicide may be the answer."[8] Dr. Linehan goes on to suggest that suicide prevention is the first priority of all psychotherapy for patients with borderline personality disorder.

A core component of treatment for those who have suicidal and borderline symptoms is a comprehensive strategy that encourages developing alternative problem-solving methods, embracing life, and removing incentives for suicidal behavior.

Self-injury is one of the more perplexing symptoms of borderline personality disorder. The gut reaction most of my students have when they first hear about self-injurious behavior is, "How can someone do that?" Even for the person with borderline personality disorder, the urge to self-injure often feels foreign. Although lumped together into one criterion with suicide in the psychiatric manual, the goal of the self-injurer isn't to die. People give many reasons to describe why they engage in self-injurious behavior (SIB). The most common theme I've seen, though counterintuitive, is that the action gives immediate release and relief, helping them to feel better. Other reasons include to express self-hatred, to cope with memories of abuse, to express rage, to punish themselves, to distract themselves from painful emotions, to block out feelings, or to simply experience feelings.

One Web site asks the questions: "Why do you SI [self-injure]? How does it make you feel?"[9] One of the most succinct responses of the many given on the Web site is this:

> 1. I feel like a pressure cooker that's going to explode. Cutting and bleeding sufficiently is like letting out the steam. If I do this to my satisfaction, I feel immediate relief, as if injected with Valium or something. It helps stop the inner turmoil for a while. 2. To feel real when I feel numb. 3. It becomes an addiction.
> *[female, age 38, 13.5 years SIB]*

Another shares:

> I cannot adequately describe in words my emotional state prior to a cutting. The feelings are overwhelming—usually severe feelings of rejection, self-hatred, or anger. Cutting presents a way to make the pain show and be felt on the *outside* where I can deal with it.
> *[female, age 33, Ph.D., SIB since teens]*

Often, the person who commits SIB is not always fully aware of the reasons. Many do it while in a partial or complete state of dissociation (criterion 9). The above 33-year-old female adds:

> I do not know why I cut, but it scares the hell out of me. Most of the time I am feeling very rejected or angry or I am seething with self-hatred.

Still another notes:

> I injure myself to try to calm down, to try and escape the painful memories of my abuse, to try and take control of my emotions, to try and feel safe, to stop the nightmares and daymares, to try and feel. *[female, age 23, college student, 17 years SIB]*

Often self-injurious behavior is used to overcome feelings of emptiness:

> I personally find I'll cut if I'm feeling empty inside . . . cutting is a simple way of feeling real and checking if you can still feel. *[male, age 19]*

Despite the "positives" of SIB, most people who do it find it a very distressing symptom—and a shameful and embarrassing one. It can, however, be addicting. Research has found that SIB releases endorphins, the body's own morphine and the substance responsible for "positive addictions" such as "runner's high." Like other addictions, it is not an easy habit to break. In treatment, it's wise to anticipate a series of gains, followed by relapses before achieving abstinence.

Criterion 6: Highly Unstable Mood

For the person with borderline personality disorder, it is not uncommon for feelings to swing from thrilled, excited, and on top of the world to suicidally depressed in the space of a few hours. Someone with BPD may experience overwhelming anxiety, then feel fine. These mood swings are considered by some to be the *sine qua non* of the disorder. One person with borderline personality disorder captures the pain of the fluctuating moods in a poem:

Joy—why does it not remain?
Pain and depression engulf me in their icy grip.
I long for the light-heartedness that I enjoyed,
brief as it was.
Why does the heaviness and discontentment have to
return—again, once more?
Inside I scream in anguish, but no one knows.
Do they see it in my eyes, hear it in my voice?
And if they do, do they really understand—do they care?
I want it to go away, all the torment, aching and misery.
I reach out for help, but they don't understand.[10]

Some children are born with highly irritable temperaments, fussy and colicky as infants. Their parents may set future patterns into motion by responding with excessive discipline or helplessness and neglect. Either reaction, though understandable, can worsen an already difficult situation. Inborn emotional instability can also be intensified by environmental factors. Emotionally unstable role models, either at home, among peers, or in the media, can also worsen volatile, ever-changing emotions. Depressed parents, lacking in energy and feeling overwhelmed, tend to be neglectful, both to themselves and their children.

Criterion 7: Feelings of Emptiness

If you have never experienced feelings of emptiness, it's very hard to describe such inner hollowness. If you have experienced it, there's almost no need to describe it. It's like seeing the color blue. If you've seen blue, you know what it looks like. Imagine trying to describe blue to someone blind from birth. Words fail. The only way to describe the emptiness felt by those with BPD is through analogies and metaphors.

As a therapist, I once empathetically experienced a client's feelings of emptiness. I was in a session with a woman who had borderline personality disorder. I recall becoming truly attuned to her feelings. As I listened to her speak in a gentle, hollow monotone, a distant, far-away voice, connected to me yet disconnected, present yet absent, I remember suddenly experiencing a feeling of terror—terror in re-sponse to the emptiness and nothingness I was feeling. I felt a power-ful urge to pinch myself, to make sure I was awake and not dreaming, to feel *anything*. The boundaries of my body blurred. I could no longer feel my skin surrounding and containing me. It was as if I could just melt into the air and disappear against my will, until my very willpower was being drawn into the vacuum and dissipated. Nothingness. Hollowness. Emptiness. As if I no longer existed and never had existed. I wanted to fight for my life, but I didn't know how. I wanted to flee, to run, to get away from the client who brought about these feelings. Then the moment passed. As quickly as the feel-ing came over me, it faded away, leaving an in-delible imprint, but leaving all the same.

> *M*any self-injurers claim that feeling anything, even pain, is better than emptiness or nothingness.

Later, I discussed the case with my then-supervisor, first-rate clinician Dr. Paul Margolies, and we explored the implications of that experi-ence. It is awesome, Paul pointed out, that peo-ple are able to deal with feelings like that. For me, it was a fading glimpse, a passing moment. For my client, it was her life, her routine experience. Since then, I've developed a deep respect for those who make it through each day while experiencing such feelings.

My empathetic reaction was nearly identical to the reactions clients with borderline personality disorder describe. Similar to my urge to pinch myself, many self-injurers claim that feeling anything, even pain, is better than emptiness or nothingness. They also describe the feelings of fear and terror, the threat of nonexistence (different from, but clearly related to, a fear of death), and the feelings of ex-treme vulnerability I experienced.

One woman with borderline personality disorder describes her emptiness in the following poem:

Empty
thoughts stopped.
Dreams ended.
Nowhere to go
from here.
Can't make something out of emptiness
except maybe a hole
to toss pent-up feelings into.
But I have no feelings anymore.
Can't think of anything
at all.[11]

Feelings of emptiness are often associated with the extreme behaviors seen in borderline personality disorder. Abandonment fears often peak at times when the person feels empty, so he won't want to be left alone. Desires to commit suicide, drink, take drugs, binge, or act impulsively are often provoked by the overwhelming urge to escape feelings of emptiness.

Criterion 8:
Easily Provoked to Anger

Individuals with borderline personality disorder can be provoked to a fit of rage over things that seem trivial to others. They can react with a level of anger that, to most everyone else, is inappropriate to the situation. For example, Doug, a hospitalized spinally injured client, became enraged, verbally abusive, and violent over something that anyone else would have reacted to with simply a complaint to the hospital's administration.[12]

> *Individuals with borderline personality disorder can be provoked to a fit of rage over things that seem trivial to others. They can react with a level of anger that, to most everyone else, is inappropriate to the situation.*

In general, anger is an emotion that serves several valuable functions for us. It lets us know when someone is mistreating us. It's a visceral response from deep within us saying, "Stop that, you're hurting me, I don't deserve that, knock it off!" There is also a veiled threat in anger, which says, "If you don't knock it off, I'll make you regret it!" It helps us to feel powerful in situations where we might otherwise feel powerless. Anger is related to the "fight" part of the fight-or-flight response and is probably deeply rooted in the fabric of our biology as a mechanism that allowed us to survive when forceful action was required.

Rage, on the other hand, is rarely adaptive, particularly in modern life. In a rage, one is out of control and desperate. It is the response of a cornered animal, fighting for its life, not caring how much damage is done in the process. Anger, properly expressed, is often healthy to a person and her relationships; rage is usually destructive. Rage relates to poor "modulation" of emotions. The individual with BPD is often unable to regulate and tone down the kind of powerful feelings that arise in all people.

As most people mature, they learn to get over their initial emotional reactions to events. But individuals with borderline personality disorder hold on to their "upsetness" long after the event or threat has passed.

Modulation is an essential life skill most people acquire by experiencing soothing responses from others and by observing others who modulate their emotions in difficult circumstances. As most people mature, they learn to get over their initial emotional reactions to events. But individuals with borderline personality disorder hold on to their "upsetness" long after the event or threat has passed.

In addition, it's possible that the person with BPD was either born with an extremely fiery temperament that is difficult to regulate, had poor soothing from others in his early developmental environment, or had poor role models for modulating emotions. Or he could have experienced any combination of these elements.

Criterion 9: Paranoid or Dissociative Symptoms

In this last symptom listed in the *DSM-IV,* individuals with borderline personality disorder who feel overwhelmed by stress can become fearful that others are against them or out to harm them. They can also experience dissociative symptoms—loss of awareness, time, location, or their identity. These symptoms can be extremely distressing. Dissociation can be experienced as "I'm losing my mind" or "I'm having a nervous breakdown." These symptoms are associated with other disorders, such as schizophrenia and dissociative identity disorder (multiple personality disorder), but in borderline personality disorder the symptoms last only a few minutes, a couple of hours, or, less frequently, several days.

One individual with BPD describes a dissociative experience in a poem entitled "Numb":

> Sometimes I forget
> I'm here,
> listening to your filthy words.
> Sometimes I forget
> you're screaming
> so loudly, it makes my ears ring . . .
> But sometimes I remember,
> and it hurts
> again.[13]

As implied in the poem, dissociative disorders are often associated with periods of abuse. Dissociation is an adaptive response by people experiencing something overwhelming that they are powerless to change. A person who is being sexually abused, for example, may "disappear" mentally during the abuse and may even have difficulty remembering it later. If the abuse is mild and infrequent, less harm may result. In addition, individuals who had other validating and supportive relationships are less likely to have long-term harm. For individuals who were more severely abused, who have strong biological dispositions, or had little support, however, dissociation can become a way of coping that becomes deeply ingrained and can later interfere with functioning. In a dissociated

> *Dissociation is an adaptive response by people experiencing something overwhelming that they are powerless to change.*

state, these individuals may not have access to the many other coping skills they have developed over the years. They may act, think, or feel like a young child, while those around them expect adult behavior. Or they may feel they need to act like a child in order to stay safe. Under stress, or in circumstances that remind an individual of a traumatic event, the person becomes prone to dissociation.

Although dissociation may sound strange, it's actually a completely normal and common phenomenon experienced to a lesser degree by everyone. Have you ever been listening to a boring lecture and suddenly realized your mind was elsewhere, such as on your weekend plans, an upcoming date, or the list of things you have to do? Did you miss part of the lecture, even though you were in the room with a perfectly good set of ears? If you answer "yes," then what you had was a dissociative experience. To the extent that such "spacing out" occurs at

---

Why Is the Disorder Called "Borderline"?

Years ago, followers of psychoanalyst Sigmund Freud divided patients' functioning into three different levels: normal, neurotic, and psychotic. The psychotic patient, who was withdrawn, self-absorbed, and out of contact with reality, was considered beyond the reach of psychoanalysis. The neurotic patient, who was anxious or depressed, responded well. Analysts noticed, however, that there were individuals who seemed neurotic but did not fit very well into either the category of neurotic or psychotic, and who did not generally do well in "talking" treatment alone.

Psychoanalyst Adolf Stern is credited with first conceptualizing borderline personality disorder in its present form. In a seminal paper written in 1938, he described what he called the "borderline group of neuroses," indicating that they were at the border between neurosis and psychosis.[14] He described 10 characteristics, many of which are consistent with modern notions of BPD. We no longer think of

inopportune times, extends for several days, or interferes with one's daily life, however, dissociation can be a serious problem.

WHAT CAUSES BORDERLINE PERSONALITY DISORDER?

BPD is caused by a combination of biological, psychological, and social factors. Let us examine each of these separately.

The Biology of Borderline Personality Disorder

Nearly any parent of more than one child knows that noticeable differences are present, practically from the moment of birth. One child was a calm, easy child; another, a fussbudget; the third, a terror. These

borderline personality disorder as indicating a "border" of any kind, but the name has stuck.

Today, we consider borderline personality disorder to be a distinct pattern in its own right. Probably, the most prominent feature of BPD is the emotional roller-coaster that individuals experience. As a result, some prominent theorists have suggested alternative designations: "cycloid," referring to the rapidly cycling emotions, and "erratic," describing the unpredictability of behavior. "Labile-impulsive disorder," which is an accurate and concise description, has also been put forward. Recently, the American Psychiatric Association has engaged in serious discussions about changing the name of the disorder. However, since the next edition of the *Diagnostic and Statistical Manual of Mental Disorders* is not due out until 2010, a name change is unlikely to occur before then. In support of the current designation, the name "borderline" does evoke an image of being "on the edge," which effectively captures part of the borderline phenomenon: the chaotic emotions endured by individuals with the disorder.

inborn characteristics are known as *temperament*. Temperament can be defined as "the individual's constitutional disposition to activity and emotionality."[15] The powerful impact of biology on our interests, talents, predilections, and personality is humorously illustrated in the cartoon below.

The past 10 to 15 years have brought many exciting developments in our understanding of the neurobiology of personality disorders. Despite what parents were observing, not long ago there was virtually no biological study of personality. That's because personality was thought to be a function of the environment—unlike depression, schizophrenia, and other disorders, which were believed to have biological underpinnings.

Separated at birth, the Mallifert twins meet accidentally.

Reprinted with permission from The New Yorker Collection 1981, *Charles Addams, cartoonbank.com.*

This blind spot to the contribution of biology to personality disorders is understandable, from an historical perspective. People in the United States have a strong belief that anyone can be anything he or she wants to be, if the person has the drive, desire, and will. Even our Declaration of Independence—which states that "all men are created equal"—tends to minimize the role of biology in individual differences. John B. Watson, one of the most influential psychologists in U.S. history, once wrote, "Give me a dozen healthy infants, well-formed, and my own specified world to bring them up in and I'll guarantee to take any one at random and train him to become any type of specialist I might select—doctor, lawyer, artist, merchant-chief, and yes, even beggarman and thief, regardless of his talents, penchants, tendencies, abilities, vocations, and race of his ancestors."[16] Watson's position is clear: The environment is the primary determinant of one's life course. Simultaneously, Freud's "psychic determinism" took root. Although Freud was a neurologist, he came to believe that people's problems were primarily rooted in early childhood experience, especially how they were raised by their parents, and how they resolved their early conflicts.

Growing scientific evidence suggests that Freud and Watson overestimated the role of the parents/environment, and underestimated other factors. The data strongly suggest that parents react to children according to their temperaments, as do many others in the individual's environment. Of the portion that cannot be attributed to biology, many factors, such as the child's peer interactions, relationships with teachers and clergy, and cultural factors, play a huge role in shaping the ultimate personality of the individual.

> The belief that biology plays only a minor role in personality is quite mistaken. Scientific evidence is mounting that biological factors are crucial.

In fact, the belief that biology plays only a minor role in personality is quite mistaken. Scientific evidence is mounting that biological factors are crucial. In the words of psychiatrist and personality-disorders expert Dr. Ken Silk:

If a clinician attempts to piece together the origins of any given in-terpersonal behavior or behavioral pattern, current evidence would support perhaps equal or nearly equal contributions from genes and environment, though this balance does not apply equally across all personality traits. Although this approximate 50/50 split provides a Solomon-like answer to an age-old debate, clinicians do not yet have evidence as to how environmental matches, for example the combi-nation of specific traits in a parent or caretaker, can modify, mollify, or exacerbate an inborn trait in an offspring.[17]

It is extremely unlikely that someone with a placid, passive, unen-gaged, aloof temperament would ever develop borderline personality disorder. The individual may develop a personality disorder—perhaps *schizoid personality disorder*—or may not develop a disorder at all. However, to become labile and erratic demands that one have procliv-ities in that direction.

Brain Activity, Brain Anatomy, and Neurological Functioning

The largest portion of the brain is the *cerebrum*, the upper section, where we interpret information coming in from our senses, control voluntary movements, and think. The cerebrum has two halves (the left and right hemispheres), and is divided up into four lobes. The *frontal lobe*, located near the forehead, is involved in consciousness, judgment, planning, emotional responses, voluntary movement, and language. The *parietal lobe*, which is located immediately behind the frontal lobe, is involved in visual attention, touch perception, and sen-sory integration. The *temporal lobe*, which is located underneath the frontal lobe and part of the parietal lobe, controls hearing, memory, and some aspects of categorization. Finally, the *occipital lobe*, which is all the way in the back of the cerebrum, controls vision. A coating of gray matter, called the *cerebral cortex*, covers the cerebrum. Under-neath, the *white matter* holds nerve fibers that transmit messages be-tween gray cells and other nerve centers in the brain and spinal cord. The *prefrontal cortex*, at the front of the cerebrum, controls concentra-tion, planning, and problem-solving. (See figure 1.1.)

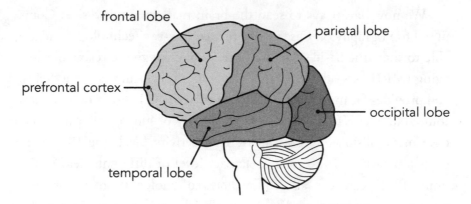

Figure 1.1—*The Brain*

The *limbic system*, located in the center of the brain, is sometimes called the "emotional brain" (see figure 1.2). It consists of the *amygdala*, *hippocampus*, *thalamus*, *hypothalamus*, and parts of the *brain stem*. The hypothalamus is the part of the brain involved in appetite, libido, and sleep; the hippocampus processes and sorts memories, moving them from short-term storage to long-term storage.

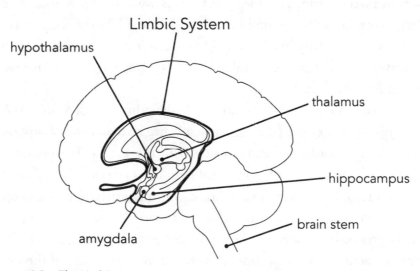

Figure 1.2—*The Limbic System*

We now have ways to scan the brain that are noninvasive. Computed tomography (CT) scans are related to x-ray technology, and are able to show the basic structure of the brain. Magnetic resonance imaging (MRI) uses adjusted radio waves and powerful magnetic fields, and provides far more detailed images than the CT. Positron emission tomography (PET) scans detect the activity of glucose. Because glucose metabolism is a good measure of activity level, the PET scan gives a measure of the relative activity level of different areas of the brain. PET scans can also follow "tagged" molecules to assess their activity; for example, studies using specially tagged serotonin molecules can help illustrate what happens to serotonin in the brain. Unlike other scans, which look at brain *structure*, PET scans look at brain *function* or activity. Using these scans to compare people with borderline personality disorder to those without it, we can determine the structural and activity differences in the brain.

Peter Goyer and his associates studied a group of 17 patients who had a personality disorder diagnosis.[18] Six of the patients had BPD, another six had antisocial personality disorder (which is associated with impulsivity and aggressiveness), and the remaining five had other personality disorders. An auditory stimulus was used to provoke a reaction in the brain, and then PET scans were taken. A moderately large correlation was found between a lifetime history of aggression and reduced activity in the frontal lobes. Later work by Goyer and associates showed that these findings held up when gender and age were taken into account.[19]

More recent work has supported these findings. Paul Soloff, M.D., and his associates used PET scans with five patients with borderline personality disorder and eight healthy controls. He had two conditions for each subject: placebo and fenfluramine (a serotonin-enhancing medication). In the placebo condition, control participants had greater activity in portions of the frontal and temporal lobes compared to the BPD group. In response to fenfluramine, control participants had increased activity in the prefrontal cortex on the right side of the brain and several areas on the left side. In no case was there increased activity in the brains of the subjects with BPD. Soloff concludes concisely, "Patients with BPD have diminished response to serotonergic stimulation in areas of the prefrontal cortex associated with regulation of impulsive behavior."[20]

Further, in a study done by Marco Leyton, Ph.D., and his associates, participants with borderline personality disorder were compared to 11 individuals who had no current or prior psychiatric history using PET scans and MRIs.[21] The individuals in the study were tested with a task that required restraining one's impulses. As expected, the individuals with BPD were significantly more impulsive than the control subjects. Similar to the earlier studies, differences were found, especially in the serotonin-rich areas of the brain. Similar to the findings of Goyer et al., lower levels of brain activity were seen near the frontal lobe area. The authors concluded that low serotonin synthesis capacity in the relevant pathways of the brain may promote impulsive behavior in individuals with borderline personality disorder.

There are also interesting neuroanatomical differences between individuals with and without BPD. Twenty-one women with borderline personality disorder were compared to an equal number of women who had never had a psychiatric disorder.[22] Subjects were matched on several important demographic variables: gender, race, handedness, years of education, and age. In addition, analyses controlled for overall size of the brain, so one cannot conclude that group differences were due to one group being generally smaller or having smaller brains than the other group. The volume of the hippocampus, a part of the brain that is critical for memory, was found to be nearly 16 percent smaller in the borderline group. The average volume of the amygdala (which is related to emotional functioning and social behavior), was over 7.5 percent smaller in the BPD group. The researchers tested whether these differences were related to prior abuse experienced by the individuals with borderline personality disorder.

The evidence was unclear; further research is needed to determine if the smaller hippocampus and amygdala are related to abuse.

In sum, brain-scan studies show that individuals who have difficulty with impulse control and aggression have reduced levels of activity in their brains in a number of key locations. This effect held up, whether one used lifetime history of impulsive or aggressive acts or current impulsivity on an assigned task to define impulsivity. Increases in aggression are associated with a low level of activity in the frontal cortex, as well as reduced activity in several areas within the limbic system. Aggression has also been associated with low levels of serotonin. It is as if the frontal lobes are a fence, and the impulses are a wild horse. If the frontal lobes are impaired—if the fence is too low or too weak—the wild horse will escape. Impulsivity and aggression are also associated with the limbic system, which is involved in the integration of the emotions with sensory information from the environment. The information is then sent to the frontal lobes, which get involved in the interpretation of that data. It is similar to an intelligence operation (spying) for a country. As in spying, accurate data must be gathered, sent to headquarters, and interpreted in order to have an accurate picture of what is happening and to respond appropriately. If a spy takes unwise, impulsive actions, the mission is also imperiled. In the person with BPD, mild to moderate impairments in several systems that are involved in the gathering, delivery, and interpretation of data make mistakes more likely. In chapter 4, we will discuss how medications that increase serotonin levels decrease aggression and impulsivity.

> *Brain-scan studies show that individuals who have difficulty with impulse control and aggression have reduced levels of activity in their brains in a number of key locations.*

Other subtle processing problems have been found, based on four neuropsychological studies of individuals with borderline personality disorder. Consistently, researchers found difficulties with visual discrimination and filtering, and difficulties with recall of complex material. There also appear to be problems in visuomotor integration and figural memory. These problems occur, on average, in a mild to moderate and diffuse way; that is, in most areas of neuropsychological functioning, individuals with borderline personality disorder have normal results. These problems are subtle, and could easily be missed in any given individual. Neurological examinations and EEG studies show a high rate of subtle neurological dysfunction in individuals with BPD.[23]

Thus, brain functioning and learning style may contribute to many of the difficulties that we see in borderline personality disorder. For example, difficulties in visual discrimination and filtering are likely to lead to difficulties interpreting information from the environment. When the person with BPD sees something, he may not be able to select what is important from what is unimportant (poor filtering), which makes the situation confusing. Filtering problems are associated with *field dependence* (being overly influenced by context, rather than one's "internal compass") and having poor boundaries, which are clinical features of borderline personality disorder. Diffuse dysfunction noted in the various studies may also be related to dissociation, which is common in individuals with borderline personality disorder, whether or not they have a history of abuse.

> *Brain functioning and learning style may contribute to many of the difficulties that we see in borderline personality disorder.*

Individuals with BPD have been found to have difficulty with both verbal and visual memory, especially complex material. Difficulty with recall of complex material may make it difficult for people with BPD to learn from their experiences. This is consistent with the clinical observation that many people with BPD make the same mistakes over and over. Information that is not properly encoded will lead to misinterpretations indefinitely. It is like the student who does not properly hear or understand a lesson from class, and dutifully records the misinformation in her notes. She studies for the exam, and is able to produce what she had written in her notes. Of course, however, she still gets the item wrong on the exam. Encoding is a critical element of learning. Memory retrieval problems can lead to similar observed difficulties. In this case, the metaphorical student may have copied the information properly in her notes, but, try though she may, she is unable to recall it. The result on the exam is the same. We do not yet know whether individuals with BPD have difficulty with retrieval, recall, or both; either way, it can create difficulties for the individual, especially if the problem is not recognized. Since memory *seems* to happen automatically, especially in social situations, many people assume that the person who makes certain kinds of errors is being willful, is not listening, or has a variety of character flaws. In fact, it could be that the individual has difficulty processing information. Processing problems can also impact an individual's self-image. Kathleen O'Leary, M.S.W., and Rex Cowdry, M.D., note that "such a memory deficit may contribute to difficulties borderline patients experience in maintaining a continuous sense of self and using the past to respond to present events and predict future consequences."[24]

> *Difficulty with recall of complex material may make it difficult for people with BPD to learn from their experiences. This is consistent with the clinical observation that many people with BPD make the same mistakes over and over.*

Neuropsychological findings regarding individuals with BPD have important treatment implications. O'Leary and Cowdry note:

Regardless of etiology, a psychoeducational approach in treatment may be useful. It may prove therapeutic for a clinician to suggest that cognitive processing problems are part of this disorder, and that a patient may have "misread" a scene or "forgotten" some important elements in a story. As in all psychoeducational approaches that use a biological or neurological framework to understand a disorder, the goal is not to absolve patients of responsibility for their actions or lapses, but rather to increase patients' awareness of their own predilections so that they can cope with their vulnerabilities and change their behavior.[25]

Using strategies such as performing self-ratings, taking notes, and journaling to enhance recall can improve the adjustment of the affected individual. In some cases, a therapist may want to use these strategies with the therapeutic relationship itself. For example, the client might take notes during a session that is tape recorded. The client can then review his notes and compare it to the tape recording. This is laborious and would not be a routine treatment, but this can help to illustrate processing difficulties and misinterpretations in a useful and informative way.

The Role of Psychological Factors

Many psychological factors can enhance the risk of developing borderline personality disorder. The most widely researched or discussed are a history of traumatic abuse, the invalidating environment, and cultural factors.

One of the most compelling facts research has revealed is that adults who have borderline personality disorder usually experienced some form of significant abuse, such as sexual or physical abuse, as a child. Incest and other forms of sexual abuse are particularly implicated. Studies show that approximately two-thirds to three-quarters of people with BPD have a history of being abused sexually.[26] But note that not all people who are sexually abused develop borderline symptoms. And not all people with the disorder have a history of abuse. At this point, the causal connections remain complex.

One of the most recognized theories of how abuse relates to borderline symptoms is Marsha M. Linehan's theory of the "invalidating environment." Invalidation means that someone is telling you that your feelings, thoughts, and perceptions aren't real or don't count. Such invalidation, according to Dr. Linehan, can contribute to

> One of the most recognized theories of how abuse relates to borderline symptoms is the theory of the "invalidating environment." Invalidation means that someone is telling you that your feelings, thoughts, and perceptions aren't real or don't count.

the development of borderline personality disorder. Consider the girl whose interests in mechanical pursuits don't fit society's gender stereotyping, who is punished or told her interests are bad or wrong; or the boy who's told he should be able to control his emotions and that his yearning for nurturance is a show of weakness. Consistent invalidation leads to confusion and poor self-esteem.

Sexual abuse is the ultimate invalidation. Your well-being is irrelevant to the abuser, who is gratifying his or her needs. As described by Dr. Linehan: "Sexual abuse, as it occurs in our culture, is perhaps one of the clearest examples of extreme invalidation during childhood. In the typical case scenario of sexual abuse, the person being abused is told that the molestation or intercourse is 'okay,' but that she must not tell anyone else. The abuse is seldom acknowledged by other family members, and if the child reports the abuse she risks being disbelieved or blamed."[27]

Another form of invalidation connected to abuse occurs when a child does come forward and reports the abuse and is not believed. Evidence suggests that this invalidation may have the most powerful impact of all.

When you encounter someone with borderline personality disorder, it may be tempting to assume his parents were neglectful or abusive and to feel accusatory toward the family. This can be a huge mistake.

The experience of sexual abuse connects many of the symptoms of BPD into a coherent pattern. For example, children who've experienced incest at the hands of a relative at an early age and continuing into their teen years will often use dissociation (criterion 9) to mentally escape from a frightening, confusing situation.

They are also likely to use splitting (criterion 2), in order to continue to have a relationship with the relative. Unable to make sense of the belief that the relative is supposed to love them and is there to protect them (which the adult will often say, and perhaps even delude himself or herself into believing) and the obvious selfishness and one-sidedness of the relationship, children swing between feelings of love and feelings of hate and revulsion. People who've experienced sexual abuse often feel dirty, tainted, and ashamed. This low self-esteem affects their relationships across time, leading to dependency and fear of abandonment (criterion 1), suicidal feelings (criterion 5), and depression (criterion 6).

When you encounter someone with borderline personality disorder, it may be tempting to assume his parents were neglectful or abusive and to feel accusatory toward the family. This can be a huge mistake. As we have seen in this chapter, the biological and environmental risk factors for BPD are varied and complex. Children may have strong biological vulnerabilities to the disorder. Many different environments can give rise to the development of BPD. And many families consist of good parents or caring siblings who have struggled over the years to help the individual with BPD get treatment and develop a stable life. In these cases, it can be the family members who feel traumatized by the process. Borderline personality disorder affects both the individuals with BPD and those who care about them.

> *If we were to design a society most likely to create borderline personality disorder among its citizens, our current American society would be almost ideal.*

Social and Cultural Factors

Evidence shows that borderline personality disorder is increasing in frequency. This may be due, in part, to increased awareness and diagnosis of BPD by clinicians. There are also forces at work that are genuinely increasing the number of new cases. Since our biology has not changed much in the past 50 years, much less 500 years, we must look to social forces as a viable cause. In fact, if we were to design a society most likely to create borderline personality disorder among its citizens, our current American society would be almost ideal.

One of the few constants in today's world is an ever-accelerating pace of change. The majority of American families are affected by this fast pace. In our highly mobile society, it is becoming less likely that children will grow up in one stable environment, in one home, in one city, or even in one family. It is reasonable to call this pace of change "dizzying."

Formerly stable institutions, such as marriage, are no longer so stable. More than 50 percent of marriages end in divorce. Second marriages have an even higher failure rate. Some parents are opting not to marry each other at all. The breakup of parents—married or not—makes it more difficult for the developing child to internalize stable role models. It is not uncommon for a divorcing couple to line up on opposite sides of a courtroom, each painting themselves as all-good and the other as all-bad. The developing child can internalize this kind of real-life splitting. Divorce can also undermine internalized images that would have helped stabilize the growing individual.

Children of divorce may unconsciously wonder: "If my family can be torn apart, what can I count on? Why not just live for the moment? I thought of my parents as being one way, and they turn out to be totally different. How can I trust my impressions of people?" The greater incidence of single-parent families with only one child or families in which children have few siblings has led to a decline in potential support systems. The absence of grandparents, nearby or in the home, is another lost support system. Other institutions that may have corrected instabilities in family life, such as strong neighbor and community ties, are also in decline.

Instead of being stay-home mothers, most women with children are now engaged in full-time careers, either by choice or by economic necessity. But few fathers have chosen to stay home with their children. Where in the past older relatives once stepped in as caretakers, today's families are often devoid of such multigenerational influences and benefits.

Today, children are often raised by an array of "others," including day-care workers, baby-sitters, and aides working in early education programs. Some of these workers are well-educated, while others are young and inexperienced. Some are excellent, while others are insufficient. Some are nurturing, while others are neglectful. But none can truly provide the intense love and close trusting bond of a good parent.

Working parents often come home relatively late, exhausted from workday demands. They have difficulty spending the few precious moments they have with their children providing firm, consistent discipline. Instead, they often assuage their guilt by being lax or lavishing the child with gifts. In some families, both parents are so invested in their careers and pursuits that they come to view their children as inconvenient.

Television and other video media also have a profound impact on personality development. Role models and heroes have become increasingly violent, unstable, and outwardly sexual. Studies have compared two theoretical models of the effects of viewing violence on television and videos: *modeling* refers to the viewer or listener learning and imitating violence; *catharsis* refers to a harmless form of release of preexisting aggressive urges that results from watching or listening to violent programming. The vast preponderance of the evidence supports the modeling hypothesis: People who see more violence behave more violently. It is reasonable to surmise that similar effects will be found for video games. In addition to violence, the influx of sexual images in the media both reflects and furthers society's sexualization.

> *Television and other video media also have a profound impact on personality development. Role models and heroes have become increasingly violent, unstable, and outwardly sexual.*

Finally, emotional shallowness and instability often dominate TV programs. Problems develop and are resolved in 30 to 60 minutes, often as a result of a dramatic, 2-minute confrontation. The sincere expression of feelings and negotiations that comprise real conflict resolution does not happen on TV. It is reasonable to theorize that as our children watch television they are learning how to be impulsive, cynical, sexually unrestrained, explosively angry, and melodramatic—that is, *more borderline*. In the words of Dr. Millon:

> TV may be nothing but simple pablum for those with comfortably internalized models of real human relationships, but for those who possess a world of diffuse values and standards, or one in which

parental precepts and norms have been discarded, the impact of these "substitute" prototypes is especially powerful, even idealized and romanticized. And what these characters and story plots present to vulnerable youngsters are the stuff of which successful half-hour "life stories" must be composed to capture the attention and hold the fascination of their audiences—violence, danger, agonizing dilemmas, and unpredictability, each expressed and resolved in an hour or less—precisely those features of social behavior and emotionality that come to characterize the affective and interpersonal instabilities of the [person with borderline personality disorder].[28]

Another phenomenon pervading American culture that encourages the development of borderline personality behaviors is the "empty self." According to psychologist Philip Cushman: "It is a self that seeks the experience of being continually filled up by consuming goods, calories, experiences, politicians, romantic partners, and empathic therapists in an attempt to combat the growing alienation and fragmentation of its era."[29] Alienated from family and community life, we experience emptiness, loneliness, and meaninglessness—cornerstones of the borderline personality. The answer promoted by powerful forces within our culture is to buy more in order to feel better. Of course, these items never really fill the void, so we continue to experience the emptiness and the drive to fill it. Our national character was once one that valued community. Now, we are a nation that values spending and consuming. Where we were once a society of creators, we are now a society of consumers—impulsive, cynical, depressed, and increasingly enraged by simply waiting—on the road, in line, and online.

In sum, our present culture is a mixed bag. Some of its aspects are healthy. Other aspects are toxic in their encouragement of borderline personality characteristics in our population. Yet, as more people explore values, practices, and lifestyles that enhance inner peace, a sense of maturity and groundedness, a healthy self-image, and a purpose in life, we may as a nation begin to enjoy greater psychological health.

CHAPTER 2

Diagnosis
Looking for Answers

"WHAT'S THE FIRST step?" Carol asked.

"Well, you need to find out if you have borderline personality disorder," said Alexis.

"How do you do that?"

"You could go to a therapist for an evaluation. I went to a psychologist, Dr. Weiss, who was really nice. She gave me some diagnostic tests. I answered a few pages of true-false questions, and then she gave me the inkblot test."

"What was that like?" asked Carol.

"Actually, I kind of got into it," Alexis said. "It was like every answer I gave about the inkblots was important. Dr. Weiss was able to tell all kinds of things about me—that I had difficulty controlling my emotional reactions and my feelings of dependency. She asked me to confirm other things that came out on the tests, like my mood swings and feeling bad about myself. Her questions were so on target. Then she showed me the actual diagnostic manual, with the symptoms of borderline personality disorder. She waited until I'd read it, and then she said, 'Does this sound like you?'"

"How did you feel, Alexis?"

"I felt—understood. And surprised at how close a match the description in the book was to my experience. I also felt, for the first time, like I wasn't alone—I mean if it was in this book, other people must have it, too."

THE PREVALENCE OF BORDERLINE PERSONALITY DISORDER

Other people do have borderline personality disorder—enough people for BPD to be called "a common disorder" among the general population. In fact, it's estimated that at least 2 percent of the general population has BPD, with the reported incidence in women two to three times higher than in men. And up to 15 percent of the population struggles with some aspect of the disorder—nearly one person in seven.[1]

The personality disorder seems to emerge in early adulthood and is characterized by unstable emotions, low self-esteem, impulsiveness, depression, "flying off the handle," and anger. Many of the symptoms of BPD echo the turmoil of adolescence, such as identity problems, existential anguish, poor judgment, risky behavior, pessimism, extreme sarcasm, feelings of emptiness, suicidal thoughts, and rebelliousness alternating with overdependency. Due to these similarities, it's important to evaluate long-term patterns of affect and behavior in diagnosing BPD, especially in young adults.

> It's estimated that at least 2 percent of the general population has BPD, with the reported incidence in women two to three times higher than in men.

For some people with BPD, the illness tends to run its course by middle age. In these cases, individuals with BPD have developed greater impulse control, mature judgment, careers, and stable lives. But for others, the disorder may continue to wreak havoc on their personal and professional lives well into their senior years. Given this possibility and the anguish inherent in the disorder, it's essential that people who think they may have BPD reach out for help from the therapeutic community for diagnosis and treatment.

Why More Women Are Diagnosed with BPD

Several theories seek to explain why women comprise 66–75 percent of BPD diagnoses. Some of these explanations are:

1. Psychosocial factors may make women more vulnerable to the disorder.

2. Biological factors may make women more vulnerable to the disorder.

3. Clinicians can be biased, leading them to diagnose women as borderline and men as antisocial.

4. Women with borderline personality disorder are more likely to come to the attention of mental health practitioners and get diagnosed than are men with BPD.

5. The *DSM-IV* criteria may reflect gender bias.

One explanation for why far more women than men are diagnosed with borderline personality disorder is based on the fact that many individuals with BPD have been sexually abused. In our society, girls are sexually abused far more frequently than boys are. If sexual abuse contributes to causing BPD—and I believe that it does—then differential rates of abuse can explain part of the gender difference in diagnosis. As suggested by Dr. Linehan, sexual abuse is a form of invalidation that can lead to BPD in the biologically predisposed individual.

Women's cultural role and social status may also play a part. In our society, women tend to earn less money and hold less authoritative positions than men. There is strong evidence that socioeconomic status contributes to the development of personality disorders. Likewise, studies have shown that parents' low income, occupational status, and education predicts the development of personality disorders in their children.[2]

This finding is consistent with a study by professor and researcher Lynn Collins, which linked social status to the development of psychological symptoms.[3] Collins showed her classroom students (the research participants) a film of the Stanford Prison Experiment, a brilliant study on the impact of social role on the development of psychopathological symptoms. Researchers in Zimbardo's study randomly placed students at Stanford University into two groups, labeled "guards" and "prisoners." During the experiment, the "guards" became more authoritarian. The "prisoners" became alternately submissive and defiant. In less than a week, the researchers had to terminate the experiment. The guards had become so domineering and abusive that continuing the experiment would have been unethical.[4]

Collins then had her students rate the "prisoners" and "guards" for symptoms of mental disorders from a comprehensive checklist. What they found was that the prisoners exhibited symptoms of depression, anxiety, and helplessness—symptoms traditionally more prevalent in women. Conversely, the guards displayed aggression, arrogance, and other symptoms of antisocial and narcissistic disorders—diagnoses given predominantly to men.

What is especially powerful about this study is that, because both the guards and the prisoners were male, biological differences between men and women could not have been part of the explanation for the findings. In addition, because the students were placed into groups at random, it is unlikely that the way they were raised or other factors explained the differences in the ratings of the guards and the prisoners. The likeliest explanation for their behavior is that their assigned social role influenced their identity and their behavior.

Similarly, there is a powerful argument that the traditional social roles of women, as described, for example, by Juanita Williams and by Beverly Skeggs, have a significant impact on borderline personality development.[5] Because of women's traditionally subordinate role in our culture, they are more prone to anxiety, depression, and feelings of helplessness than men. Similarly, submissiveness and fear of abandonment are more consistent with women's social role than men's.

Another contributing factor in the higher percentage of women diagnosed with BPD is that clinicians are not entirely free from gender biases when making diagnoses. The simplest way to study this phenomenon objectively is to send two case descriptions, which have some ambiguities in what the proper diagnosis should be, to a group of clinicians, changing only the gender in the description, and see how they diagnose the cases.

Researchers Dana Becker and Sharon Lamb sent out two case descriptions that had some features of borderline personality disorder and some features of post-traumatic stress disorder to a gender-mixed group of social workers, psychologists, and psychiatrists. The only difference between the two cases was that one was identified as male, the other as female. The clinicians were asked to rate the case on how closely it matched each of 14 different *DSM-IV* diagnoses. The results were that the cases designated "female" received a higher BPD rating than did the cases designated "male."[6]

It could be that women are more often diagnosed with BPD because those applying the criteria too often do so in a gender-biased manner. This was alluded to by the lead character in the film *Girl, Interrupted*. The movie is based on the true story by Susanna Kaysen about her experience as a young woman diagnosed with borderline personality disorder following a suicide attempt.[7] At one point, she challenges the psychiatrist's diagnosis of her as "promiscuous." She points out to him that if she were male, her sexual behavior would not be considered promiscuous. I believe these kinds of gender-biased judgments play a role in characterizing

> *It could be that women are more often diagnosed with BPD because those applying the criteria too often do so in a gender-biased manner.*

women's behaviors and symptoms as borderline, and failing to apply the same label to men who present similar behaviors and symptoms.

Another reason that women more often receive the diagnosis of BPD is that, in general, women are more likely to seek psychological help for most conditions, especially for depression and anxiety. For men in our culture, asking for help is seen as a sign of weakness or dependence; for women, asking for help bears no such stigma. Therefore, women tend to have a positive view of seeking help, regarding it as an opportunity to connect with another person.[8] It is probable that some of the difference in diagnosis rates between men and women is due to women's greater comfort in going for help, especially with a mental health issue.

Finally, it could be that men who should be diagnosed with borderline personality disorder are not. Men who have highly impulsive behaviors often wind up in the legal system, with a diagnosis of antisocial personality disorder. Recent research with (male) spouse abusers, for example, has found that many meet the criteria for borderline personality disorder.[9]

GETTING AN ACCURATE DIAGNOSIS

Unlike Alexis's positive diagnostic experience described at the beginning of this chapter, not everyone with BPD is so quickly and accurately diagnosed, not everyone gets psychological testing, and not everyone is shown a page in the *DSM-IV*. But at some point, most people who experience the anguish of borderline personality disorder and go to get help for it undergo a diagnostic evaluation of some kind. And, like Alexis, when the result is the correct diagnosis—and the meaning of the diagnosis is properly explained—the client usually feels gratified and validated.

> *Obtaining a proper diagnosis is the first step toward obtaining proper treatment. When the diagnostic process goes awry, improper treatment usually results.*

Obtaining a proper diagnosis is the first step toward obtaining proper treatment. When the diagnostic process goes awry, improper treatment usually results. In her telling autobiography, *Let Me Make It Good*, Jane Wanklin describes a lengthy and harrowing series of misdiagnoses.[10] In 1976, when she was 21 years old, psychiatrists misdiagnosed her with schizophrenia, hospitalized her, and gave her antipsychotic medication. In the hospital, her punishment for "acting out" included the use of physical restraints. Feeling invalidated and overwhelmed, her feelings of desperation grew even worse.

With her undiagnosed and untreated borderline personality disorder raging out of control, Jane spent years going in and out of hospitals, mired in substance abuse, self-injury, and obsessive or ambivalent relationships. She also became bulimic and anorexic. As with many other young women with eating disorders, she was attempting to be "perfect" by attaining the perfect weight and body. With her all-or-none, black-and-white thinking, it went way too far. Watching her life wane away under her self-imposed starvation, she turned back from her suicidal path and decided to give life another chance.

After some 12 years of misdiagnosis, Jane discovered she had borderline personality disorder. Properly diagnosed, she began taking steps towards recovery. It wasn't easy at first. Not everyone reacts well to hearing a diagnosis, even when it comes from a sincere, well-meaning professional. Here's what Jane wrote about the experience:

> One afternoon, a small, dark, delicately featured young woman walked on the ward, carrying a thick folder . . . she introduced herself as Dr. Farida Spencer, the ward psychologist, and fixed me with her large, brown eyes and shy smile. She then informed me that she had the results of my test and what followed was nothing short of a nerve-splitting bombshell.
>
> "Well, you're definitely not schizophrenic. We checked the results several times, and it's been determined that you suffer from an illness known as borderline personality disorder."
>
> I was incredulous. "What the hell kind of label is that to dump on someone? You make me sound like some kind of pathetic joke!" All of a sudden, I no longer had the "prestige" of being safely insane and worthy of a certain amount of quirky "respect." I was now listed as being on some borderline of a ridiculous sham of a "diagnosis" that made me sound insignificant and disgusting. Personality disorder? "You mean, I'm like, just nasty and stupid, with some defect in my basic, fundamental makeup?"
>
> Undaunted, Dr. Spencer continued, saying that the tests showed that I felt empty and devoid of purpose and that out of the checklist of 10 borderline symptoms, I displayed a staggering eight. . . . Some of these included severe depression, suicidal tendencies, drug abuse, eating disorders, cutting, and indications of a certain amount of psychosis.[11]

Jane's reaction, by the way, is a cautionary tale to those of you who might want to share with your loved one that you think he or she may be suffering from borderline personality disorder. (Do note that even though Jane was initially hostile, she accepted the diagnosis by the end of the meeting.) A warning can't be much more forceful than Paul T. Mason and Randi Kreger express it:

> The fantasy goes like this: The person will be grateful to you and go rushing to therapy to conquer their demons. Unfortunately, this doesn't usually happen. Almost everyone we interviewed told us that their loved one instead responded with rage, denial, and a torrent of criticism. Frequently, the possible borderline accused the family member of being the one with the disorder.[12]

My experience is that most people accept the diagnosis very well. I usually present a diagnostic impression, such as "I believe you have borderline personality disorder." Sometimes I show the individual test results, such as the "Borderline" scale of the Millon Clinical Multi-axial Inventory, Third Edition (MCMI-III). I then show the individual the criteria in the *DSM-IV*, and ask, "Does that sound like you?" I cannot recall a bad reaction to this. However, I am a therapist. Ways for you to share your own thoughts with your loved one are discussed in chapter 9, "Family Perspective of Borderline Personality Disorder."

THE DIFFICULTY OF DIAGNOSING BORDERLINE PERSONALITY DISORDER

Jane's experience of being initially misdiagnosed and then of reacting negatively to hearing she had BPD is, unfortunately, not rare. Many people with borderline personality disorder are misdiagnosed.

Personality disorders are complex patterns of behavior, and are inherently difficult to diagnose. Often, the client comes in for an emergency, such as a suicide attempt; the clinician is concerned with stabilizing the individual and may miss the longer-standing personality patterns. In other cases, a person comes in to be treated for an acute disorder such as depression or anxiety, and leaves therapy prematurely, before a diagnosis can be made. Sadly, some clinicians simply are not adequately trained in personality disorders and do not detect them.

Jane's initial contact with the mental health system occurred after a transient psychotic episode, during which she was hearing voices coming out of her stereo. Some individuals with borderline personality disorder may be vulnerable to transient psychotic episodes. Hearing voices, however, is more typically a sign of schizophrenia than of borderline personality disorder. After a time on antipsychotic medications at the hospital, Jane's symptoms cleared up to some degree, and she eventually was sent home. In the mind of the clinician, the most likely scenario was that this person who heard voices had schizophrenia—a logical conclusion. Following the standard treatment for schizophrenia, she became better, though not entirely well, and was discharged. The error is understandable.

In addition to a potential for being confused with schizophrenia, BPD has a high degree of overlap with numerous other disorders, which makes it more difficult to diagnose. According to the *DSM-IV*, borderline personality disorder often coexists with mood disorders, substance abuse, eating disorders, post-traumatic stress disorder, and attention-deficit/hyperactivity disorder. In making a differential diagnosis from other conditions, the clinician is directed to consider six other personality disorders (histrionic, narcissistic, antisocial, schizotypal, dependent, and paranoid; see sidebar, "What Is a 'Personality Disorder'?").

*B*PD has a high degree of overlap with numerous other disorders, which makes it more difficult to diagnose. It often coexists with mood disorders, substance abuse, eating disorders, post-traumatic stress disorder, and attention-deficit/hyperactivity disorder.

REDUCING YOUR RISK OF MISDIAGNOSIS

You can reduce your risk of being misdiagnosed in many ways. One is to meet with a clinician who has experience working with people with personality disorders. Another is to undergo psychological tests that

What Is a "Personality Disorder"?

According to the *DSM-IV*, a personality disorder is defined as "an enduring pattern of inner experience and behavior that deviates markedly from the expectations of the individual's culture, is pervasive and inflexible, has an onset in adolescence or early adulthood, is stable over time, and tends to lead to distress or impairment."[13] Everyone has a personality style. The sine qua non of a personality disorder is that the attitudes and behaviors are inflexible. Most people can modify what they do, depending on the situation, and interpret their environment in accord with the situation. The person with a personality disorder sees things the same way, and demonstrates a narrow range of behavior, much of the time. For example, people with borderline personality disorder may persistently see others as potentially abandoning them, and are very frequently emotionally erratic. Those with narcissistic personality disorder are pervasively arrogant, and often unaware that they are alienating others with their grandiose behavior.

The *DSM-IV* defines a total of 10 personality disorders, as follows:

- *Paranoid personality disorder* is a pattern of distrust and suspiciousness such that others' motives are interpreted as malevolent.

- *Schizoid personality disorder* is a pattern of social detachment and lack of emotional expression.

- *Schizotypal personality disorder* is a pattern of acute discomfort in close relationships, cognitive or perceptual distortions, and eccentricities of behavior.

can improve diagnostic accuracy. Clinicians are properly wary of self-diagnoses by clients based on a book or article they've read. Yet, bringing this book to your session or mentioning that you've read a self-help book on borderline personality disorder and you believe it

- *Antisocial personality disorder* is a pattern of disregard for, and violation of, the rights of others.

- *Borderline personality disorder* is a pattern of instability in interpersonal relationships, self-image, and affects, and marked impulsivity.

- *Histrionic personality disorder* is a pattern of excessive emotionality and attention seeking.

- *Narcissistic personality disorder* is a pattern of grandiosity, need for admiration, and lack of empathy.

- *Avoidant personality disorder* is a pattern of social inhibition, feelings of inadequacy, and hypersensitivity to negative evaluation.

- *Dependent personality disorder* is a pattern of submissive and clinging behavior related to an excessive need to be taken care of.

- *Obsessive-compulsive personality disorder* is a pattern of preoccupation with orderliness, perfectionism, and control.

- *Personality disorder not otherwise specified (NOS)* is used when traits from several different personality disorders are present or the personality pattern is not included in the classification (such as passive-aggressive personality disorder).[14]

Two additional personality disorders are being researched for possible future inclusion in the *DSM-IV.* These are the depressive personality disorder and the passive aggressive personality disorder (also called negativistic personality disorder).

describes you should lead the clinician to, at the very least, consider a BPD diagnosis.

Some clinicians, fearful of stigmatizing a patient, are hesitant to give a diagnosis of borderline personality disorder.

DIAGNOSTIC PROCEDURES

Diagnosis of psychological conditions, similar to the diagnosis of medical conditions, is both an art and a science. In some cases, the diagnosis is clear and simple. In other cases, however, diagnosis can be very tricky, and draws on the skill, experience, and intuition of the diagnostician. Arriving at any personality diagnosis, including BPD, requires gaining an understanding of the client, a process that engages both the mind and the heart of the clinician.

Psychological tests are designed to help the clinician understand the client better. Objective psychological tests are like interviews that are very carefully studied. You should be aware that some clinicians place low emphasis on diagnosis and may even believe that diagnosis has or should have little place in the psychotherapy process. People who have an existential-humanist orientation or who are client-centered therapists may not use personality disorder diagnoses (see chapter 3). They are practicing in a tradition that has very different roots from those that gave rise to the *DSM-IV*. Even though these forms of therapy do not employ *DSM-IV* diagnoses, scientific evidence shows that this type of therapy can be as effective as other forms of therapy for BPD. You should not avoid a therapy merely because it is not concerned with *DSM-IV* diagnosis.

In any case, you will have an easier time finding the best treatment once you've found out that you have borderline personality disorder. Here are some ways you can find out.

The Clinical Interview

Most clinicians rely heavily on interviewing as a means of gaining knowledge about the client. The interview technique works quite well. It tends to be comfortable for both the practitioner and the client. Some people find taking tests frightening because they are not familiar with the tests and do not know what they will reveal. In the clinical interview, practitioners can use the many skills acquired in their training and experience to help the client feel at ease. When I interview a client, I can pace the interview, encourage the client to be more or less revealing, provide her with an opportunity to explain her predicament in her own words, and so on. If all goes well, and it usually does, the client leaves the interview feeling better than when she came in.

Often, it is hard to make a definitive diagnosis of borderline personality disorder, or any other personality disorder, on the basis of one interview. This is because there are various symptoms to consider. I need to take into account all of the symptoms listed in chapter 1, such as frantic efforts to avoid abandonment, intense and unstable interpersonal relationships, identity diffusion, impulsivity, emotional instability, and so on. In addition, many clients will come in and say, "Doctor, I'm feeling depressed." But I have yet to see a client who comes in and says, "Doctor, I have a personality disorder."

It is impossible in a clinical interview to ask every client about every symptom. Therefore, as a clinician, I must follow up leads that the client gives to me. With borderline personality disorder, very powerful clues include a history of self-injury or suicide attempts. Also, if the person has problems with substance abuse, I ask about other possible symptoms of borderline personality disorder, just in case. If the person has none of those symptoms, I must discern the more subtle patterns of relationships (intense and unstable), feelings (such as rage and fear), and behaviors (impulsivity, for example) that define the disorder.

In making a proper diagnosis, there are many nuances. For example, Betty, a former client, used to ride her bicycle late at night into unsafe neighborhoods in order to purchase stolen jewelry. Is this a self-damaging, impulsive act? Is this thrill-seeking? Does it provide her with income from selling the jewelry? Or was this young woman's risk-taking an attempt to elicit attention and concern, perhaps from her parents? Before I make an accurate diagnosis, I must ferret out the meaning of the symptoms and make sure they fit the criteria. In Betty's case, her risky actions were so self-endangering and self-destructive that her parents placed her in a hospital. I did not have a sufficient number of sessions to make a definitive diagnosis, but I believed that borderline personality disorder was likely.

The biggest problem with relying solely on the clinical interview is the risk of missing something important in the client's history. Once the clinician is "on the trail" of a diagnosis, it becomes likely he or she will get it right, but it is also possible to overlook a diagnosis. When a clinician learns that a client suffers from depression, he or she may begin to treat it and fail to discover that the person has, in addition, an anxiety disorder, post-traumatic stress disorder, and/or a personality disorder.

The current managed care environment, unfortunately, encourages "quick-and-easy" approaches. Usually, the client comes in complaining of depression, anxiety, or substance abuse. A managed care organization may approve only four to ten sessions to try to treat the problem. Often, personality disorders are not covered. Therefore, the clinician is pushed to define a particular problem narrowly, treat it, and discharge the client. Although insurance companies claim to be saving money, it is often more expensive to treat narrow symptom patterns, such as depression, over and over, than it is to treat the personality disorder itself. Suicidal behavior, with its trips to the emergency room, can be very expensive.

Psychological Tests That Aid Diagnosis and Treatment

In part because of the limitations of clinical interviews, psychological tests have been developed to increase the accuracy and validity of diagnoses. Most psychological tests used by clinical psychologists help determine a diagnosis and evaluate areas of concern. A client's strengths and skills can also emerge through these tests.

Psychological tests fall into two broad categories: *objective* tests and *projective* tests. Objective tests are generally designed in true-false or rating-scale formats. For example, an objective test might present the statement "I feel sad and blue most of the time" and ask you to respond "true" or "false," or to rate the item on a 5-point scale (ranging from "completely true" or "somewhat true" to "false" or "somewhat false").

The MCMI-III, and the Minnesota Multiphasic Personality Inventory are examples of objective tests, and are discussed in detail in this chapter.

Projective tests use ambiguous material that the client is asked to interpret. The interpretation you, as the client, give illustrates how you look at the world. The most famous projective test is the Rorschach Inkblot Test. Other projective tests include the Thematic Apperception Test (TAT) and various figure drawings.

Some people find taking projective tests anxiety provoking because the material is unfamiliar. They may be concerned about what the tests will reveal about them. Others become intrigued for exactly the same reason. The individual's approach to the test itself provides important clinical information. Openly discussing your concerns with the examiner is important and can be helpful in the ultimate success of your testing and treatment.

> *Most psychological tests used by clinical psychologists help determine a diagnosis and evaluate areas of concern. A client's strengths and skills can also emerge through these tests.*

Throughout this section, you may notice that I sometimes use the term "psychologist" rather than "clinician." This is because only psychologists are licensed to administer most of the standard psychometric tests. Many different practitioners can administer some exams, such as vocational interest inventories. Diagnostic tests that involve personality disorder, anxiety, and depression, for example, often can only legally be interpreted by clinical psychologists with doctoral degrees.

When taking a psychological test, it is helpful to be open and honest. Go with your gut and say the first thing that comes to mind. The tests help to speed up the process of getting to know you, and they increase the odds of covering all the bases. Keep in mind that spending the few minutes to a couple of hours to complete some tests can make your entire treatment more effective and helpful to you.

Millon Clinical Multiaxial Inventory

The Millon Clinical Multiaxial Inventory, Third Edition (MCMI-III), developed by Theodore Millon, Ph.D., consists of 175 true-false items and requires about 25 minutes to complete. In addition to assessing personality disorders, it also evaluates depression, anxiety, post-traumatic stress disorder, and mania, among other conditions.

The MCMI-III can also give the clinician information about many subtle variations of borderline personality disorder. For example, some individuals with BPD are very dependent on others, relying on them to make important decisions about their life. Although they may feel ambivalent about this dependence, they nonetheless feel helpless and anxious when alone.

Others with borderline personality disorder manifest independence. Their primary emotion is anger, not helplessness or depression. They evince a tough exterior and a devil-may-care attitude. In this instance, the MCMI-III shows the clinician different possible mixtures of personality disorder features: borderline plus dependence in the former case; and borderline plus antisocial in the latter. This diagnostic test can also help the clinician distinguish between disorders in which the differences are subtle, such as post-traumatic stress disorder versus borderline personality disorder, or a major depression versus the milder and more chronic dysthymic disorder.

Minnesota Multiphasic Personality Inventory

The Minnesota Multiphasic Personality Inventory, Second Edition, (MMPI-2) is a 567-item true-false test, which takes an hour to 90 minutes to complete. The MMPI-2 provides the clinician with similar information as that of the MCMI-III. In addition to its diagnostic value, the test also reveals one's ability to tolerate stress, as well as other tendencies and proclivities. During my graduate training, I showed an MMPI profile (the printout of the scale scores, set up as a graph) of a 16-year-old boy to my supervisor. He reviewed the profile and said, "Rebellious type?" I nodded. "Wears an earring?" he continued. I nodded again. Back in the mid-1980s, earring-wearing boys were pretty rare, so for him to have seen that in the profile was impressive. The supervisor went on to describe the likely major issues in this boy's life and potential ways to create a rapport with him—all of which were uncannily accurate. This is an example of how immensely helpful the information provided by the MMPI-2 can be.

The Rorschach Inkblot Test

The famed Rorschach test, published in 1921 by Hermann Rorschach, consists of 10 inkblots. You are asked only one question: "What might this be?" You then describe to the psychologist what you see. The process is akin to the game of describing what one sees in the billowing image of a cloud in the sky.

By looking at the pattern of your answers, psychologists can infer various characteristics and possible conditions. People with depression, mania, anxiety, personality disorders, and other conditions tend to give particular kinds of responses, which have been catalogued for comparison purposes. The test also detects positive attributes, such as complex thinking and problem solving. By seeing patterns in the answers, the psychologist can determine areas of strength and weakness.

> The Rorschach test is, and always has been, controversial. Yet, experienced clinicians can extract important and useful information from it, sometimes in a manner that is uncanny.

The Rorschach test is, and always has been, controversial. Yet, experienced clinicians can extract important and useful information from it, sometimes in a manner that is uncanny. I like the Rorschach test because it helps me to see the world the way the client does. I almost always find at least some, and often a great deal of, information that is accurate and useful. The Rorschach test also helps raise questions that I can then discuss with the client. In addition, as the Rorschach is both ambiguous and novel, it helps me discover how someone handles new situations.

Thematic Apperception Test

The TAT (Thematic Apperception Test), developed by the great American psychologist Henry Murray, consists of a series of cards with pictures on them. You are asked to make up a story about each card. The stories you tell illustrate to the examiner how you see the world.

Unlike the Rorschach test, there is no established scoring system for the TAT. The content of the stories is the source of the valuable information in this test. Like the Rorschach, the TAT not only provides diagnostically useful information, it is also a good indicator for themes to discuss in therapy.

Structured Interviews and Clinician Rating Scales

Structured interviews are generally considered the best diagnostic instruments in the field. In order to show that a researcher's sample gen-

---

Test Yourself: Do You Have Borderline Personality Disorder?

Answer the following statements as true or false:

1. I often become terrified that people close to me will leave me.

2. My relationships are really intense, involving a lot of passion, anger, or both.

3. I have cut or injured myself in response to feeling stressed out or depressed.

4. I have a history of changing my ideas about who I am going to be, such as changing to completely different jobs, completely different ways of dressing, or changing my major in college many times.

5. I get angry, or even furious, more easily than most people do.

6. Many times I have done things without thinking about them first that have gotten me into trouble, such as taking drugs, spending too much money, or having sex with someone I barely know.

7. Sometimes I feel empty inside.

8. I can love someone one minute and hate them the next.

9. I don't really know who I am.

10. I tend to do risky things on the spur of the moment.

uinely consists of people with borderline personality disorder, a structured interview is generally considered the most accurate and reliable form of assessment. The most commonly used structured interviews for personality disorders include the SCID-II (Structured Clinical Interview for *DSM* Axis-II), the SIDP-IV (Structured Interview for Diagnosing Personality Disorders, *DSM-IV* Edition), and the Personality Disorder Examination (PDE).[15] The Diagnostic Interview for Borderline Patients (DIB) is specifically designed for individuals with borderline personality disorder.[16] Structured interviews generally take

11. I have made one or more suicide attempts or serious gestures (such as cutting my wrists or taking an overdose).

12. My mood can change from minute to minute, from being depressed to being just fine or even on top of the world, or from being nervous to being completely confident.

13. When I think somebody close to me is going to leave me for good, I'll do anything to keep them involved with me.

14. I have to admit I can be pretty moody.

15. Sometimes I feel as if I don't even exist, as if I have to pinch myself to know that I am here.

16. I have a hot temper.

17. Sometimes I blank out or space out, and forget a block of time for a number of hours, even when I'm not on drugs or alcohol.

18. Sometimes I feel like I can't trust anyone, and that people are just looking for ways to hurt me or trip me up.

Scoring: Score one point for each "true" response. The higher your score, the more likely it is that you may have borderline personality disorder. This "test" has not been scientifically validated. In a clinical interview, however, I would consider a client with a score of 9 or more—meaning they answered "true" 9 or more times—as likely to have borderline personality disorder.

about 45 to 90 minutes to administer. They have an enormous advantage over unstructured interviews: The clinician asks all of the relevant questions, and therefore does not neglect any important areas. As previously discussed, the greater risk is usually that a clinician will overlook an important area, not that they will misinterpret the symptoms that they see.

Currently, using structured interviews is not standard practice. I rarely use them. The main reason, at least for me, is that I like to create as personal an environment as I can for my clients when I first meet them. While having a client fill out a form in a waiting room is one thing, it is another to spend our entire first meeting reading questions to them. In research, however, the use of structured interviews is very common, in order to maximize the odds of making an accurate diagnosis. Nonetheless, whether you receive testing or a structured interview when you go to your therapist, you should consider yourself fortunate. The information provided is invaluable.

COEXISTING CONDITIONS

Several conditions occur much more frequently in people with borderline personality disorder than they do in the general population. These are called coexisting, or comorbid, conditions in the medical/psychological literature. Depression and anxiety disorders (including post-traumatic stress disorder) are common in people with BPD. There are several theories about why this is so. One theory is that the personality disorder precedes the depression or anxiety, and makes a person more vulnerable to it. In another theory, the conditions are all related, perhaps at a biological level; some of the same biological substrates that lead to depression, perhaps, are those that lead to emotional instability in BPD, and therefore the two conditions will coexist with some regularity. A third theory is that having a personality disorder shapes the course of depression and anxiety, making them more severe or making them last longer.[17] Each of these is presumably true to some degree. Whatever the reason for their frequent covariation, it is important to look at depression and anxiety in a discussion of borderline personality disorder.

Depression

If you have borderline personality disorder, chances are you know what it feels like to be depressed. Symptoms of depression include feeling sad and blue, loss of usual interest and pleasure in activities you once enjoyed, loss of energy, and changes in sleeping patterns. Before you can be confident that one of the treatments below will help you, you need to know you have depression, or at least some of its symptoms.

If you are feeling depressed, you are in good company. According to the *DSM-IV*, about 5 to 25 percent of all people in the United States will have at least one bout of major depression in their lifetime. At any given moment, about 20 million people are experiencing major depression. When all of the different kinds of depression described below are added up, this number could easily double. The total cost of depression in this country, including the cost of treatment and lost productivity (such as losing time from work), adds up to roughly $43 billion per year.

For people with borderline personality disorder, the rates of depression are much higher. According to a literature review on the frequency of comorbid conditions with borderline personality disorder, 24 to 87 percent of individuals with borderline personality disorder have affective disorders as well.[18] If you have borderline personality disorder, your chance of having a bout of serious depression at some point in your life is very high.

The *DSM-IV* lists six kinds of depression:

Major depression is an acute, severe depression. I have seen people with major depression who barely got out of bed, often for several weeks or longer. Many people are not aware there are physical signs of depression. These signs include difficulty sleeping and eating too much or too little. (See sidebar, "Criteria for Major Depressive Episode.")

Dysthymic disorder is milder but more chronic than major depression. In dysthymic disorder, the person experiences a depressed mood most of the time for a minimum of two years.

Seasonal affective disorder is a type of depression that hits in the winter, when there are low levels of sunlight. An effective treatment is to expose the individual to full-spectrum artificial light

Criteria for Major Depressive Episode

A. Five (or more) of the following symptoms have been present during the same 2-week period and represent a change from previous functioning; at least one of the symptoms is either depressed mood or loss of interest or pleasure.

❏ Depressed mood most of the day, nearly every day, as indicated by either subjective report (e.g., feels sad or empty) or observation made by others (e.g. appears tearful). Note: In children and adolescents, can be irritable mood.

❏ Markedly diminished interest or pleasure in all, or almost all, activities most of the day, nearly every day (as indicated by either subjective account or observation made by others).

❏ Significant weight loss when not dieting or weight gain (for example, a change of more than 5 percent of body weight in a month), or decrease or increase in appetite nearly every day. Note: In children, consider failure to make expected weight gains.

❏ Insomnia or hypersomnia nearly every day.

❏ Psychomotor agitation or retardation nearly every day (observable by others, not merely subjective feelings of restlessness or being slowed down.

❏ Fatigue or loss of energy nearly every day.

that emulates sunshine; this is called phototherapy or light therapy. Other antidepressant therapies, such as those covered in chapters 3 and 4, are also effective for SAD.

Adjustment disorder with depressed mood is what we used to call *reactive depression*, when something stressful or overwhelming happens in your life and you become depressed.

❑ Feelings of worthlessness or excessive or inappropriate guilt (which may be delusional) nearly every day (not merely self-reproach or guilt about being sick).

❑ Diminished ability to think or concentrate, or indecisiveness, nearly every day (either by subjective account or as observed by others).

❑ Recurrent thoughts of death (not just fear of dying), recurrent suicidal ideation without a specific plan, or a suicide attempt or a specific pan for committing suicide.

B. The symptoms do not meet the criteria for a mixed [manic-depressive] episode.

C. The symptoms cause clinically significant distress or impairment in social, occupational, or other important areas of functioning.

D. The symptoms are not due to the direct physiological effects of a substance (e.g., drug abuse, a medication) or a general medical condition (e.g., hypothyroidism).

E. The symptoms are not better accounted for by bereavement, e.g., after the loss of a loved one, the symptoms persist for longer than 2 months or are characterized by marked functional impairment, morbid preoccupation with worthlessness, suicidal ideation, psychotic symptoms, or psychomotor retardation.[19]

Bipolar disorder, which is also called *manic-depression*, is characterized by alternation between periods of depression and periods of
extreme excitement or irritability, called manic episodes. It is estimated that bipolar disorder affects about 1 percent of the population, or about 3 million people.

Cyclothymic disorder is like bipolar disorder on a diet. There are
mood swings, but they are much less extreme than in bipolar disorder. Individuals alternate between feeling they are on a natural
high and feeling very depressed.

One good way to find out if you are depressed is to take a stan-
dardized test. A well-known, widely used test is the Center for Epidemiologic Studies-Depressed Mood Scale, also called the CES-D.

A score of 16 suggests the presence of depression. At least one study
shows that a score of 34 suggests a rather severe depression.[20] Please
use this scale only as a helpful guide; you should not self-diagnose depression, but rather should seek professional consultation if you suspect you have depression on the basis of your test results.

Anxiety

Anxiety can be described as "feeling nervous." Although people may
think of depression as being the most common mental health problem, anxiety disorders are actually more prevalent. According to the
National Institute of Mental Health's Epidemiologic Catchment Area
study in 1993, during a 1-year period, 12.6 percent of the population,
or 23.2 million people, had anxiety disorders (compared to 17.5 million with depression). As with depression, the rate of anxiety disorders is much higher in people with borderline personality disorder. In
a study of 504 inpatients with personality disorders, conducted at
Harvard by Mary Zanarini, Ed.D., and her associates, 88.4 percent of
379 patients with borderline personality disorder simultaneously had
an anxiety disorder.[21]

There are many types of anxiety listed in the *DSM-IV:*

Center for Epidemiologic Studies-Depressed Mood Scale (CES-D)

Using the scale below, indicate the number which best describes how often you felt or behaved this way—DURING THE PAST WEEK.

0 = Rarely or none of the time (less than 1 day)
1 = Some or a little of the time (1–2 days)
2 = Occasionally or a moderate amount of the time (3–4 days)
3 = Most or all of the time (5–7 days)

_____   1. I was bothered by things that usually don't bother me.
_____   2. I did not feel like eating; my appetite was poor.
_____   3. I felt that I could not shake off the blues even with help from my family or friends.
_____   4. I felt that I was just as good as other people.
_____   5. I had trouble keeping my mind on what I was doing.
_____   6. I felt depressed.
_____   7. I felt that everything I did was an effort.
_____   8. I felt hopeful about the future.
_____   9. I thought my life had been a failure.
_____ 10. I felt fearful.
_____ 11. My sleep was restless.
_____ 12. I was happy.
_____ 13. I talked less than usual.
_____ 14. I felt lonely.
_____ 15. People were unfriendly.
_____ 16. I enjoyed life.
_____ 17. I had crying spells.
_____ 18. I felt sad.
_____ 19. I felt that people disliked me.
_____ 20. I could not get "going."

Scoring: Add up the score for all items except 4, 8, 12, and 16. Items 4, 8, 12, and 16 are scored "backwards"—if you rated it a 3 when you took the test, give yourself 0 points, if you rated it a 2, give yourself 1 point, if you rated it 1, give yourself 2 points, and if you rated it 0, give yourself 3 points. Total these and add them to the rest of your scores.

A score of 16 or higher suggests depression; a score of 34 or higher suggests a rather severe depression.

Source: National Institute of Mental Health

Generalized anxiety disorder indicates feelings of restlessness and tension that pervade a person's life. The key feature of generalized anxiety disorder is that, although the person feels nervous and worried, there is usually no specific target or event that is the focus of the anxiety. For example, it's not that the person just worries when there is a big presentation at work—the person worries all the time. At any given moment, about 3 percent of the population has generalized anxiety disorder.

Phobias, on the other hand, are extremely focused and specific fears. Social phobia, also called social anxiety disorder, is an extreme fear of embarrassment that leads to avoidance of social situations. Agoraphobia is a fear of places where escape may be difficult (such as crowded places, public transportation, bridges, or elevators) or where help may not be available if one has a panic attack (as in being home alone). Specific phobias are fears of specific situations or objects, such as fear of closed-in places (claustrophobia), spiders (arachnophobia), or heights (acrophobia). The famous Hitchcock movie *Vertigo* dramatizes a case of acrophobia. Phobias are relatively prevalent, and as many as one in 10 people will experience a phobia in their lifetime.

Obsessive-compulsive disorder is often marked by people engaging in repetitive actions, which they know are irrational or unnecessary, as a means of relieving or avoiding anxiety. Common examples are repetitive hand-washing and repeatedly checking door locks to be sure they are locked and appliances to be sure they are turned off. Obsessive-compulsive disorder, relatively rare, can be quite complex to treat; it often involves both behavior therapy and medication.

Post-traumatic stress disorder (PTSD) is the response to an overwhelming or terrifying event, and includes nightmares, flashbacks (re-experiencing the event while awake), and avoidance of experiences that remind you of the event. The individual also generally experiences a high level of arousal, a feeling of being on edge, which may manifest itself as problems sleeping or an exaggerated startle response. Although PTSD is probably best known as an affliction among soldiers as a result of their war experiences, it can occur in civilian life following assault, rape, or environmental disasters, such as floods and hurricanes. If you experienced sexual or physical abuse, you may have chronic symptoms of PTSD. It is estimated that approximately one person in eight will experience PTSD at some point in his or her life.

Panic attack is a sudden, unexpected fear, accompanied by a number of bodily responses, which may include rapid heart rate, dizziness, chills or hot flushes, and pain or heaviness in the chest. The person having a panic attack may feel that he or she is losing control or "going crazy," that nothing is real, and that there is a sense of impending doom or an urge to flee. When experiencing their first panic attack, most people think they are having a heart attack, and they fear they are about to die. Panic attacks, especially when they are severe and chronic, can cause other problems. The sufferer may try to control panic attacks by avoiding places where the panic attacks occur, learning to avoid one place after the next, until finally the person is almost homebound with agoraphobia.

Many medical conditions cause anxiety or symptoms similar to anxiety. Some of these conditions include emphysema, heart disease, thyroid conditions, pheochromocytoma (an adrenal gland tumor), vertigo, menopause, and epilepsy. Also, the use of stimulants (cocaine or speed), yohimbe (an aphrodisiac), alcohol, antihistamines, or steroids can cause anxiety symptoms. It is best to have a medical examination to rule out these problems before concluding that your self-diagnosis of anxiety is accurate.

One other factor to consider is caffeine use. I have seen countless patients who describe having insomnia, trembling hands, and nervousness. When I ask them about caffeine use, some report drinking

The Hamilton Anxiety Scale

Rate each item from 0 to 4.

0 = Absent
1 = Mild (less than 50% of the time or causes little interference)
2 = Moderate (more than 50% of the time or causes moderate interference)
3 = Severe (substantial or marked interference more than 50% of the time)
4 = Extremely Severe (as bad as could be, very disabling)

_____ Anxious mood (worry, irritability, apprehensiveness)
_____ Tension (startle, crying, fatigue, trembling, unable to relax, restlessness)
_____ Phobic fear (such as of strangers, being alone, animals, traffic, crowds, other situations)
_____ Insomnia (difficulty falling or staying asleep, disturbing dreams, tired on waking)
_____ Poor concentration or memory
_____ Depression (low mood, low interest, less pleasure, waking early)
_____ Muscle symptoms (aches, stiffness, pain, jerks, grinding teeth, unsteady voice)
_____ Sensory symptoms (ringing in ears, blurred vision, hot or cold flashes, weakness, tingling)
_____ Heart symptoms (racing, skipping, pounding, chest pressure, choking, sighing, can't catch breath)
_____ Abdominal symptoms (stomach pain, nausea, rumbling, heartburn, loose bowels, constipation, sinking feeling)
_____ Urinary and sexual symptoms (frequent or urgent urination, lower sexual desire, orgasm problems, erectile problems, premature ejaculation)
_____ Autonomic symptoms (flushing, paleness, light-headedness, headaches, goose bumps, sweating)
_____ Restlessness

Scoring: Add your score from each item to get a total score.
What your score means:

0–10: minimal anxiety (self treatment is appropriate)
11–20: mild to moderate anxiety (may need professional help)
Over 20: moderate to severe anxiety (professional help is advisable)

Source: Adapted from M. Hamilton, "The Assessment of Anxiety States by Rating." _The British Journal of Medical Psychology,_ 32, 50–55. © The British Psychological Society. Reprinted with permission.

the equivalent of one to two pots of coffee per day! Weaning the person down to one cup in the morning and another in the early afternoon, and eliminating all caffeine after about 4:00 P.M. often solves the problem. For some people, other caffeine-containing items are the culprits; chocolate and most teas contain a good deal of caffeine. A good hot-drink alternative is caffeine-free herbal tea.

For the purposes of this book, the most critical factor is not which kind of anxiety you may have, but to determine if you have anxiety and to look at remedies that may be helpful. The Hamilton Anxiety Scale is a good tool to help you to identify your level of anxiety.

CHAPTER 3

Psychotherapy

How many therapists does it take to change a light bulb?
Just one, but the light bulb really has to want to change.

A new era has begun in which the treatment of borderline
patients can be undertaken with both more optimism and more
appreciation for the effectiveness of multiple modalities.

—*JOHN GUNDERSON, M.D., AND PAUL LINKS, M.D.*[1]

THE MAIN TREATMENT for borderline personality disorder is psychotherapy, which offers real hope of learning to live life in a new way. The disorder has been linked with certain biological factors and genetic predispositions, which interact with learning and other environmental factors. And so, the therapeutic process is often supplemented with medications, such as antidepressants and other biological interventions.

But does psychotherapy for borderline personality disorder really work? A recent review of the scientific studies that focused on information a consumer would want to know—such as the decrease in the symptoms and the rate of recovery from personality disorders—is very encouraging.[2] The researchers reviewed 15 outcome studies and combined the findings (approximately 50 percent of the total sample had borderline personality disorder, and the remainder had a mixture of other personality disorders). This procedure, called meta-analysis, is more accurate than considering the results of any one study. An individual study can reflect special characteristics of a particular sample (such as a small group of people who were more motivated than average) or the special prowess of a particular therapist or two. But when scientists look at a number of studies simultaneously, the patterns that emerge are more likely to be the kind of outcome you can expect.

The review found that psychotherapy resulted in large improvements in clinician ratings of client functioning, such as whether the client was suicidal, able to function at work, or was in touch with reality. Improvements were approximately as large on client self-report scales, which rate improvement in depression, anxiety, contact with reality, and other important issues.

> *A recent review found that psychotherapy resulted in large improvements in clinician ratings of client functioning, such as whether the client was suicidal, able to function at work, or was in touch with reality.*

What if you decide not to seek treatment? How big a difference does therapy really make? In what was perhaps the most interesting part of their research review, the scientists calculated the rate of improvement in the therapy studies with those of "natural history" studies. Natural history studies do not include an intervention, such as therapy; the study simply takes measurements over a period of years. It is a safe bet that participants with borderline personality disorder were receiving some kind of therapy, but we do not know exactly what. They may have received only some inpatient therapy following suicidal behavior, or perhaps some outpatient therapy or counseling.

The comparison review found that for each year 3.7 percent of the "natural history" group recovered, and 25.8 percent of the psychotherapy group recovered. In other words, with specialized treatment, approximately seven times as many people recovered with treatment as without. Also, more of the recovery occurred early on.

After 1.3 years of treatment, 50 percent of the treated group had recovered (compared to the 10.5 years it took for the natural history group to achieve a 50 percent recovery). After 2.2 years, 75 percent of the treated group had recovered (compared to 17.3 years in the natural history group). In other words, without treatment, it takes 5 to 7 times as long to recover from BPD.

In this case, "recovered" means that the individual no longer meets the *DSM-IV* criteria for the disorder. For example, someone who had six symptoms—but now has four—is considered "recovered." However, this does not mean psychotherapy has nothing more to offer them, nor does it mean the individual is "cured." Nevertheless, moving from the category of being diagnosable with six *DSM-IV* criteria for BPD to not being diagnosable with only four symptoms marks the individual's progress and the therapy's success.

> *A good estimate of the amount of time you'll need in therapy if you have borderline personality disorder is about 2 years.*

The research review also points to an estimate of how long the individual with borderline personality disorder may need to stay in therapy, which is about 2 years. (The scientific studies reflect a slightly more positive outcome than what might actually occur in treatment. An average of 21 percent of participants in the scientific studies dropped out, and it is likely that these individuals would have been the ones to meet with poorer-than-average results, had they finished the study.) Some individuals may take longer to recover, while others see substantial benefits after such short-term treatment as 6 months to a year. Some of those people return to therapy later, benefiting even more from extensive, intensive, or thorough treatment.

TYPES OF PSYCHOTHERAPY

There are many different types of psychotherapy. In this chapter, I describe the main schools of thought and what you can expect from them, along with scientific data. My goal is to provide information that can help you select the best treatment for you. No one therapy is right for everyone. Don't be discouraged if you tried psychotherapy before, and it didn't work. Try again. Perhaps a different approach would be helpful. Even with similar approaches, one therapist may connect with you better than another. Never is the saying more apt: If at first you don't succeed, try, try again.

In this regard, borderline personality disorder is no different from some medical diseases. Many people with diabetes, arthritis, or other chronic conditions who cannot tolerate a particular medication find relief with another medication, or they try other medical treatments before discovering that regular exercise and yoga bring relief. What's the difference between those who succeed in gaining relief and those who don't? Many times, the key is hope. Those who have hope that they will ultimately recover ultimately do—not so much because they hope they will, but because they keep trying treatments until they find one (or more) that works.

> Ultimately, the relationship between therapist and client is collaborative. Both of you share the goal of helping you to get well.

As you read this chapter, consider which approach is most comfortable for you or most consistent with your own. Go with your gut. Ask your therapist questions to assess whether you are right for one another. Consider the student-teacher relationship, for example: It's not enough to have a good teacher, unless the student makes a good effort to learn as much as possible. So, make a commitment to find a good therapist, then do your best to learn as much as possible during each session. Ultimately, the relationship between therapist and client is collaborative. Both of you share the goal of helping you get well. Later in the chapter, I offer pointers on spotting potential pitfalls, as well as maximizing the positives in the therapeutic relationship.

Dialectical Behavior Therapy

Dialectical behavior therapy (DBT) is the brainchild of clinical psychologist Marsha M. Linehan, Ph.D., whose original interest was in

Psychotherapies

Psychodynamic: Focuses on your early relationships, as well as your inner conflicts (especially how they manifest themselves in your relationship with the therapist).

Cognitive-Behavioral: Helps you to change your negative feelings by challenging your negative thoughts, and building new and productive skills and behaviors.

Client-Centered: Built on the premise that the power to heal rests within the person. The therapist's main task is to create an environment within which the client's natural healing emerges. The therapist is generally warm and empathic in order to facilitate healing.

Family Systems: Family therapists assume that the best way to help someone heal is to engage the whole family. They generally focus on relationships and interaction patterns.

Group: Skill-building groups tend to be educational in nature and lead to the acquisition of new skills (such as assertiveness or mindfulness). Process groups focus on interactions among the group members and tend to lead to insights about how we affect one another.

people who were suicidal. The program is called "dialectical" because Dr. Linehan noticed certain paradoxes in treatment. For example, a therapist must accept a client as she or he is, initially. On the other hand, the therapist also works to help the client change. But how can your therapist want you to change, even as she accepts you as you are? It's a paradox, and resolving these seemingly contradictory efforts is how the therapeutic process moves forward.

In this case, the client and the therapist join together against borderline personality symptoms to resolve the paradox. This is one of

DBT's greatest keys to success. In philosophy, a dialectic is when opposites (such as acceptance and need for change) move together over time. This is why Dr. Linehan chose to name her treatment for BPD dialectical behavior therapy.

Of all the treatments for borderline personality disorder, the one that has probably generated the most excitement is DBT, which is a highly specific form of treatment for BPD. The data supporting DBT is very encouraging. In studies, people with borderline personality disorder treated with DBT reduced their rates of suicide attempts, parasuicidal behavior (that is, suicidal gestures, such as superficial cuts on the wrist, indicating the person does not want to die), depression, substance abuse, and binge eating.[3] In addition, dropout rates from DBT groups are much lower than for other treatments. One study found that after one year's treatment, only 16 percent of clients dropped out of DBT in comparison to about 58 percent of clients who left standard treatment.[4] In another study by Dr. Linehan, DBT was more successful in reducing borderline symptoms than standard treatment by BPD experts associated with prestigious institutions.[5]

> *Of all the treatments for borderline personality disorder, the one that has probably generated the most excitement is dialectical behavior therapy. DBT is a highly specific form of treatment for BPD.*

In one series of studies, Dr. Linehan and her associates compared 20 participants in a DBT program to 21 individuals who received "treatment as usual" (TAU).[6] TAU is a common control condition. Basically, it means that the person was left untreated by the researchers (only receiving the measures used in the study). This control group is representative of what average people with BPD do: Perhaps they get treatment, perhaps not.

As it turned out, 12 (55 percent) of the subjects were in individual psychotherapy, and 3 (15 percent) were in group psychotherapy. Subjects were randomly assigned to treatment conditions, so we have no reason to believe the groups differ in any meaningful way other than the kind of treatment they received. Also, interviewers were "blind" to the status of the participant (that is, they did not know who was in the DBT group and who was in the TAU group). Some of the results are displayed in table 1.

Although the sample size is fairly small, the results suggest very powerful effects. In addition to presenting the study's statistics, I calculated the ratio of the TAU scores divided by the DBT scores. After 18 months, while the average person in the TAU group had 2.1 parasuicidal episodes, the number was 0.1 episodes in the DBT group (which translates to one episode per 10 individuals). In other words, there were 21 times as many parasuicidal episodes per person in the TAU group. On average, individuals in the DBT group received about one-and-a-half days of psychiatric treatment during the 18 months, while those in the TAU group received 16 days—10 times as many. Despite this apparently large difference, the finding was not statistically significant, because of the relatively small sample size and the high degree of variability among those studied. Other studies,

Table 1.   Comparison of Symptoms, DBT vs. Treatment As Usual

Variable (After 18 Months of Treatment)	Average Score, DBT Group	Average Score, Treatment As Usual (TAU) Group	Ratio
Parasuicidal episodes	0.10	2.10	21.00
Medically Treated Episodes	0.05	0.75	15.00
Psychiatric Hospitalization (days)	1.56	16.00	10.26
Anger	30.97	37.46	1.21
Global Assessment Scale	48.18	32.14	1.50
Employment Performance	1.47	2.27	1.54

Source: Adapted from M. M. Linehan, H. L. Heard, and H. E. Armstrong, "Naturalistic Follow-Up of a Behavioral Treatment for Chronically Parasuicidal Borderline Patients," *Archives of General Psychiatry* 50 (1993): 971–974.

however, have supported that DBT reduces the number of days in the hospital.

The Global Assessment of Functioning (GAF) scale, a clinician rating of overall functioning, was significantly (about 50 percent) higher in the DBT group (see figure 3.1). There were also significant differences in anger, employment performance, and self-reported social adjustment. Follow-up at 24 months generally indicated continued improvements.

The GAF scale scores give an overall view of the progress of individuals in the DBT program, versus those in the TAU group. At 18 months, the TAU group had an average score of 32, which then improved to 36 at the 24-month follow-up. Both scores are in the 31 to 40 range, which indicates "Some impairment in reality testing or communication . . . or major impairment in several areas," according to the *DSM-IV*.[7] The DBT group was at a score of 48 after 18

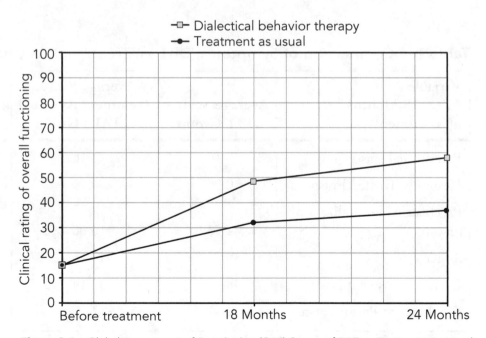

Figure 3.1—*Global Assessment of Functioning (GAF) Scores of DBT vs. Treatment As Usual*

Source: Adapted from M. M. Linehan, H. L. Heard, and H. E. Armstrong, "Naturalistic Follow-Up of a Behavioral Treatment for Chronically Parasuicidal Borderline Patients," *Archives of General Psychiatry,* 50 (1993): 971–974.

months, which is in the upper end of the 41 to 50 range, which indicates "serious symptoms . . . or any serious impairment in social, occupational, or school functioning."[8] After 24 months, they had
improved to 57, which is in the range of "moderate symptoms," and
not far from the range of "mild symptoms." Overall, I consider these
results most encouraging. DBT represents an enormous step forward
in our treatment of BPD.

Pre-scores are estimates, based on Dr. Linehan's description that
all of the study participants initially had parasuicidal episodes. In the
TAU group, at 18 months and 24 months, the
scores (32 and 36) indicate impairment in reality
testing or several major life areas. In the DBT
group, the scores at 18 and 24 months (48 and
57) indicate serious symptoms, followed by moderate symptoms.[9]

Dr. Linehan believes an invalidating environment is the main cause of borderline symptoms,
especially in cases where there is a biological predisposition to the disorder. An invalidating environment may be one in which, as a child, you are
repeatedly told or made to think that you do not really feel the way
you do and that you shouldn't feel the way you do. This consistent
pattern of invalidating your feelings may lead you to be confused
about what your true feelings really are. It is possible, however, that to
a very sensitive child, even normal interactions may feel invalidating.
The treatment is to learn certain skills in functioning, while experiencing appropriate validation during psychotherapy.

The "dialectic" in DBT occurs when concepts are arranged in
contrast to one another. In Linehan's words, "Constant attention to
combining acceptance with change, flexibility with stability, nurturing
with challenging, and a focus on capabilities with a focus on limitations and deficits is the essence of this strategy. The goal is to bring
out the opposites, both in therapy and the patient's life, and to provide conditions for syntheses."[10]

Dr. Linehan believes an invalidating environment is the main cause of borderline symptoms, especially in cases where there is a biological predisposition to the disorder.

In a key insight, Linehan recognized that these disparate elements must be in a constant and dynamic balance, both within the person and within the therapeutic relationship.

What to Expect from DBT

When you enter a DBT program, you are offered a one-year renewable contract. Therapy usually lasts a minimum of 2 years. You must agree to abide by some rules. All clients are in both individual therapy and group skills training. If you miss four therapy sessions in a row, you are discharged from the program. Therapists function as a team and share information with each other. They obtain mutual support. BPD is a tough disorder, and it can be frustrating and demoralizing for therapists. I believe one of the reasons DBT is so successful is because it creates a positive work environment for the therapists, with lots of support and mutual consultation.

Rules around suicide attempts are also part of the initial treatment contract. You must agree to work towards reducing or eliminating self-harming and suicidal behaviors. If you attempt to commit suicide, you generally will not receive potentially rewarding treatment, such as extra sessions or special attention. Dr. Linehan believes that all rewards for being suicidal must be removed. Instead of gaining attention and support for making an attempt, you will lose these "rewards." On the other hand, calling your therapist for help in using your coping techniques, instead of making a suicide attempt, is lavished with support and praise. This seems healthier, doesn't it?

Like many things in life, borderline personality disorder is a paradox. For the person with BPD, life as it stands is unbearable and hard to accept. In order to get well, however, the first step in treatment is what Linehan refers to as "radical acceptance." Linehan says:

> By "acceptance" here, I mean something quite radical—namely acceptance of both the patient and the therapist, of both the therapeutic relationship and the therapeutic process, exactly as all of these are in the moment. This is not an acceptance in order to bring about change; otherwise, it would be a change strategy. Rather, it is the

therapist's willingness to find the inherent wisdom and "goodness" of the current moment and the participants in it, and to enter fully into the experience without judgment, blame, or manipulation.[11]

Therefore, change strategies, such as skills building and problem solving, are balanced by validation from the therapist. The therapist views even the most problematic behaviors, such as suicidal behaviors, as attempts by the person with the disorder to cope with pain, not as "manipulation." Embracing the client's perspective, and truly understanding where she is coming from, is a cornerstone of treatment. Further, the process involves respect for the client's inner wisdom and faith in the client's ability to ultimately prevail. The foundation is for client and therapist to accept reality as it is in this moment.

> *The therapist views even the most problematic behaviors, such as suicidal behaviors, as attempts by the person with the disorder to cope with pain, not as "manipulation."*

There are four sets of skills that clients learn in a group format. The first are core mindfulness skills. Mindfulness refers to being present in the moment. It is derived from Eastern meditation practices. Mindfulness skills help you to stay calm, focused, and centered. The second set of skills are interpersonal effectiveness skills, such as maintaining self-respect in relationships and learning to obtain what you want and need. The third set of skills, emotional regulation, helps you learn to reduce your emotional vulnerability, to pay attention to bodily cues that are giving you signals about how you feel, and how to lead a healthy and balanced life. Finally, distress tolerance skills help you cope with life's crises, by learning how to self-soothe. Skills include using one or more techniques such as imagery, relaxation, encouragement, and prayer.

One important advantage of going to a DBT program is that the therapists are specialists in borderline personality development. The other treatment approaches reviewed in this chapter are more general, so you must confirm that the therapist has experience and comfort in treating BPD.

DBT Skills for BPD

Core Mindfulness Skills: Be present in the moment by staying calm, focused, and centered.

Interpersonal Effectiveness Skills: Maintain self-respect in relationships by obtaining what you want and need.

Emotional Regulation Skills: Reduce your emotional vulnerability by paying attention to bodily cues giving you signals about how you feel. Lead a healthy and balanced life.

Distress Tolerance Skills: Cope with life's crises through self-soothing techniques, such as imagery, relaxation, encouragement, and prayer.

Cognitive-Behavioral Therapy

Cognitive-behavioral therapy (CBT) is the synergistic combination of two forms of therapy: cognitive therapy and behavior therapy. Cognition refers to thoughts, beliefs, judgment, reasoning, and perception. Behavior refers to conduct, action, and response.

A mountain of scientific evidence has proven both forms of therapy effective. In addition, ongoing scientific research and clinical papers have enabled cognitive-behavioral therapy to become even more efficient and effective on a continuous basis.

The application of CBT to personality disorders in general, and to borderline personality disorder in particular, is relatively new, dating back to the mid-1980s. Most of the research in cognitive-behavioral therapy focused on Dr. Linehan's dialectical behavior therapy (DBT) model, a related treatment based on CBT. Despite the lack of specific outcome studies with cognitive-behavioral therapy, it is most likely quite successful. Scientific studies of CBT with depression, anxiety, and other conditions show outstanding effectiveness. It is an inherently briefer therapy than psychodynamic psychotherapy (see page 89), although you should still anticipate spending at least a year or two in treatment.

Clinical trials are under way to test Jeffrey Young's schema therapy with people who have personality disorders. Some of the key schemas (thought patterns) that Dr. Young views as most commonly associated with BPD are listed in table 2.

Table 2.   Maladaptive Themes Learned in Early Childhood by People with BPD

Early Maladaptive Schemas	Typical Beliefs
Abandonment/ Instability	I worry that people I feel close to will leave or abandon me.
Mistrust/Abuse	I have been physically, emotionally, or sexually abused by important people in my life.
Emotional Deprivation	Most of the time, I haven't had someone to nurture me, share himself/herself with me, or care deeply about everything that happens to me.
Defectiveness/Shame	I am unworthy of the love, attention, and respect of others.
Dependence/ Incompetence	I do not feel capable of getting by on my own in everyday life.
Undeveloped Self	I feel that I do not really know who I am or what I want.
Insufficient Self-Control/ Self-Discipline	I often do things impulsively that I later regret.
Subjugation	I feel that I have no choice but to give in to other people's wishes, or else they will retaliate or reject me in some way.
Punitiveness	I am a bad person who deserves to be punished.

Cognitive Therapy

Cognitive therapy was developed, more or less simultaneously, in the late 1950s and early 1960s by Aaron T. Beck (cognitive therapy) and Albert Ellis (rational-emotive therapy). The basic premise of cognitive therapy is that the way we think powerfully shapes our feelings and behaviors. Problems with mood, such as depression, can be directly traced to specific thought content and particular types of logical errors.

Cognitive therapy focuses on errors in thinking that people with a particular set of symptoms are likely to make. For example, when you are depressed, you may only remember depressing events from your past. You may also catastrophize, blowing something out of proportion. When you drop a glass container on the floor and think, "I'm so clumsy, this is horrible, I can't stand it," this is catastrophizing. A common error in the thinking of individuals with BPD is dichotomous thinking. Dichotomous thinking refers to the tendency to think in black-and-white, all-or-none terms, as in good or evil, perfect or flawed, success or failure. Another error in logic is emotional reasoning. Emotional reasoning is believing that something is true because you have a particular feeling. For example, feeling bad is mistaken as proof that you are bad.

> *The basic premise of cognitive therapy is that the way we think powerfully shapes our feelings and behaviors. Problems with mood can be directly traced to specific thought content and particular types of logical errors.*

Such dysfunctional thinking can then be changed using Socratic dialogue. For example, if you were to say, "My boyfriend dumped me and my life is over," a cognitive therapist would explore the validity of those statements and your logic. She might ask, "Have you ever broken up with someone before?" and "Have you ever been happy since then? Is there any meaning to your life other than your relationship with your boyfriend, anything at all?"

Errors in thinking tend to lead to negative outcomes. For example, using emotional reasoning, even if the feeling involved is a good one, leads one away from reality, and therefore towards potential disappointment. Feeling invincible, I head down the expert ski trail when I am only a beginner—well, you can see where this is going! Making judgments based on accurate, realistic assessments of the world is most likely to leave us feeling rewarded and satisfied.

Behavior Therapy

The basic principle of behavior therapy is that behavior can be modified by changing the rewards, or the contingencies, that motivate the behavior. In addition, behavior therapists place a strong emphasis on learning. Their supposition is that maladaptive behavior has been learned and can thus be "unlearned."

Consider the perplexing behavior of self-injury, such as cutting oneself. You would think that the pain experienced from cutting would be a sufficient deterrent. But from the behavior therapist's standpoint, the behavior occurs because reinforcers or "rewards" are maintaining it. The pure behavior therapist is not particularly interested in the past or in the symbolic meaning of the behavior. The main focus is on reinforcers. For example, the client says that before an episode of self-cutting she feels tense, depressed, and frustrated. After the event, she feels calm and relieved. She also finds that cutting herself elicits attention from her family, significant others, and medical personnel.

The behavior therapist and the client create a plan addressing each reinforcer. How can you relieve tension, decrease frustration, decrease depression, and receive attention without self-cutting? Framed in this way, answers emerge. Relaxation training reduces tension. Meditation or the development of coping skills can increase frustration tolerance. Enjoying activities can decrease depression, as can cognitive therapy. Medications or herbal remedies can also reduce depression and anxiety. Receiving attention in new, healthier ways may involve changes in family and other interpersonal relationships. The therapist can work with the client to make these changes in small increments.

Behavior therapy has been effective in treating self-injurious behavior. Notice that diagnostic labels do not mean much to the behavior therapist, who targets the self-injurious behavior itself for change.

> *D*iagnostic labels do not mean much to the behavior therapist. These therapists convert "borderline personality disorder" to a series of small, discrete symptoms that are handled one at a time.

Each problematic behavior is similarly handled, in turn. Behavior therapists convert "borderline personality disorder" into a series of small, discrete symptoms that are handled one at a time.

By definition, behavioral interventions target behavioral change, which can be easily observed; they therefore lend themselves quite easily to scientific study. Thus, a vast number of studies have proven the effectiveness of behavior therapy for psychological conditions. There are no scientific studies using behavior therapy alone to treat borderline personality disorder, per se, but there are studies showing its efficacy with depression, anxiety, self-injury, and other symptoms of BPD.

Behaviorists use some of the following techniques discussed below.

Behavioral Contracting

Behavioral contracting is just what it sounds like. The therapist draws up a written contract in collaboration with the client, outlining behaviors and rewards. Behavioral contracting can be very helpful in treating symptoms of borderline personality disorder. Your first, and possibly most important, contract is to agree in writing to appropriate rules for psychotherapy itself. You can also use contracting to reward yourself for healthy behaviors, such as setting boundaries with others, and to lose rewards for engaging in harmful behaviors, such as drug abuse or self-injury.

Homework

Most behavioral and cognitive-behavioral therapists give homework. Don't groan: Therapy homework is like getting free therapy sessions. If you meet with your therapist once per week, and you do a homework assignment every night in between, you are basically getting six "extra sessions." Homework assignments depend on the goals of treatment. Homework I commonly assign includes: Practice relaxation techniques three times per week; meditate each day for 30 minutes; and record thoughts and feelings daily in a journal. When I do assertiveness training, there is usually a homework assignment to be assertive with someone—whether it be politely and firmly turning away a salesperson, or telling a loved one what you need in an assertive manner.

Homework, like exercise, sounds like a great idea, but many people find it difficult to do. An important part of your relationship with your therapist is handling missed homework assignments. Many clients don't do their homework then feel guilty. As a therapist, I feel disappointed when clients don't do their homework. It helps me to remind myself when I haven't done my homework, such as exercising or eating properly.

> *Therapy homework is like getting free therapy sessions. If you meet with your therapist once per week, and you do a homework assignment every night in between, you are basically getting six "extra sessions."*

I then focus on what interfered with the client's assignment. When homework is not done, it is often a sign that we need to change the assignment. If a person doesn't journal three times per week, maybe she can do it once a week. Or perhaps she could take a poetry class, which would provide more structure. The client and therapist need to brainstorm together to come up with a homework plan that works.

Psychodynamic Psychotherapy

When most people think of psychotherapy, what comes to mind is psychoanalysis or psychodynamic therapy. Classical psychoanalysis, developed by Sigmund Freud, involves the client lying on a couch and free-associating (saying whatever comes into her or his mind). Free association and dream analysis are the main components of psychoanalysis.

I recommend *against* using psychoanalysis to treat borderline personality disorder. Dr. Adolf Stern, credited with coining the term "borderline" in his seminal 1938 paper, noted that such patients

Therapy on the Cheap:
Counseling Centers and Clinics at Universities

If you are attending a college or a university, you may be able to get free psychotherapy at the campus clinic or counseling center. Much of this therapy is done by graduate students supervised by licensed, doctoral-level clinicians. Although most students have relatively little experience, they usually have small caseloads and can compensate by spending more energy and time on each case. Be patient with these student therapists. They may make errors or not seem to understand you in one session, then seem right on target the next time. The reason is simple: Between sessions, they probably met with their supervisor, or did more reading or research on your issues. I have supervised students who are superb therapists, some of whom had many years of clinical experience as masters-degree level therapists doing clinical rotations to earn their doctoral degrees. I have also supervised students with private practices, in which they charge $75 to $100 per session, while giving therapy away for free at the campus clinic or counseling center.

appeared to be treatable but did not respond well to psychoanalysis—and could become psychotic (lose touch with reality) under psychoanalysis. Classical psychoanalysis requires the client to make extensive use of "free association"—saying whatever comes to mind, without censorship. Such a lack of structure tends to be difficult for people with BPD because the free association often leads to extremely painful thoughts and feelings that they may not be able to handle. Although Stern believed psychoanalysis was necessary for the general population (comparing it to a required surgical procedure), he noted that for individuals with BPD:

> A negative therapeutic reaction is nevertheless inevitable; in some, the reaction is extremely unfavorable, and, cumulatively, may become

Universities and professional schools often have clinics available to the public, unlike the counseling centers for students. These are usually billed on a "sliding scale." Individuals with low income may pay a very small amount (as little as $2 per session), while people with relatively high incomes (for example, $50,000 per year) might pay close to the "going rate" (such as $50 to $75 or more per session). Insurance may or may not cover the costs, as the student therapist is generally unlicensed, and insurance companies have moved away from allowing the supervisor's license to "count" for billing purposes.

The biggest drawback to these clinics for individuals with borderline personality disorder is that student rotations generally last for a year or less, and adequate treatment of BPD generally takes 2 years or longer. You may go through several therapists before completing therapy. Although continuity of care is generally preferable, people have been successfully treated by rotating therapists. The "silver lining" is the opportunity to learn to form new relationships and to work through different relationships with different people.

dangerous; patients may develop depression, suicidal ideas, or make suicide attempts.[12]

Basic psychoanalytic method has not changed much since Dr. Stern made that statement, and nothing indicates there would be good outcomes now. The word "inevitable" is chilling in this context. Under the dictum "do no harm," then, those with BPD should avoid psychoanalysis.

However, there are other well-validated treatments, including psychodynamic ones, that we know are helpful. Psychodynamic psychotherapy, which evolved from changes in the psychotherapeutic approach made by practitioners since Freud's time, includes Jungian, Adlerian, object relations, and self-psychology. There are important differences between and among the various psychodynamic approaches. In terms of BPD treatment, the most important issue is that psychodynamic approaches tend to provide the client with significant structure. As we've noted, the lack of structure in free association during classical psychoanalysis may be more than the individual with BPD could handle. In contrast, psychodynamic approaches provide ways for the therapist to be more interactive and supportive of the client with BPD.

What to Expect in Psychodynamic Treatment

Psychodynamic theory suggests that events in a child's life before age 5 are critical. Our beliefs about whether the world is a safe place take root before we can talk, reason, or think critically. If we are held, loved and properly nurtured, we develop the general belief that all is well in the world, a perception that rapidly generalizes. On the other hand, if we are ignored, we view the world as neglectful and uncaring. At this early age, our thoughts connect in all kinds of ways, based on what we're exposed to.

Perhaps the most significant contribution of the psychodynamic way of thinking is the focus on the unconscious. Our minds are likened to an iceberg. The tip of the iceberg, less than 10 percent, is visible above the surface of the water; the bulk of it is submerged (the way an ice cube floats in a glass of water). Similarly, the vast majority of what occurs in our minds takes place in the unconscious, according to psychodynamically oriented practitioners.

Awareness of what is really going on is gained by analyzing dreams (which Freud called "the royal road to the unconscious") through a detailed analysis of your actions and other symbolic aspects of your behavior and beliefs. Psychodynamic therapy may involve multiple meetings per week, usually over a period of several years.

Ultimately, in order for psychodynamic treatment to be successful, the therapeutic relationship must be brought "into the room." This means that the therapist will talk with you about the current relationship between the two of you: how you feel about her, and how this relates to feelings you have had with significant others in your life. Working through feelings in the "here and now" can be very powerful and therapeutic. For example, a client's feelings about women, which he developed in his relationship with his mother, had an effect on his relationship with his female therapist. On the one hand, he professed that "therapy is great." On the other hand, he routinely interrupted his therapist while she talked, was late for appointments, and even became enraged at her. The therapist's job is to point out such inconsistencies and work through them with the client. Caught "in the moment," when the feelings are most real and intense, is often the best time to gain insight and make lasting change.

*A*wareness of what is really going on is gained by analyzing dreams through a detailed analysis of your actions and other symbolic aspects of your behavior and beliefs.

Dr. Otto Kernberg, a leading figure in psychodynamic psychotherapy, modified Freud's technique to improve its use as a treatment for borderline personality disorder. The main modification is the active, open discussion of behaviors that will interfere with psychotherapy. The therapist who follows Dr. Kernberg's suggestions will develop a contract with you about how to handle situations likely to arise and interfere with psychotherapy. For example, at the beginning of treatment, you and your therapist will arrange how to handle missed sessions and suicidal crises.

Dr. Kernberg calls the treatment "transference focused psychotherapy" (TFP) because of this focus on the analysis of the transference. He and his associates have been able to "manualize," or standardize the treatment, so that others can be trained in the method in a consistent fashion. States Dr. Kernberg, "We have abundant clinical experience—over 20 years at our institute—of the dramatic effectiveness of transference focused therapy. . . . I think that is an encouraging, hopeful note for the future." The treatment attempts to resolve the actual personality disturbance of the individual, rather than reduce symptoms. Dr. Kernberg notes that a good candidate for this kind of treatment should have "at least normal" intelligence, lack severe antisocial behavior, be motivated for treatment, and be capable of accepting help. To find a TFP therapist or for information on participation in Dr. Kernberg's research programs at New York Hospital–Cornell University in White Plains, New York, see "Transference Focused Psychotherapy" in appendix A.

Client-Centered/Humanistic Therapy

Client-centered therapy, developed by Dr. Carl Rogers in the 1950s, sees human beings as fundamentally driven toward growth and self-fulfillment. When someone is unfulfilled or stuck (as in cases we label depressed, anxious, or personality-disordered), the therapist's job is to allow the client a safe space within which to find her way. Like Dorothy in *The Wizard of Oz*, the person has the means within herself to find her way back home. The therapist's job, then, is to understand the person and accurately reflect back what she is thinking and feeling. Within that context, the client finds her own solutions to her own problems. The therapist is completely undemanding of the client, not demanding that you change or "get well." The therapist sees you as a being with free will and free choice. (There is one exception, which is that therapists are required by law to prevent you from harming yourself or others.)

> *Like Dorothy in* The Wizard of Oz, *the person has the means to find her way back home. The therapist's job is to understand the person, and reflect back what she is thinking and feeling.*

There are many other humanistic therapies, including Gestalt therapy, psychodrama, and logotherapy. Their shared foundation is a belief in the human spirit, faith in the underlying potential for growth, a commitment to understanding each individual from his or her own standpoint, and trust that the answers lie within the client, not the therapist. The mindfulness meditation classes I teach (covered in chapter 5) have very similar underlying assumptions and emphasize values similar to the humanistic therapies.

Very little scientific research focuses on the application of client-centered and humanistic psychotherapies to borderline personality disorder. Most practitioners who are humanistically oriented do not place a high value on the process of labeling and diagnosis, so most do not write about BPD. Many do not believe that scientific method is a particularly good way of capturing the complexity of human experience. Nonetheless, the one scientific study conducted was extremely encouraging. After receiving client-centered therapy, over 85 percent of the clients who started out with BPD were no longer diagnosable at the end of the four-year study. Researchers reported an overall reduction in symptoms of 35 percent, and suicidal behavior dropped to almost zero. Scores on the Diagnostic Interview for Borderlines, a measure of BPD symptoms, fell by 77 percent.[13] At least in this one study, client-centered therapy fared at least as well as the other established therapies for BPD (such as psychodynamic psychotherapy or dialectical behavior therapy).

It is logical that client-centered/humanistic therapy would work well with BPD. If Dr. Linehan is correct, and a central problem with BPD is the invalidating environment, then a therapy that stresses validation should be helpful. In choosing a client-centered/humanistic therapist, the key, once again, is to ask the proper questions of the prospective therapist, to find out if she or he is comfortable with clients who have BPD (see sidebar, "Choosing a Therapist," page 96).

Family Therapy

Family therapy generally subscribes to the philosophy that problems are a function of issues within the family. Thus, the problem does not reside in the individual, but in the dynamics of

In family therapy, your "borderline personality disorder" is not the target of the intervention. The problem does not reside in the individual, but in the dynamics of the family.

the family. As a result of this thinking, your "borderline personality disorder" is not the target of the intervention. The family therapy model views your behavior in light of the effect it has on the family, and the effect that the behavior of family members has on you.

To illustrate, let's say that you attempt to commit suicide, and this brings the family into therapy. The family therapist does not focus on trying to find out what is wrong with you, or why your thinking is disturbed, or what your problematic genetics might be. Instead, the therapist wants to know what message was being communicated by your actions and to whom in your family you were trying to communicate. Who wants you dead? How was that communicated? With whom were you angry? Did the family respond with love and attention, thereby rewarding the suicide attempt? Do they only love you when you are dysfunctional? When you are competent? Are you abandoned?

One might think family therapy is a good place to work through previous abuse. It can be, but it is not a good place to receive healing

Choosing a Therapist

Here's a list of questions to ask a potential therapist and pointers on what to look for in selecting a therapist:

1. *How long have you been in practice?*

Recent graduates are usually more in touch with the latest approaches and research, while seasoned clinicians benefit from experience in how to understand, relate to, and treat clients. Typically, it takes about 5 years of clinical experience or more for therapists to be in top form.

2. *What is your theoretical orientation?*

In this chapter, you will learn about the different theoretical orientations out there: psychodynamic, cognitive-behavioral, client-centered/humanistic, and family-systems. Use this information to help you choose a therapist that would be a good match for you.

3. *Do you have experience treating people with borderline personality disorder?*

You'll want to be sure the therapist you choose has experience treating individuals with BPD. Therapists who specialize in border-

and validating messages from the family. Therapists who work extensively with families in which abuse has taken place maintain that apologies or admissions almost never surface in family sessions. Instead, the old dynamics of denial and invalidation are likely to replay themselves. Dr. Lorna Smith Benjamin, in *Interpersonal Psychotherapy of Personality Disorders*, describes a case of a young woman who was abused by her brother. In a family session, which was taped, the young woman repeatedly tried to get her point across, while being undercut by her mother. By listening to the tape, she gained perspective on the pattern in her family, which helped her to break free and make her own decisions.[14]

line personality disorder have much better success with individuals who have BPD. However, if a therapist with little or no such experience is part of a treatment team (or is supervised by someone) that specializes in BPD, you will probably get good or excellent treatment. But you should avoid a solo therapist with little or no experience treating BPD.

4. *What is your treatment plan?*
The therapist should be able to answer this question clearly and confidently with a general outline of what your treatment will entail.

5. *What are your degrees and what is your training?*
Doctoral-level psychologists have a Ph.D. or Psy.D. degree, and are qualified to do psychotherapy and psychological testing. Psychiatrists have an M.D. degree and are qualified to do psychotherapy and prescribe medications. Masters-level psychologists (M.A. degree) and masters-level social workers (M.S.W.) are qualified to do psychotherapy. I recommend, in general, working with therapists who have a doctoral, or at minimum master's, level degree.

Families in which abuse has taken place are often stabilized around the denial of the occurrence of the abuse. To break through the denial may mean to destroy the family, a consequence that the key people in the family may be unwilling to accept. All of this is often not occurring at a conscious level; rather, the unconscious of each participant is playing a key role. There is powerful motivation for the family members to persuade the client that she is crazy, and that the abuse never happened. If the client accepts this role in the family, she must continue to be out of touch with reality; if she asserts reality, the family may reject her. Under such circumstances, family therapy is quite difficult. Often, as illustrated by Dr. Benjamin, a single family meeting to gain perspective is helpful, perhaps even the cornerstone of effective treatment, but it will not be the place where feelings in the family are resolved.

> *It is difficult to overstate how important family dynamics are in maintaining behavior, beliefs, and feelings.*

It is difficult to overstate how important family dynamics are in maintaining behavior, beliefs, and feelings. During a clinical internship at a specialized family therapy clinic, I recall seeing a client, Maria, a 60-year-old woman who was suicidally depressed. Maria felt chronic pain in her lower back and left leg for which she took a commonly prescribed, narcotic-like medication. She was married to a physically and verbally abusive man for many years. Her son grew up to be an alcoholic, like his father. Her daughter was a drug abuser who dropped off her child without notice for Maria to baby-sit and stole Maria's pain medication for recreational use, leaving Maria with inadequate medication. Feeling helpless, sad, and desperate, Maria filled one prescription of her medication and went to a second pharmacy to try to fill another prescription, in order to have enough medication to commit suicide. Fortunately, the computer system alerted the pharmacist, and he did not fill her second prescription.

I saw Maria in individual therapy for about 12 weeks, at which time we had a family session with her daughter. I was in the room with Maria and her daughter, while therapists observing behind a one-way mirror called in to provide me feedback and questions. During the session, Maria set boundaries with her daughter, which included advance notice of baby-sitting requests. Maria also took measures to safeguard her medications. Maria had previously set limits with her son, refusing to let him live with her if he continued to drink.

The week after this session, Maria was like a new woman. Her depression, which had lessened over time with therapy, vanished. Shortly thereafter, she began to date "a gentleman" who treated her kindly—a rather new experience for her. Maria felt confident that if he became nasty or abusive, she could set boundaries or end the relationship. Maintaining a healthier distance from her children, she was free to finally live her own life.

Recent studies suggest that including the family in treatment improves outcomes. The researchers state: "In our judgment, when the family is available and motivated, the treatment of choice is family psychoeducation, with family (systems or dynamic) intervention where possible, in combination with pharmacotherapy and/or individual psychotherapy as needed."[15]

Similarly, according to British psychiatrists Anthony James and Margaret Varecker, "Family therapy is regarded by many . . . as the treatment of choice for adolescents diagnosed as having borderline personality disorder because of the intense relationship difficulties these youngsters experience within their families."[16]

I spoke with a family therapist experienced in working with borderline adolescents and their families, who is conducting important research. Daniel Santisteban, Ph.D., at the Center for Family Studies at the University of Miami, received funding from the National Institute of Drug Abuse to study drug-abusing adolescents who had intense family therapy sessions, had a great deal of conflict, were high utilizers of services, and who were not doing very well in treatment. Closer examination of this subset of adolescents uncovered that they had many borderline personality disorder features, and many had BPD.

The 3-year project, which has just been completed, looked at the efficacy of family treatment for adolescents with substance abuse problems and BPD. The study used a combination of structural family therapy (based on the work of Salvador Minuchin) and brief strategic therapy (based on the work of Chloe Madones and Jay Haley), and added the skills training modules from dialectical behavior therapy (Marsha Linehan's model).

According to Dr. Santisteban:

> We're really teaching the adolescents the skills to be able to express, to identify and clarify their own needs, and then to be able to express them in some adaptive way to their parents. And, of course, to have goals in mind that they're working towards so that when their impulsivity kicks in they can have something to offset it. . . . And then we do the family work to help the family to accept the kid's new behavior, and to be more supportive and validating in that context.

In Dr. Santisteban's particular sample, some parents lacked communication skills, resulting in invalidating messages. Often, one or both parents had severe depression. As is well known in depression, the person is often neglectful of self and others. The depressed parents tended to respond only when the child engaged in extreme behaviors, thereby reinforcing the misbehaviors. Other family problems included family conflict and parental and sibling substance abuse. In families in which physical or sexual abuse has occurred, there is often a great deal of anger against the non-offending parent. In Dr. Santisteban's study, the offender was always out of the family system at that point (through divorce or separation, for example).

In addition to family therapy, the project provided individual therapy (with the same therapist), plus the skills training module (with a different therapist). Thus the adolescent received 3 hours of therapy once per week. The therapists provided clear guidelines about the sharing of information; anything dangerous to self or others would be shared with parents or appropriate authorities. Many of the adolescents needed medication, either for impulsivity, ADD, or depression. Many of the families needed to learn how to handle conflict without blowing up or detaching completely. A high proportion of the borderline teens were not in school, so parents were also taught how to support and advocate for their children. Therapists and parents then worked to reconnect the children to school.

Although the data analysis is not complete, there were several successes in the program. Substantial reductions were seen in hospitalizations, suicide attempts, substance abuse, depression, and anxiety in the adolescents. What was the biggest surprise for Dr. Santisteban?

> The . . . big surprise with the adolescents was how easy they were to work with. I had worked mainly with borderline adults. I found that the kids were still very flexible. Their need for attachment was clear; it was still there, you could work with it. I think by the time you're an adult borderline you have got all these layers of defenses around that need for attachment and connection, but it's out there with the kids. They attached to us very quickly as therapists in a fairly healthy way, and there was still a lot of hope in terms of how we could turn around family interactions and family relationships, because they weren't disconnected yet. By the time there's an adult borderline, they're often disconnected from their families for years and years, and it's just hard to start that up again. But when you catch them early there's still a lot of hope for making those connections again. And we were all pleasantly surprised by that.

The earlier one can intervene with borderline personality disorder, the better the outcome is likely to be. In addition, where there is chaos—either from raising a child with borderline tendencies, due to preexisting parental psychopathology or other issues—addressing the dynamics in a family context can be extremely productive. Otherwise, if only one person in the family makes a change, and that change is not supported or others misunderstand it, the change can rapidly come undone.

> *The earlier one can intervene with borderline personality disorder, the better the outcome is likely to be.*

Unfortunately, few, if any, scientific studies on the use of family therapy with BPD prove that it works. It is therefore important to

Making the Most of Your Insurance Benefits

Many people feel helpless in the face of insurance companies. Don't! You can advocate for yourself. Mark Johns, M.A., is director of Outpatient Services at PsycHealth Ltd., a company that manages utilization of benefits. According to Johns, you can take several steps to maximize your insurance reimbursements and the available services you can receive:

1. Document, document, document! Begin by getting pre-authorization for services. Document from whom you received every authorization, so you can trace back to who gave you approvals and when.

2. The key concept for gaining approval for treatment is "medical necessity." Is a treatment medically necessary? Why? What will be the outcome of treatment? That is what insurers want to know. You can use several pieces of information from this book to argue in favor of medical necessity. Research cited in this book has shown that there are biological problems associated with BPD, especially frontal lobe dysfunction (see chapter 1). Various forms of psychotherapy and medication have been found to be effective treatments, as measured by decreased parasuicidal behavior, decreased hospitalizations, and improved mood (this chapter and chapter 4). The consequences of leaving the disorder untreated are recovery rates 5 to 7 times slower than with treatment (see page 75). Currently, because of legislation requiring parity between mental and physical health in insurance policies, pressure can be placed on insurance companies to provide mental health care when it is medically necessary.

3. If you get denied, call your company. Fight back, using the argument of medical necessity outlined above. Engage your health

care provider, such as your mental health clinician or your primary care physician, to argue that the sessions are medically necessary.

4. Research has demonstrated enormous cost savings for treating BPD, rather than letting it run its natural course. Most of the cost savings come from reduced hospitalizations and decreased utilization of emergency room services (due to suicide attempts). Dr. Linehan's research on DBT programs specifically documents cost savings; in one study she documented a savings of nearly $9,000 during the first year of treatment, using DBT rather than treatment as usual.[17] This argument can often sway insurers.

5. Educate yourself, your primary care physician, and your insurance case manager (if you have one) about BPD. Let her or him know how important it is that you receive treatment, and how the research shows that there is much that can be done.

6. Get your hands on your "Certificate of Coverage," which is your contract with the insurance company. Know what you are entitled to under the contract.

7. Joining a PPO (participating provider organization), rather than an HMO (health maintenance organization), generally provides you with a wider choice of providers. If you already have a therapist, even if she or he is not part of the PPO network, you can probably get partial coverage of costs. Most HMOs do not provide out-of-network coverage.

Also, keep your eye out for new legislation. It is likely that some kind of "Patients' Bill of Rights" will be passed in the near future. If so, you may be able to sue your insurance company, or force them into binding arbitration, when they deny you coverage.

check with the therapist regarding his or her level of comfort and experience working with people with BPD. The same questions one would ask about individual therapy should be asked of family therapists.

Group Psychotherapy

Group psychotherapy has long been used as an effective psychotherapeutic modality. Group and individual treatment have different advantages and disadvantages. Individual therapy has the benefit of privacy, and the confidentiality that goes with a relationship with a therapist. Groups, on the other hand, have several advantages that cannot be replicated in individual therapy. Groups offer contact with people who may have problems similar to yours. It feels good to know you're not alone and that others can relate to what you're going through. People in support groups often share creative solutions and coping skills with other group members.

For purposes of this discussion, I divide group therapy interventions into two types: skill-building groups and process groups. Skill-building groups are places where individuals learn new ways to cope or interact with the world. Common themes include interpersonal skills, social skills, assertiveness, and stress management. Although

---

Psychodrama

Some forms of therapy can only occur in groups. One such therapy is psychodrama, a type of treatment developed by Jacob L. Moreno in the 1940s. The basic premise is that by enacting situations or dramatizing certain events, you can gain new insights to help you function more effectively and experience an emotional release (catharsis) that may help you feel better. In order to do psychodrama, you need a "director" (the therapist) and several players, as well as an "audience" (all of whom are members of the group).

sharing is encouraged and there is a lot of interaction, they feel a bit like a classroom—with topics to cover and specific techniques to learn. In a process group, the interaction that occurs in the moment is the topic of the group.

Perhaps the most powerful aspect of group treatment is feedback in the here-and-now with group members. Process groups are designed to increase the likelihood of this happening. If your relationships become unglued because you are afraid of becoming close to someone for fear you will get hurt, this pattern will likely play itself out in the group. You may get angry with a group member towards whom you are starting to feel friendly. You may joke around to fend off warm feelings. The therapist can point out these patterns.

In my experience, however, the magic of groups is the feedback from other members. There is enormous power when a group member says, "Hey, how come you always make a joke whenever I say something nice about someone? It makes me feel embarrassed and discounted!" If you respond by saying, "I don't do that," three other people in the group may shake their heads, with one remarking, "I've also seen you do that." In almost all cases, the group remains supportive of you, while asking you to take a look at your behavior and the impact it has on others. This honest feedback can be extraordinarily valuable. In a skills group, role-playing can also bring this level of "realness" into the room.

Most groups have ground rules that help them to be safe and productive. Group therapists usually encourage members to keep shared information confidential. Of course, once others are involved, the therapist loses control over confidentiality; members are warned that their confidentiality is only safe to the degree that all in the group maintain it.

The therapist may instruct members to not be judgmental, to foster a spirit of inclusiveness, to treat one another with respect and dignity, and to confront one another with honesty and sincerity. Some process groups require stable membership in order to work, so there are ground rules regarding regular attendance.

Like individual therapy, group approaches draw on different theories that guide their functioning. There are behaviorally oriented groups that teach skills (such as those used in Dr. Linehan's DBT model). There are cognitive-behavioral groups that focus on challenging irrational beliefs, changing thought patterns, and practicing new behaviors. There are psychodynamic groups that aim to uncover unconscious motivations and develop insight.

You should ask your potential group leader the same questions about his orientation as you would ask a potential individual therapist.

> Like individual therapy, group approaches draw on different theories that guide their functioning.

As with individual therapists, you should also ask him about his experience and comfort level with people with BPD. There may be challenges integrating into a group if you have BPD. If you suddenly express a great deal of rage, for instance, it may be difficult for the group to handle. If the leader has experience with people with BPD, he can let you know if it will work out for you in her group. For skills groups, these problems tend to be greatly reduced, since the material is usually less emotionally provocative.

University of Toronto's Elsa Marziali and Heather Monroe-Blum describe a treatment called "interpersonal group psychotherapy" (IGP). IGP is an approach that involves helping clients to find their own solutions. Like Dr. Linehan's approach, IGP is supportive, and the client's view of reality is respected and affirmed. As in DBT, IGP emphasizes tolerance of ambiguity and painful feelings. Unlike Dr. Linehan's model, however, IGP does not use skill training or advice. Unlike psychodynamic approaches, the therapist does not give statements Freudian (or similar psychological) interpretations. Rather, the main technique is akin to client-centered/humanistic therapy.[18]

Drs. Monroe-Blum and Marziali conducted a randomized clinical trial with a psychotherapy group they developed. Participants were given either 30 sessions of interpersonal group psychotherapy (IGP) or "treatment as usual" (TAU; open-ended individual psychodynamic therapy). The study started with 110 individuals who were diagnosed with BPD; 31 dropped out upon being randomly assigned to a treatment condition (21 from the IGP group, and 10 from the TAU group).[19]

The researchers measured a number of outcomes after 12 and 24 months, including depression, overall adjustment, and social functioning. They found that those treated in group therapy had approximately equivalent outcomes to those who received individual treatment on the outcomes they measured, but the groups required far less therapist time per person. In the IGP group, scores on symptom measures had declined after 12 months, and had declined further at the 24-month follow-up. At 24 months, depression and general psychiatric symptomology scores had declined by over 40 percent; behavioral dysfunction scores had declined by over 25 percent; and social impairment scores were lower by nearly 12 percent. Overall, there was a 60 percent cost savings using IGP, as opposed to individual therapy.

Several different group therapy approaches have demonstrated effectiveness for people with BPD. The skills-building groups developed by Dr. Linehan in her DBT model appear to be highly effective, and have been used by treatment providers who do not do the full DBT program. Patients clearly report valuing insight-oriented groups when there is enough time to establish the group process.[20] A psychodynamically oriented day-treatment program used in an 18-month randomized double-blind study relied heavily on group treatment, and produced impressive outcomes.[21] Group psychotherapy has been shown to help clients who received day treatment to continue to improve after discharge more than individuals who were not given group psychotherapy.[22]

In a review of studies of inpatient group psychotherapy, University of Michigan Medical Center clinicians Tamar Springer, Ph.D., and Ken Silk, M.D., noted that group therapy is helpful during brief inpatient stays (2 weeks to 3 months), when it has specific goals and provides support. Groups that focus on insight and confrontation, however, are ineffective for brief inpatient stays.[23]

Overall, the evidence regarding group psychotherapy for BPD is rather limited. Further research is needed to shed light on how clients fare in mixed groups, in which not all of the clients have BPD. Some argue it is preferable to have a mix,[24] while others have developed groups specifically for individuals with BPD.[25] To my knowledge, there is no data on psychodrama with individuals with BPD; intuitively, this strikes me as a potentially powerful and useful form of treatment for individuals who tend to "act out" their feelings. All in all, however, the existing data is encouraging, and group psychotherapy should be given due consideration for anyone with BPD.

THE THERAPIST-CLIENT CONTRACT

The first and perhaps most important contract you will have with the therapist is the outline of the therapeutic relationship itself. Several aspects of borderline personality disorder can potentially interfere with the therapeutic relationship. You're more likely to succeed in therapy if you take these issues into account. The client and the therapist must unite against the problematic patterns that cause the client distress. To avoid inappropriate behaviors, the therapist and the client must agree on some ground rules to ensure a successful outcome. The following guidelines provide these ground rules.

> One of the most disturbing elements of borderline personality disorder is the tendency to attempt suicide during times of stress. For the client, suicide attempts are acts of desperation.

Agreement on How to Handle Suicide Attempts

One of the most disturbing elements of borderline personality disorder is the tendency to attempt suicide during times of stress. From the standpoint of the client, of course, suicide attempts are acts of desperation. Suicidal behavior is highly upsetting to both therapist and client, however, so a predetermined plan is essential.

A sensible suicide policy is one created and agreed to when both client and therapist are calm and relaxed—rather than during a crisis.

Many contracts specify that when the client feels suicidal, he is responsible for calling the police or an ambulance, or going to the emergency room. The client can then call the therapist's pager. The contract also specifies the time allowed for a return call. Many therapists have a "same day" policy, although some have emergency numbers to call, or group practices in which someone else is on call. Therapists will often go to the hospital to help with an admission, although this is not always possible. Therapists sometimes agree to visit a client in the hospital. In most cases, a therapist will schedule an extra appointment or two with you after a suicide attempt in order to help you to stabilize. This practice, however, should be evaluated throughout therapy. The best approach is to avoid rewarding suicidal behavior.

It is wise to consider the therapist as only one part of a large health care net that is there to provide you with service. Placing more responsibility than that on the therapist guarantees that he or she will eventually burn out or disappoint someone who is in a critical situation. Emergency rooms, emergency numbers such as 911, and the police are all equipped to provide immediate service to you. It's unrealistic to expect your lone therapist in private practice to replace these systems.

If you think you would benefit from more service—a therapist who would guarantee to be available, to return your every phone call immediately, to be there to admit you, to give you sessions whenever you want—I respectfully, but fervently, disagree. This "perfect" relationship merely plays into the fantasy that someone else can, through round-the-clock care and nurturing, make you well. The reality is that you must do most of the work; your therapist is only a guide.

> It is a fantasy that your therapist can make you well. The reality is that you must do most of the work; your therapist is only a guide.

Missed Sessions and Canceled Appointments

Most therapists have some policy about payment for missed sessions (not attending a session and not calling to cancel). Some charge for missed sessions. Others allow one miss, then charge for subsequent ones. A few issues regarding BPD and missed sessions are critical. Individuals with borderline personality disorder are very likely to miss sessions—far more likely than individuals with other disorders. This may reflect problems with impulse control, feelings of guilt and shame, or problems with substance abuse, all of which are associated with BPD. In addition, individuals with BPD are more likely to take being charged for a missed session very personally—as a sign that the therapist does not care, that the therapist is harsh or punitive, or that the therapist is greedy or malicious. These feelings are related to "splitting" (the psychodynamic word for "dichotomous thinking"), in which the therapist is viewed as all-good or all-bad, all-giving or greedy, all-caring or indifferent. The reality is that the therapist cares to a certain degree, perhaps even very deeply—but this is also how the therapist makes a living. Another client could have filled and paid for the hour you skipped. Most therapists I know will accept 24 hours notice, although if sessions are missed frequently, the therapist may renegotiate the contract.

One complication of charging for missed sessions is that such payments are typically not covered by insurance. Therefore, a client who attends a session might pay a $15 co-pay, while a missed session might cost $100 out of pocket! These contingencies should be clarified and specified in advance of their occurrence. Money is tied into very deep feelings, such as convictions about what is right and wrong, status in society, and relationships within the family. Perhaps you believe that psychotherapy should be free for everyone, and you resent having to pay for it. Perhaps you feel that if you are paying someone to listen to you, it means that he doesn't care about you. Maybe you want to "test that out" by seeing how long the therapist will continue to see you while you withhold payment. Exploring these feelings and fantasies, along with the symbolic meaning of money, can be productive. Due to the strong feelings involved, however, it is best that the policy for payment be clarified up front.

Premature Termination of Therapy

One of the most disheartening things about treating individuals with BPD is their inclination for abrupt termination of therapy. It is hard to describe the exact feeling, but I think most therapists feel a sense of loss and disappointment. Chances are the client is abandoning the therapy and the therapist the way he feels he has been abandoned. If the therapy is going well when the client drops out, I suspect the client is responding to either a fear of success or a fear of intimacy. Of course, if the therapy is not going well, the client may rationally choose to end treatment.

However, it is true that people with BPD are more likely to drop out of therapy. A study by Dr. Linehan shows that almost 75 percent of clients with BPD in the "treatment as usual" group dropped out of therapy prematurely.

People with borderline personality disorder are prone to prematurely terminate therapy for several reasons. By definition, their relationships are "brief and intense," and this often applies to the therapy relationship as well. The client comes in, shares an enormous amount of deeply personal information in the first few sessions, and then is gone. It is possible the client may feel too ashamed or overwhelmed to face the therapist after revealing all her innermost thoughts and feelings.

> One of the most disheartening things about treating individuals with BPD is their inclination for abrupt termination of therapy. Chances are the person is abandoning the therapy and the therapist the way he feels he has been abandoned.

Individuals with borderline personality disorder often have issues with boundaries because their own personal boundaries were violated early in life, in cases of physical, verbal, or sexual abuse. When clients with poor boundaries open up and share too much information too quickly, they may feel vulnerable and experience an urge to flee the therapy. Also, individuals with poor boundaries may misperceive a therapist who sets necessary therapeutic boundaries as cold, indifferent, or uncaring. She may unrealistically expect her relationship with the therapist to be a friendship. When a friendship does not materialize, she may terminate the therapy.

Individuals with BPD tend to be impulsive. A client may drop out on the spur of the moment, when he senses discomfort or boredom during treatment. He may get drunk or stoned as a way of making himself unable to attend a session. On the other hand, ending therapy is the correct thing to do at times. The therapist may not be the right one for you. The type of therapy may be a poor match. For example, you may start out with a psychodynamically oriented psychotherapist and find yourself longing for something more structured, such as cognitive behavioral therapy or even a structured 2-year program of dialectical behavior therapy.

How do you know when you are fleeing therapy for poor reasons, or leaving for good ones?

Dr. Lorna Smith Benjamin has an excellent suggestion. She contracts with BPD clients to agree to wait three sessions before terminating. In other words, if a client has an urge to stop going to therapy, he would go to three more sessions in order to discuss why he is stopping, his expectations, and his dissatisfactions. If after these three sessions he is still determined to stop, then he can go. This prevents impulsive or otherwise untoward stoppages. Whether or not you or your therapist implement a "three-session rule," the principle of talking extensively with the therapist about your feelings, needs, expectations, and (perhaps most important) your goals is the key to an appropriate termination of treatment or a transition to a new type of treatment.

Confidentiality

When you go to a therapist—whether a psychologist, psychiatrist, counselor, or social worker—you are entitled to confidentiality. What you say remains in the room with the practitioner. There are two notable exceptions. If you are a danger to yourself (suicide risk) or if you are a danger to others (assault risk), the practitioner is required by law to do what is necessary to try to stop you. If you are a suicide risk, the practitioner will usually try to contract with you (secure a credible promise that you won't make a suicide attempt without calling, at which time you will accept voluntary admission to a hospital), or initiate a psychiatric hospitalization. If you threaten to harm someone, the clinician is bound to call the police and the potential victim, if there is enough information.

Usually, the therapist explains confidentiality and its limits during the first session. I generally do so before letting the client utter word one about why he is there to see me. If the first thing he says is "I have a gun and I'm going to shoot my girlfriend and then myself," then we both know confidentiality is a problem.

Another limitation on confidentiality is that insurance companies often have access to reports and other records, in order to justify continuation of care. Usually, the client signs a release of information allowing the insurer that access. For most of us, this access is not particularly troubling, although people who are in sensitive positions, such as government officials or CEOs of companies, may prefer to pay out of pocket in order to maintain their privacy.

> When you go to a therapist—whether a psychologist, psychiatrist, counselor, or social worker—you are entitled to confidentiality. What you say remains in the room with the practitioner.

A different confidentiality issue arises in cases where the therapist is receiving supervision or peer supervision. Clinicians talk about their cases with one another in order to provide better care, though the client's identity is disguised. For example, I might say to a colleague, "Every time I suggest a particular client talk about her mother, she changes the subject. But if we don't talk about her mother, we won't get anywhere." Clearly, my client cannot be identified from this conversation, from which I may gain valuable advice to help you during our next session.

If I am consulting with someone who can identify you, such as a psychiatrist who prescribes your medications, I must get a signed, written release from you. I do so routinely with my clients, as do most therapists, so that I can provide you with the best care possible. I cannot work optimally with you if I do not know about your medications. The same is true of your physician if she is unaware of your progress in psychotherapy. This is considered standard practice. For example, Medicare requires by law that I obtain consent and contact your physician, unless you sign a form forbidding me to do so. Such interchanges are extremely helpful. Ethical violations, some of which are discussed here, occur much more frequently when the therapist is isolated and has little or no contact with colleagues.

As a therapist, I am bound by confidentiality to keep your secrets, but you do not have any such obligation to me. Therefore, both on practical grounds and therapeutic ones, most therapists disclose very little about themselves to clients. Therapeutically, you are not there to help me with my problems. And because I am not going to be a role model for very many things that you do, self-disclosure on my part is not often helpful to you. I selectively share only information that is highly relevant and useful. With clients I am treating for chronic low-back pain (with specialized techniques, such as relaxation training or hypnosis), I may share that I, too, suffer from a chronic low-back pain problem. This disclosure reassures the client that I have a reasonable idea of what it is like to have a pain problem.

Few therapists share issues that are deeply personal and certainly do not do so frequently. And yet you, as the client, are expected to share your deepest secrets with someone who cannot or will not share back. If this causes you discomfort, bring it up with your therapist. Doing so may lead to a fruitful discussion on the nature of your relationship with the therapist and its limits, and perhaps to a discussion of your frustrations with limitations in other relationships. In reality, you have substantial protection regarding your confidential information. A therapist who violates confidentiality faces potential sanctions through ethical review by professional organizations, and possibly through legal review by state licensing boards. An indiscreet therapist could potentially face a malpractice suit or lose the right to practice—obviously major deterrents to violating confidentiality.

On a practical level, the therapist who shares personal information with clients is quite vulnerable. While a therapist who violates your confidentiality is risking his license and therefore his livelihood, there is no consequence if you violate the therapist's confidentiality. Thus, beyond the therapeutic considerations, in order to avoid being hurt or embarrassed, therapists must necessarily refrain from the level of self-disclosure that they expect of their clients.

You have substantial protection regarding your confidential information. A therapist who violates confidentiality faces potential sanctions through ethical review by professional organizations, and possibly through legal review by state licensing boards.

Client-Therapist Intimacy

The therapeutic relationship, by its nature, is warm and supportive. As a client, you may find yourself sharing your most intimate secrets. These may involve details about which you feel deeply ashamed, such as lies you've hidden from others, feelings of being a phony, harm you've done to others, or harm done to you, such as sexual abuse. Through it all, the therapist listens patiently, and remains connected to and supportive of you, even if your behavior has been unacceptable or you've been victimized in a way that our society stigmatizes. Over time, you may feel that your therapist understands you better than anyone else in the world does—and he may. You may find that your therapist is consistently the most compassionate and kind person you know. You may find yourself falling in love with your therapist. You may feel sexual attraction. You would not be the first, and you won't be the last.

Although strong feelings may occur in therapy, sex between a client and a therapist is never okay. It is the end of the therapeutic relationship. It is a clear violation of the ethical standards of psychologists as set forth by the American Psychological Association, and of similar guidelines for licensed psychiatrists, counselors, and social workers. It doesn't matter whether the therapist or the client made the "first move." A therapist who engages in sexual contact with a client stands to lose his or her license.

A discussion of sexual and other intimate feelings toward the therapist is generally productive. Often, the issue involves fantasies about a "perfect" relationship based on the unique characteristics of the therapeutic relationship. Therapists are dedicated to finding solutions to your problems and to helping you meet your needs—a unique situation that is not replicated in day-to-day relationships with spouses, friends, and family. Recognizing that there is no such thing as a perfect person or a perfect relationship can be an important step in the client's healing process.

> *Although strong feelings may occur in therapy, sex between a client and a therapist is never okay. It is a clear violation of the ethical standards of psychologists.*

People with borderline personality disorder may be more at risk regarding sexual encounters with therapists. Many people who have a history of being sexually abused, for example, become seductive or have a deep-seated belief that they must respond sexually when they are with an authority figure. Let me be clear: It is the therapist's duty to behave responsibly and professionally. However, you may be able to seduce him or her. Don't. It will inevitably be harmful.

If you have sexual feelings toward your therapist, discuss them. If your therapist suggests that you two become sexually involved—make sure you clarify what the therapist means to avoid a potentially terrible misunderstanding. If the therapist is actually suggesting sex, you must immediately terminate therapy. You may also wish to report the therapist to a governing agency. You can contact the state licensing board or the main professional agency in the field (American Psychological Association for clinical and counseling psychologists, American Psychiatric Association or American Medical Association for psychiatrists, or the National Association of Social Workers for social workers).

You should be aware that a "psychotherapist" is quite different from a psychologist, psychiatrist, or social worker. Although it varies by state, a psychotherapist often does not need any particular training and is not governed by state licensing. I have particularly strong concerns about unlicensed, minimally trained individuals, when it comes to sensitive ethical areas such as confidentiality and restrictions on sexual contact. I recommend always going to a licensed professional.

CHAPTER 4

Medications for Borderline Personality Disorder

IN THIS CHAPTER, you will learn about the most widely used medications for individuals with borderline personality disorder. While there is no specific medication for BPD *per se*, medications can be very helpful in treating some of its symptoms and comorbid conditions such as depression, anxiety, and impulsivity. In addition, antipsychotic medication can manage any transient psychotic episodes that sometimes may occur with BPD.

If you have BPD, talk with your clinician about what prescription medicines might be helpful. (Some of the medications available for use in the treatment of BPD are listed in table 3.) Several types of clinicians can now prescribe psychotropic medications. Physicians (medical doctors), of course, are the traditional bearers of prescription privileges; among physicians, psychiatrists are the specialists in mental health and usually have the best expertise with psychotropic medications. In addition, psychiatric nurse practitioners and some pharmacists have prescription privileges. There is now a pilot program in the military granting prescription privileges to a few specially trained psychologists, so you may soon be able to get medications from some psychologists as well. Be sure to find a practitioner with experience treating individuals with mental health conditions, especially BPD.

Medication is just part of the answer to the problems besetting individuals with borderline personality disorder. BPD expert Ken Silk, M.D., notes that the response to medication among those with BPD tends to be less than the literature, which has indicated a positive success rate in alleviating symptoms, leads one to expect. Perhaps this inconsistency is the result of the select populations in these studies. For example, a comprehensive review of scientific studies showed drop-out rates between 42 and 62 percent in many landmark medication-effectiveness studies on individuals with BPD.[1] Those participants who remained in the studies may have been more motivated, or may have been the ones who had the best response to the medications— perhaps leading to study results showing a better response than is typical.

MEDICATIONS FOR BORDERLINE PERSONALITY DISORDER

Psychiatrist Paul Soloff, M.D., of the University of Pittsburgh's Western Psychiatric Institute and Clinic, has done the most comprehensive review to date on the effectiveness of medication for individuals with borderline personality disorder. He divides BPD into symptoms falling into three dimensions, or areas, that are treatable with medications: cognitive-perceptual, affective dysregulation, and impulsive-behavioral dyscontrol. It is important to note that interpersonal psychopathology of BPD patients is best treated with psychotherapeutic approaches, though medication may facilitate the patient's ability to participate in the therapy.

COGNITIVE-PERCEPTUAL DIMENSION

The cognitive-perceptual dimension refers to problems with thought processing and perceptions, such as ideas of reference, mild paranoid

Table 3.   Medications Used in Borderline Personality Disorder

Medications	Generic	Brand name(s)
Antipsychotic Medications	chlorpromazine	Thorazine
	fluphenazine	Prolixin
	haloperidol	Haldol
	loxapine	Loxitane
	perphenazine	Trilafon
	thiothixene	Navane
	trifluoperazine	Stelazine
Atypical Antipsychotics	clozapine	Clozaril
	olanzapine	Zyprexa
	quetiapine	Seroquel
	risperidone	Risperdal
	ziprasidone	Geodon
Antidepressant Medications		
Tricyclic Compounds	amitriptyline	Elavil, Endep, Tryptanol
	desipramine	Norpramin, Pertofrane
	doxepin	Adapin, Sinequan
	imipramine	Tofranil, Tipramine
Selective Serotonin Reuptake Inhibitors (SSRIs)	citalopram	Celexa
	fluoxetine	Prozac
	paroxetine	Paxil
	sertraline	Zoloft
MAO Inhibitors	phenelzine	Nardil
	tranylcypromine	Parnate
Other Antidepressants	amoxapine	Asendin
	bupropion	Wellbutrin
	maprotiline	Ludiomil
	mirtazapine	Remeron
	nefazodone	Serzone
	venlafaxine	Effexor

(continues)

Table 3.   Medications Used in Borderline Personality Disorder, *continued*

Medications	Generic	Brand name(s)
Mood Stabilizers	carbamazepine lithium carbonate valproic acid, valproate, divalproex	Tegretol Depakene, Depakote
Antianxiety Medications: Benzodiazepines		
Long-Acting Agents	chlordiazepoxide diazepam flurazepam	Librium Valium Dalmane
Intermediate-Acting Agents	clonazepam lorazepam	Klonopin Ativan
Short-Acting Agents	alprazolam oxazepam	Xanax Serax
Antianxiety Medications: Nonbenzodiazepine	buspirone	BuSpar

thinking, illusions, or, rarely, hallucinations (perceiving things that are not really there, such as hearing voices no one else hears). Cognitive-perceptual problems are treated with antipsychotic medications. Dr. Soloff notes that antipsychotics are the most studied of the medications used with BPD. They are not only effective in reducing ideas of reference, paranoid ideation, and illusions, but also are helpful with anger, hostility, irritability, and parasuicidal behavior.

Antipsychotic Medication

Psychosis means a loss of contact with reality. People who have a psychotic disorder may experience hallucinations with any of their senses. Most frequent are auditory hallucinations, especially hearing voices when no one is speaking. These voices sometimes take the form of "command hallucinations," in which the voices "order" the patient to do something (often violent or self-destructive). Although clinicians must take precautions with individuals experiencing command hallucinations, clients usually do not act on these commands.

The next most frequent are visual hallucinations (seeing things that are not really there). My experience is that the most common visual hallucinations are seeing figures, such as "the devil," or seeing movement (of people) in the shadows. Tactile hallucinations (such as feeling a crawling sensation on the skin) or olfactory hallucinations (such as smelling a foul odor) are relatively rare.

> *P*sychosis *means a loss of contact with reality. People who have a psychotic disorder may experience hallucinations.*

Delusions differ from hallucinations in that they have more to do with your beliefs than your senses. For example, I had a client who claimed the "Chinese Mafia" was following him. When I asked him to describe what led him to this belief, he said he saw Chinese people wherever he went. The client was seeing things that were there—many East Asians lived in the neighborhood he was describing—but no one was following him. Sometimes, hallucinations can lead to delusions. Another client, who heard voices (a hallucination), believed the FBI had planted transmitters in her head (a delusion).

It's important to note that individuals with BPD do not have chronic psychosis (if they did, they would get an additional diagnosis, such as schizophrenia). And so, antipsychotic medications are used on a short-term basis to quickly stabilize them.

Antipsychotic medications (also called "neuroleptics") act to reduce both hallucinations and delusions. Two classes are discussed below: the widely used traditional or older antipsychotics, and the more selectively used "atypical" antipsychotics.

Although not a cure, antipsychotic medications, discovered in the 1950s, have been of great benefit, enabling many patients to be discharged and to live fuller lives in their community.

Studies of Antipsychotics for Borderline Personality Disorder

For individuals with BPD, antipsychotics have demonstrated improvements not only in thought disorder symptoms (psychosis), but also improvements in mood, anger, anxiety, and somatic complaints. These encouraging findings were initially discovered in open trials[2] and later confirmed in double-blind placebo-controlled studies.[3] A number of medications have been evaluated, including haloperidol (Haldol), chlorpromazine (Thorazine), perphenazine (Trilafon), trifluoperazine (Stelazine), loxapine (Loxitane), and thiothixene (Navane).

Atypical Antipsychotics

These newer antipsychotic drugs are called "atypical" because they operate on brain chemistry in a manner different than the older ("typical") medications. The older antipsychotic drugs are thought to work mainly by blocking the action of a brain transmitter called dopamine, which can be associated with hallucinations and delusions. The newer atypical antipsychotic drugs block both dopamine and serotonin in parts of the brain. This produces more effectiveness against certain symptoms, but also different side effects. Medications such as olanzapine (Zyprexa), quetiapine (Seroquel), risperidone (Risperdal), and ziprasidone (Geodon) have different side effects, most notably a huge reduction in extrapyramidal (Parkinson-like) symptoms. One other atypical antipsychotic, clozapine (Clozaril), is in a class by itself. The very first atypical antipsychotic drug, clozapine is still considered the most potent of the group; however, it has very significant side effects and must be managed by a psychiatrist skilled in its use. It is never the drug "of first choice" but may work on symptoms that prove resistant to all other antipsychotic drugs. This complex molecule affects at least nine neurotransmitters. We do not know exactly how it works, but it blocks the action of both dopamine and serotonin in the brain.

> For individuals with BPD, antipsychotics have demonstrated improvements not only in thought disorder symptoms (psychosis), but also improvements in mood, anger, anxiety, and somatic complaints.

Effectiveness of Atypical Antipsychotics

Most studies on atypical antipsychotics have been done with individuals with psychotic disorders, such as schizophrenia. Open label and randomized placebo-controlled studies have found that atypical antisychotics are effective.[4] Some studies show the atypical antipsychotics are more effective than older antipsychotics at reducing psychosis and improving overall functioning. They have also dramatically reduced extrapyramidal (Parkinson-like) side effects.[5] Oxford University researcher John Geddes and his associates performed a meta-analysis of 52 studies of atypical antipsychotics, which represented over 12,000 patients. Their results showed that amisulpride, clozapine, olanzapine, quetiapine, and risperidone reduced psychotic symptoms, compared to placebo. Dropout rates were similar between the older medications and the new ones, indicating that patients may have found the side effects of the new medications (weight gain, for example) as troubling as the side effects of the older ones (such as extrapyramidal symptoms).[6] However, for individuals who have not responded to older antipsychotics, atypical antipsychotics offer a potentially promising form of treatment. The atypical antipsychotic clozapine has been shown to have some effectiveness on symptoms that have proven resistant to other antipsychotic drugs. For this reason, clozapine may be considered the most potent of the antipsychotic drugs, but is not recommended as the first choice because of its side effects and difficulty of use. As mentioned above, it is often used as the "treatment of last resort," but one with surprisingly beneficial results in many resistant cases.

Some studies show the atypical antipsychotics are more effective than older antipsychotics at reducing psychosis and improving overall functioning.

The few studies done with individuals with BPD have been very encouraging. A recent placebo-controlled double-blind study of olanzapine with 28 women with BPD demonstrated significant improvements for a broad range of symptoms.[7] Olanzapine helped a group of 9 patients with BPD and dysthymia improve their overall functioning and decrease depression, interpersonal sensitivity, hostility, and impulsivity.[8] Clozapine has been shown to be effective in reducing self-injurious behavior and dramatically improving overall functioning in a group of 7 women with BPD.[9] Two additional open trials found global improvements and symptom reductions in 12 inpatients[10] and 15 patients with concurrent atypical psychosis with BPD.[11]

In addition to controlled studies, several case studies have been encouraging. Most exciting are cases in which self-injurious behavior has been reduced or eliminated. A highly impulsive 31-year-old woman with BPD had a remission of her self-injurious behavior when treated with risperidone.[12] Two women, ages 24 and 27, with severe BPD, eliminated their self-injurious behavior when treated with olanzapine (follow-up was conducted for at least 6 months).[13] Perhaps the most remarkable case was a 32-year-old woman who was severely self-injurious (medically hospitalized 39 times to treat the self-injuries). She had been restrained 226 times for a total of over 7,300 hours during her 6.5 years of psychiatric hospitalization. To put that number of hours in perspective, consider that a typical full-time work year is about 2,000 hours (40 hours per week for 50 weeks).

Numerous medication approaches had been tried, including low-dose antipsychotics, high-dose antipsychotics, tricyclic antidepressants, SSRIs, benzodiazepines, lithium, and carbamazepine; she also received psychotherapy. Treated with clozapine, her incidents of self-injury decreased within 2 weeks, and she was discharged in 3 months to a community-based setting. She was then transferred to an apartment. She was still doing well at a 16-month follow-up, with no self-injurious behavior since her discharge.[14] In addition to cases of self-injurious behavior, several other cases have reported positive results with atypical antipsychotics. One person with BPD and dysthymia improved after receiving a combination of risperidone and fluvoxamine (Luvox, an antidepressant) much more than she did with antipsychotics.[15] In one case, a person with obsessive-compulsive disorder and BPD improved considerably after taking clozapine, despite failing with psychotherapy, older antipsychotics, and atypical antipsychotics.[16]

Side Effects of Antipsychotic Medications

Neurological side effects, especially with the typical antipsychotics, include akinesia (difficulty moving), drowsiness, extrapyramidal (Parkinson-like) symptoms, and akathisia (motor restlessness). Seizure threshold can also be lowered, which could be a problem for individuals with epilepsy or other seizure disorders (low-potency medications, such as chlorpromazine, are more likely to produce this problem). Approximately one person in 1,000 will experience neuroleptic malignant syndrome, an uncomfortable and potentially dangerous condition characterized by fever, muscle rigidity, increased pulse, and confusion or stupor. Antipsychotics also impact the neurotransmitter acetylcholine, and thus have anticholinergic effects, such as flushing, dry skin, dry mouth, delayed ejaculation, memory problems, and confusion. In the cardiovascular system, antipsychotics can promote hypotension (low blood pressure), and some (including the atypical ziprasidone) are also associated with arrhythmias. Hormonal changes can occur, such as increased release of prolactin (the hormone that induces the body to produce milk), decreased testosterone, and reduced sex drive in both genders. They can also interfere with the release of insulin, which can be a problem in individuals who have or who are prone to diabetes. The atypical antipsychotic olanzapine can cause insulin resistance (increasing the risk of type 2 diabetes), which is not seen with risperidone. In the blood, rare but potentially dangerous conditions can occur. Clozapine is associated with reduced white-blood-cell count, a condition known as agranulocytosis; if you take clozapine, you will need to have weekly blood tests for the first six months, then biweekly for as long as you are on the medication. Agranulocytosis occurs in approximately one percent of all cases, and almost always responds to withdrawal of the medication. However, a few deaths have been associated with the medication, which is why it is not used as a first-line treatment, despite excellent

> *Neurological side effects, especially with the typical antipsychotics, include akinesia (difficulty moving), drowsiness, extrapyramidal (Parkinson-like) symptoms, and akathisia (motor restlessness).*

efficacy. In addition, antipsychotics have been associated with light sensitivity; more seriously, doses of thioridizine over 800 milligrams can produce permanent visual impairments. Some antipsychotics can lead to weight gain (olanzapine, for example).[17]

The side effects of long-term use of antipsychotics can be very serious. Tardive dyskinesia (TD) is a condition that commonly involves involuntary movements of the mouth or limbs. A standard medical text estimates a 20 to 30 percent rate of TD for typical antipsychotics, so it is not especially rare.[18] TD can be very disabling; I have seen patients who could barely walk and who had odd, twisting motions all day long.

> *The side effects of long-term use of antipsychotics can be very serious.*

Sometimes, discontinuing the medication can reverse symptoms—but if TD has set in, the condition is permanent. Atypical antipsychotics fare better with TD. Clozapine has the lowest incidence of TD; risperidone rarely causes TD at low doses, but in high doses (greater than 6 milligrams, for example), its side effects resemble the older high-potency antipsychotics (such as haloperidol), and the risk of extrapyramidal symptoms becomes greater. Work closely with your doctor to avoid getting TD.

In general, high-potency medications, such as haloperidol, tend to produce more extrapyramidal symptoms, while low-potency medications, such as chlorpromazine, are more sedating and produce more anticholinergic effects (such as dry mouth). Different medications, even if they are of the same general type, have different side-effect profiles. Many other side effects can occur. Check with your prescribing clinician, your pharmacist, and other resources, such as those listed in appendix B under "Medications." You can also get an exact list of side effects from your prescribing clinician or pharmacist.

AFFECTIVE DYSREGULATION DIMENSION

Affective dysregulation refers to unstable or unbalanced mood, including inappropriate and intense anger; mood swings; and feelings of emptiness, sadness, loneliness, and lack of pleasure in activities. The SSRIs (selective serotonin reuptake inhibitors), which are classified as antidepressant drugs, help reduce these emotional states. They offer relief to individuals with BPD by reducing depression, lability, anxiety, and anger.

These medications also have the benefit of low side-effect profiles. For these reasons, SSRIs are generally the first drugs of choice for this population. In cases where the SSRIs do not work, or the response is not good enough, an MAOI (monoamine oxidase inhibitor) can be considered. Sometimes a low-dose antipsychotic can be added, in order to further reduce feelings of anger.

> *Antidepressant medications have a long history and well-established efficacy. They usually begin to relieve depression in approximately 2 to 3 weeks.*

MAOIs have been found to be useful for atypical depression, defined by mood reactivity, excessive eating and sleeping, and lack of energy. Interestingly, the tricyclic antidepressants are often ineffective for people with BPD. In contrast, mood stabilizers, such as lithium carbonate, valproate, and carbamazepine, have been effective in some cases and offer an additional alternative.

Antidepressants

Antidepressant medications have a long history and well-established efficacy. They usually begin to relieve depression in approximately 2 to 3 weeks. Although some people experience improvements quickly, most people need to wait in order to get the full benefits of the medication.

Monoamine Oxidase Inihibitors

Monoamine oxidase (MAO) is the enzyme that breaks down monoamines; monoamines are a group of neurotransmitters, including serotonin and norepinephrine. Although they lost popularity due to their side-effect profile, monoamine oxidase inhibitors (MAOIs) may still be effective in cases where other medications are not.

MAOIs Effectiveness with BPD

At least three studies have shown beneficial effects of MAOIs with BPD. A study in 1971 showed that many individuals with "pseudo-neurotic schizophrenia" (a forerunner of borderline personality disorder) had a positive response to tranylcypromine, trifluoperazine, or a combination of the two.[19] A study of phenelzine was done with 16 women with "hysteroid dysphoria"; 14 of the 16 met the criteria for borderline personality disorder. Participants also received psychodynamic psychotherapy twice per week. Eleven of the 16 (68 percent) did well with this combination.

After 3 months, the 11 patients who did well were entered into a double-blind placebo-controlled withdrawal phase—the participants were given an inactive substance rather than the medication. Eight of the 11 (73 percent) experienced a worsening of symptoms, including relationship problems, feelings of emptiness and boredom, and self-injurious behavior.[20] Drs. Cowdry and Gardner's randomized, placebo-controlled study showed tranylcypromine improved mood and reduced suicidality and impulsivity. Dr. Soloff concludes, "The MAOI antidepressants offer global improvement for multiple presentations of mood pathology in BPD, including depression, anxiety, and anger, but also for impulsivity, suicidality, and (to a lesser extent) behavioral dyscontrol."[21]

> If you have major depression along with borderline personality disorder, tricyclics (TCAs) are effective with depressive symptoms.

Some MAO inhibitors can have severe side effects if you eat cheeses and other foods that contain tyramine. Your blood pressure can skyrocket, which can be extremely dangerous. Some recently developed MAOIs avoid this side effect. Ask your clinician to carefully explain the proper use of your medication.

Tricyclics

If you have major depression along with borderline personality disorder, tricyclics (TCAs) are effective with depressive symptoms.[22] Unlike MAOIs and SSRIs, however, TCAs have been found to have very little positive effect on other symptoms of borderline personality disorder. Among individuals with high levels of hostility, amitriptyline was found to worsen physical assaultiveness and suicidality relative to placebo.[23] Based on his review of the literature, psychiatrist and BPD expert Emil Coccaro, M.D., concludes, "It is possible that tricyclic agents may be either of little benefit, or perhaps contraindicated, in some personality disordered (for example, BPD) patients."[24]

Paul Soloff, M.D., concurs: "Although based on scanty evidence, it appears that tricyclic antidepressants have limited efficacy in BPD as a primary diagnosis."[25] Noting that there are increased behavioral problems—for example, with amitriptyline—Soloff concludes, "It would be prudent for clinicians to avoid use of tricyclic antidepressants as a first line of treatment in this population."[26]

Side Effects of Tricyclics

Tricyclic antidepressants have some potentially annoying side effects, such as dry mouth, blurred vision, urinary retention, constipation, drowsiness, dizziness, low blood pressure, and weight gain.

Selective Serotonin Reuptake Inhibitors

Some of the newer antidepressants, selective serotonin reuptake inhibitors (SSRIs) such as Prozac, have generated a lot of excitement. They reduce depression as much as older antidepressants and have much fewer side effects. Anecdotally, I have noticed that patients on SSRIs seem more enthusiastic about them than clients who are on tricyclics. In addition to feeling less depressed, clients on SSRIs seem to "brighten up" and feel cheerier. Another positive: These new antidepressants result in fewer side effects. With the advent of Prozac, it has become less stigmatizing and more acceptable to talk about being depressed. This freedom from stigma may be Prozac's most powerful antidepressant legacy.

> With the advent of Prozac, it has become less stigmatizing and more acceptable to talk about being depressed. This freedom from stigma may be Prozac's most powerful antidepressant legacy.

Studies of SSRIs and BPD

Randomized double-blind studies have shown that SSRIs are helpful in reducing depression and anxiety in individuals with BPD. SSRIs also reduce impulsivity and impulsive aggression including self-directed aggression (self-injurious and suicidal behavior), as well as anger.[27] For these reasons, SSRIs are often the first medications used with someone with BPD.

Commonly used SSRIs include fluoxetine (Prozac), sertraline (Zoloft), paroxetine (Paxil), and citalopram (Celexa). Even if you do not respond to one SSRI, another one may work.

Side Effects of SSRIs

When taking SSRIs, some people experience neurological symptoms, such as agitation or akathisia (motor restlessness). Nausea and headaches may also occur. Sexual side effects are common; women may find it difficult or impossible to have an orgasm, and men may have delayed ejaculation. For a more complete list of side effects, ask your physician or pharmacist about your particular medication, or see one of the books in appendix B under "Medications."

Mood Stabilizers

There is more than a passing resemblance between borderline personality disorder and temporal lobe epilepsy. The two conditions share similar cognitive symptoms (transient psychotic episodes) and emotional symptoms (rage and behavioral dyscontrol). There is also some similarity to bipolar (manic-depressive) disorder; in both disorders, one's mood swings wildly back and forth. These similarities have led clinicians and researchers to explore whether anticonvulsants for temporal lobe epilepsy and mood stabilizers for bipolar disorder would be effective for BPD as well.

Lithium Carbonate

Usually referred to simply as "lithium," lithium carbonate is a highly effective medication for bipolar disorder, especially in bringing manic symptoms under control. Because of its effectiveness, lithium is widely used for people with bipolar disorder. Lithium has an unusually narrow "therapeutic window." This means that the amount of lithium you need to have in your blood to get a therapeutic effect is very close to the level at which it is too high and it becomes poisonous (toxic). Simultaneously, this is also very close to the level at which the blood level is too low and is ineffective. This scenario reminds me of those concentrated saccharine drops my grandfather used to use. You could barely taste the sweetness of one drop, three drops were too sweet, but two drops were just right. Likewise, you must work closely with your prescribing clinician to make sure your blood levels are correct, by taking routine blood samples.

Studies on the Effectiveness of Lithium with BPD
Only one double-blind placebo-controlled study has been conducted of the impact of lithium on borderline symptoms. In this study of 17 patients, lithium reduced anger and suicidal behavior. The researchers speculated that the medication helped by reducing impulsivity.[28]

Anticonvulsants
Anticonvulsants, such as valproic acid and carbamazepine, were developed to treat seizures that accompany such disorders as epilepsy. It was later discovered that anticonvulsants could be useful in treating bipolar disorder.

Studies of the Effectiveness of Anticonvulsants with BPD
Small open label studies showed that valproate and divalproex sodium reduced such symptoms as irritability, anger, impulsivity, rejection sensitivity, and mood lability.[29] However, in one of the studies, the impact of medication was rather modest, and the researchers concluded that valproate may have little value in treating individuals with BPD.[30] An open trial of lamotrigine with seven patients was very encouraging. One of the seven developed a rash and had to discontinue, and three did not respond to the medicine. Three others, however, made remarkable improvements: Impulsive sexual and drug-taking

behavior and suicidality "disappeared." At the one-year follow-up, all three respondents no longer met the criteria for BPD.[31]

Double-blind studies have had somewhat mixed results, but the majority of studies have found positive effects. A 10-week double-blind trial with 12 participants receiving divalproex sodium and four receiving placebo showed that the medication helped with overall functioning, aggression, and depression."[32] A double-blind placebo-controlled crossover study of 16 female outpatients showed that carbamazepine helped to reduce behavioral dyscontrol.[33] Carbamazepine was one of the drugs tested in Cowdry and Gardner's well-known double-blind placebo-controlled study of four medications to treat BPD. They found that carbamazepine reduced behavioral dyscontrol compared to placebo. However, a study of 20 inpatients with BPD failed to find any positive effect with carbamazepine in a 30-day double-blind placebo-controlled trial; two patients in the carbamazepine group discontinued due to severe behavioral dyscontrol (wrist cutting and acts of violence).[34]

> While antipsychotics appear to have effects on many symptoms, the effects of mood stabilizers are more specific, and should be used only in select cases.

In sum, the overall trend in the studies demonstrates that anticonvulsants such as carbamazepine and valproic acid (and its derivatives, valproate and divalproex sodium) and lamotrigine have been found to be useful for treating behavioral dyscontrol in patients with unstable moods or impulsivity. While antipsychotics appear to have effects on many symptoms, the effects of mood stabilizers are more specific, and should be used only in select cases.

Side Effects of Lithium and Anticonvulsants

Lithium's side effects can include neurological symptoms (a fine tremor in the hands, mental dullness, problems with memory and concentration, fatigue), hormonal changes (low thyroid hormone, which lowers energy level and metabolism rate), kidney changes (increased thirst and urination), gastrointestinal effects (diarrhea, nausea, abdominal cramps), and weight gain. Lithium can also have significant effects on heart functioning, which should be monitored by your physician. Anticonvulsants such as carbamazepine and the valproic acid family can cause neurological symptoms (drowsiness, dizziness, ataxia, fatigue, headache, and double-vision), gastrointestinal effects (nausea, vomiting, abdominal pain, diarrhea, constipation), effects on the eyes (blurred vision, increased pressure in the eye), and genital or urinary symptoms (increased urination or retention, kidney failure, impotence). Side effects vary considerably by medication and by individual. Work with your prescribing clinician and check the resources included in appendix B under "Medications."

Antianxiety Medications

Perhaps it is a sign of our times that antianxiety medications (anxiolytics) are so popular and varied. For many years, Valium (diazepam) was the top-selling drug in the world. Xanax (alprazolam), and BuSpar (buspirone) are other widely used antianxiety medications.

> *Perhaps it is a sign of our times that antianxiety medications (anxiolytics) are so popular and varied.*

Benzodiazepines

Benzodiazepines are widely used, due to their effectiveness and safety for anxiety disorders, if taken properly. Benzodiazepines are divided into three groups: long-acting, intermediate-acting, or short-acting. As implied, the longer acting the medication, the longer it stays in your bloodstream.

Unfortunately, research has shown that short-acting, high-potency benzodiazepines, such as alprazolam, are very problematic for people with BPD. Alprazolam was one of four medications tested in Drs. Cowdry and Gardner's placebo-controlled study.[35] Fifty-eight percent of individuals with BPD who took alprazolam had severe behavioral dyscontrol (such as a drug overdose, wrist or neck cuts, or violence), compared with only 8 percent of those on placebo. However, other benzodiazepines may be useful. For example, case reports have shown that clonazepam, a long-acting benzodiazepine anticonvulsant and antimanic agent that increases serotonin levels, has improved anxiety, depression, anger, and impulsivity in people with BPD.

Dr. Soloff concludes: "Given the paucity of controlled studies on benzodiazepine use in BPD, a well-defined adverse risk profile, and the ever-present danger of abuse and dependence, the clinician would be well-advised to use caution prescribing alprazolam or other short-acting benzodiazepines for the borderline patient."[36] George Stein is more blunt: "Benzodiazepines are contraindicated in personality disorder because of their propensity to disinhibit and to induce rage reactions and states of drug dependency."[37]

Benzodiazepines have some negative properties, as well. They are dangerous when mixed with alcohol. They cause withdrawal symptoms if discontinued after an extended period of use, and they are considered habit-forming with a high risk of addiction.

Not all anxiety medications have been researched for use with BPD. One that Soloff considers promising is buspirone, which is not habit-forming and is often used for chronic anxiety.[38] Because it increases serotonin levels, in theory, it should be beneficial for most people with BPD. However, research must be done with this medication before conclusions can be reached.

IMPULSIVE-BEHAVIORAL DYSCONTROL DIMENSION

Impulsive-behavioral dyscontrol indicates difficulty controlling one's actions. Dr. Soloff lists the following examples: "suicidal threats, parasuicidal behavior, impulsive-aggression, assaultiveness, property destruction, binge behaviors (with drugs, alcohol, sex, or food), and cognitive impulsivity with low frustration tolerance."[39] The medications used for impulsive/behavioral dyscontrol are similar to those used for affective dysregulation. SSRIs, which have been the most effective with impulsive-aggressive symptoms and are usually well-tolerated, are the first-line medications.

It is logical that SSRIs, which increase the levels of the neuro-transmitter serotonin, help people control their impulses. As noted in chapter 1, serotonin activity is reduced in people with impulsivity and impulsive aggression. If the SSRI does not work out, an antipsychotic can be used. In emergencies, antipsychotics may be given first because they act right away. Lithium carbonate, anticonvulsant medications, and atypical antipsychotics have some effectiveness and can be tried in select cases.

MEDICATION ALGORITHMS

Dr. Soloff has developed several algorithms for BPD psychopharma-cotherapy. An algorithm is a systematic way of pursuing treatment. It suggests an order of medications to try, based on which are most likely to be effective and what their side effects are. For example, to treat someone who suffers from impulsive aggression, bingeing, or self-injury, (see "Algorithm 3" in appendix C) a clinician following the algorithm would first try an SSRI antidepressant. If this is only par-tially effective, the doctor should add a low-dose antipsychotic, espe-cially if anger or aggression is an urgent problem. If the SSRI is completely ineffective, antipsychotic drugs can be used as a nonspe-cific treatment for impulsive behavior. If this does not resolve the symptoms, the clinician should move on to the next level of recom-mended treatments, including MAOIs. The algorithm also covers several other pathways.[40] Appendix C also includes Dr. Soloff's algo-rithms for treatment of cognitive-perceptual symptoms (suspicious-ness, paranoid ideation, mild thought disorders, and others) and for the treatment of affective dysregulation (lability, rejection sensitivity, inappropriate intense anger, depressive "mood crashes").

Although many medications are appropriate for treating borderline personality disorder symptoms, the results have varied. Some people have phenomenal outcomes, while others see no effect or a worsening of symptoms. Most people, however, experience some improvement in symptoms, though not a complete remission. For example, a very impulsive and aggressive person who is given the best available medications (perhaps an SSRI, such as Prozac, plus a low-dose antipsychotic, such as haloperidol) will experience less impulsivity and aggression, but will still be somewhat impulsive and aggressive. Psychotherapy or stress reduction, as supplemental treatments, may help the person to become more balanced, beyond the effect of the medications.

> *Although many med-ications are appro-priate for treating borderline personality disorder symptoms, the results have varied.*

Unfortunately, we do not know as much about medications for BPD as we would like. Dr. Soloff states:

Current empirical guidelines are based on a small and inadequate database of studies. Empirical support through randomized controlled trials are lacking (or still awaiting replication) for widespread clinical practices involving the use of atypical antipsychotics, lithium carbonate, benzodiazepines, and the anticonvulsant mood stabilizers in the borderline patient. The clinician should approach each treatment as an empirical trial, with the patient as co-investigator.[41]

TO LEARN MORE

For more information on specific medications, you can refer to the list of resources in appendix B under "Medications." H. Winter Griffith's *Complete Guide to Prescription and Nonprescription Drugs 2002* and Medical Economic Company's *PDR Family Guide to Prescription Drugs* are two excellent references. A fantastic reference for the seriously curious is Stephen Stahl's *Essential Psychopharmacology*. These resources also provide basic information on medication side effects and precautions. I have had clients who worried that a side effect was a possible medical disorder or a psychological problem, so keep in mind that most side effects are often easily managed by lowering the dosage or changing medications.

CHAPTER 5

Mind-Body Therapies for Borderline Personality Disorder

MIND-BODY THERAPIES HELP you work with the body and through the body to attain new levels of integration and awareness through therapeutic experiences that may arise during art therapy, yoga, movement/dance therapy, psychodrama, or music therapy. This approach is different from mainstream psychotherapy, a mostly verbal activity in which you talk about your thoughts, your feelings, and your dreams.

The experiential learning that takes place in mind-body therapies can be extremely powerful—and sometimes almost indescribable. People who have benefited from mind-body therapies have said that some experiences seem beyond words. The body has its own wisdom and intelligence, which Western culture has, in the past, ignored or minimized. It is at this level of lived experience that mind-body therapies intervene. Many individuals, especially those with BPD, can benefit greatly from such interventions.

By its nature, BPD usually involves "acting out," or translating emotions into actions (rather than words). For example, in response to a vague but horrible feeling, a person with BPD may attempt suicide or turn to illegal drugs for distraction. In addition, many people with BPD act on impulse, even in the face of long-term negative consequences. Finally, those who self-injure may be so out of touch with their bodies that they need to hurt themselves in order to feel anything. Thus, it makes sense, in the overall treatment of BPD, to include therapies that encourage action (such as psychodrama), body awareness (such as dance/movement therapy, yoga), and emotional awareness through nonverbal means (such as art therapy). All the general rules about therapeutic relationships that apply to psychotherapists—regarding confidentiality, therapeutic contract, and client-therapist intimacy—apply to mind-body therapists.

> *The experiential learning that takes place in mind-body therapies can be extremely powerful—and sometimes almost indescribable.*

YOGA

A lamp does not flicker in a place where no wind blows;
so it is with a yogi, who controls his mind, intellect, and self,
being absorbed in the spirit within him. When the restlessness
of the mind, intellect, and self is stilled through the practice
of Yoga, the yogi by the grace of the Spirit within himself finds
fulfillment. Then he knows the joy eternal, which is beyond
the pale of the senses, which his reason cannot grasp.[1]

—*THE BHAGAVAD GITA*

Yoga is an ancient discipline. Records indicate that yoga was practiced in India as long as 6,000 years ago. By 500 B.C.E., it had developed into a mature discipline.

Of the many different types of yoga, the best known in the United States today is hatha yoga, the system of physical postures (*asanas*). According to B.K.S. Iyengar, in his classic text *Light on Yoga:*

Asanas have been evolved over the centuries so as to exercise every muscle, nerve, and gland in the body. They secure a fine physique that is strong and elastic without being muscle-bound, and they keep the body free from disease. They reduce fatigue and soothe the nerves. But their real importance is how they train and discipline the mind.[2]

Iyengar developed his own school of yoga, which bears his name. Iyengar yoga uses precise body alignments and various props and blocks to facilitate appropriate postures. Astanga yoga, or "power yoga," is physically demanding and builds strength, flexibility, and stamina. This type of yoga is becoming more popular and is offered in a number of health clubs and yoga centers.

> *It makes sense, in the overall treatment of BPD, to include therapies that encourage action (such as psychodrama), body awareness (such as dance/movement therapy, yoga), and emotional awareness through nonverbal means (such as art therapy).*

Yoga has been extensively studied in India. According to Michael Murphy, cofounder of the Esalen Institute, and Steve Donovan, director of Esalen's Study of Exceptional Functioning:

> In . . . the *Yoga Research Bibliography: Scientific Studies of Yoga and Meditation* (1989), Monro, Ghosh, and Kalish present over 1,000 citations ranging from essay-commentaries to clinical applications and pure empirical research . . . the trend is clearly toward a mounting body of evidence showing the efficacious use of yoga techniques and Hindu meditation practice in specific disorders such as hypertension, diabetes, cancer, cholesterol regulation, alcoholism, anxiety disorders, asthma, pain control, and obesity.[3]

While relatively little of this information has trickled into the West, studies show quite encouraging results for using yoga and meditation techniques to alleviate conditions related to borderline personality disorder. One study found that yoga training was about as effective in reducing symptoms of depression as the antidepressant imipramine (though less effective than electroconvulsive therapy) in a group of 45 depressed inpatients.[4] Another study found that yoga training reduced stress levels and sleep disturbance and improved self-concept, quality of sleep, and feelings of well-being in a group of 12 female college students.[5] An uncontrolled study of the impact of yogic diet and lifestyle on 25 subjects with gastrointestinal disorders demonstrated decreases in anxiety and depression.[6]

Yoga is part of Jon Kabat-Zinn's Mindfulness-Based Stress Reduction (MBSR) program. Featured in Bill Moyers's *Healing and the Mind* (both the book and the video), MBSR is one of the most effective stress-reduction programs ever developed. Among the impressive findings have been 50 percent decreases in anxiety and depression, substantial reductions in medical symptoms, improved self-esteem, and a generally improved sense of well-being.[7] As an MBSR trainer, I have seen how yoga can provide a gateway into meditation because the movements help quiet the mind. I have also noticed improvements in flexibility, health, and relaxation in those who practice yoga.

> *S*tudies show quite encouraging results for using yoga and meditation techniques to alleviate conditions related to borderline personality disorder.

My own experience with yoga is that it teaches a profound lesson. In many postures, you must hold a state of tension in at least some of the muscles in order to maintain your balance. For example, in the triangle pose, you must tighten muscles in the legs and arms in order to keep from falling over. Most of the muscles of the belly and the chest can be kept loose, however. To the extent that you can keep those muscles loose, you can promote a feeling of wholeness and relaxation even within a state of tension. When the muscles of the belly and chest are kept loose, breathing remains free and easy. There is calm, even though many muscles are tense and balance can be somewhat precarious. In this state, the lesson—that you can be relaxed during a state of tension—is actually embodied. This lesson is a metaphor for what we experience in life: the struggle to stay relaxed in situations that elicit tension.

With consistent yoga practice, your flexibility—not just physical flexibility, but mental flexibility—improves.

Yoga can be an excellent part of practically any stress management program, as it combines the benefits of exercise and meditation. Yoga also helps to improve body awareness and promotes feelings of centeredness and groundedness. In addition, classes are usually affordable and readily available in many locations.

Presently, there is no nationally recognized certification process for yoga instructors as a whole; each style of yoga typically has some type of certification. You can ask the teacher about her training and credentials. You can also contact the American Yoga Association (see "Yoga" in appendix A).

> *With consistent yoga practice, your flexibility—not just physical flexibility, but mental flexibility—improves.*

RELAXATION TRAINING

It is important to be able to induce a state of calm during periods of stress. Any person under a sufficient amount of stress can experience anxiety, panic, or depression. Therefore, learning to feel calm and focused is an important part of managing day-to-day life in our fast-paced, complex culture.

Certain activities are well-known to elicit feelings of relaxation. Autogenics training refers to mentally going through each part of the body, focusing on that part, and saying that it feels "heavy" and "warm." I do a sequence that goes from the feet to the shins/calves, thighs, pelvis, belly, lower back, upper back, chest, arms, shoulders, neck, and head. Autogenics training is best done lying down in a comfortable position. Unless you have a condition that makes it uncomfortable to lie flat, try lying on your back without crossing your arms or legs (to avoid restricting your blood circulation in any way). You can also place a pillow under your knees to avoid strain on your back, if you wish. You can make your own tape, or say to yourself silently:

"My feet feel heavy and warm, heavy and warm. My shins and calves feel heavy and warm, heavy and warm," and so on.

Of all the techniques designed specifically to promote relaxation, in my practice I have found autogenics training to be the most effective. It is extremely simple because there are no complex images to remember. The combination of allowing your body to feel heavy and imagining that it feels warm produces a deep feeling of relaxation. Of the hundreds of people with whom I've done this technique, most find feeling heavy a bit easier than feeling warm. At the end of the exercise, you may want to "reverse" the suggestion of heaviness by saying to yourself: "My body is feeling lighter and lighter, still totally relaxed, lighter, and lighter, and lighter. My body now feels light, loose, and relaxed."

> *Of all the techniques designed specifically to promote relaxation, in my practice I have found autogenics training to be the most effective.*

Once, during a stress-reduction class at an adult education center, I forgot to reverse the suggestion of heaviness at the end of an autogenics session. As a result, students moved about slowly, pushing themselves off the floor, grabbing onto chairs to pull themselves up. Since then, I have always used light, yet still-relaxed images at the end of a session.

Guided imagery is a relaxation technique in which you imagine a specific relaxing scene and your presence in it, step-by-step. I usually use the beach as a relaxing image. In a group, however, I first make sure no one is afraid of the water or has fears about being in the sun. Other scenes people find relaxing are walking through the woods or sitting by a lake or pond. Some people can only relax when they are active; in these cases, imagery of hiking, rock climbing, or other strenuous activity can be used. Such individuals often choose to actually exercise, rather than merely imagine it, in order to relax.

Permissive imagery is similar, but leaves the "place to go" (in your mind's eye) up to your imagination. I encourage people to go to their "special place," where they can feel calm and relaxed, and visualize it utilizing all five senses (seeing, hearing, tasting, smelling, and touching).

Relaxation training is widely accepted as a form of therapy with at least moderate effectiveness, a belief that is supported by substantial amounts of scientific data. Meta-analytic and other studies have shown that relaxation training can be an effective treatment for anxiety,[8] post-traumatic stress disorder (PTSD),[9] attention-deficit/hyperactivity disorder (ADHD),[10] stress,[11] insomnia,[12] and health problems such as headache, asthma, and hypertension.[13]

Relaxation is generally considered very safe. During relaxation training or hypnosis, some of my clients with trauma histories have had flashbacks or memories of the trauma. This also happens occasionally during imagery-based interventions, but this has not happened during progressive muscular relaxation. If you have a trauma history, you should start by doing relaxation training with a professional, then make a tape when you find a program that works for you. Before doing relaxation work, let your therapist know that you have experienced a trauma in the past.

> *Studies have shown that relaxation training can be an effective treatment for anxiety, post-traumatic stress disorder, attention-deficit/ hyperactivity disorder, stress, insomnia, and health problems such as headache, asthma, and hypertension.*

Many psychologists, social workers, and other psychotherapists, especially those with a behavioral orientation, are skilled in relaxation training. The therapist is often willing to make a tape for you, which you can then use for practice. *The Relaxation and Stress Reduction Workbook* by Martha Davis, Matthew McKay, and Elizabeth Eshelman (New Harbinger Press, 1995) is an incredible and practical book. The workbook has scripts that you can use to make your own relaxation tape. Additional resources are listed under "Meditation and Mindfulness" in appendix B.

EXPRESSIVE ARTS THERAPY

Expressive arts therapy refers to a group of therapies that use creative expression as a form of therapy. Dance, music, and art therapy are the disciplines most clearly associated with this approach. Psychodrama, using the acting out of roles as a form of therapy, can also be included. In expressive arts therapy, what is important is the expression—not the final product. It will help you to alleviate any self-consciousness by remembering that, while professionals in the arts are expected to produce a certain level of "perfection" for the public, people in expressive arts therapy are expected only to participate for their own self-expression. In this case, there is no right or wrong way: Simply express what is going on within you and what you are feeling in the moment. Natalie Rogers describes it this way:

> *While professionals in the arts are expected to produce a certain level of "perfection" for the public, people in expressive arts therapy are expected only to participate for their own self-expression.*

When using the arts for self-healing or therapeutic purposes, we are not concerned with the beauty of the visual art, the grammar and style of the writing, or the harmonic flow of the song. We use the arts to let go, express, and to release. Also, we can gain insight by studying the symbolic and metaphoric messages. Our art speaks back to us, if we take time to let in those messages.[14]

Some people believe that they are "not creative," and therefore may not benefit from this approach. This is an unfortunate belief that stems from culturally based judgments of what is "good" or "bad" art. True, when I go to an art museum, I do not expect to see stick figures (although these days, who knows!). However, the process of self-expression is one in which we can all engage. Self-expression is an inherently creative process; as such, it can be healing. Natalie Rogers expresses this idea beautifully:

> The Creative Connection process that I have developed stimulates such self-exploration. It is like the unfolding petals of a lotus blossom on a summer day. In the warm, accepting environment, the petals open to reveal the flower's inner essence. As our feelings are tapped, they become a resource for further self-understanding and creativity. We gently allow ourselves to awaken to new possibilities. With each opening we may deepen our experience. When we reach our inner

core, we find our connection to all beings. We create to connect to our inner source and to reach out to the world and the universe.[15]

This unfolding process improves self-awareness and allows the processing of feelings, which are cornerstones of virtually all psychotherapies.

The healing approach of expressive arts therapies is different from that of psychotherapy in that images and other artistic expressions often have primacy over words. It is a particularly important modality for people who are not adept at, not temperamentally suited to, or simply don't like expressing their feelings using words. Many people with borderline personality disorders "act out" their feelings. As discussed in the introduction to this chapter, rather than saying, "I feel horrible and rejected," some individuals will cut themselves or make a suicide attempt. Rather than talking with someone to self-soothe, such an individual may do something impulsive to distract himself. Individuals with BPD are often action-oriented, rather than verbally oriented.

The healing approach of expressive arts therapies is different from that of psychotherapy, in that images and other artistic expressions often have primacy over words.

As with the other therapies covered in this chapter, there is as yet little scientific evidence specific to borderline personality disorder in the creative arts therapy literature. For some people, especially those who do not respond well to verbal therapies, these therapies are the key to their recovery. A meta-analysis of dance therapy (an outcome review of 781 clients, critically analyzed by experts) suggests a potent treatment effect, comparable to the impact of verbal psychotherapy.[16] Though preliminary, the results suggest that the effects of dance therapy exceed those of traditional verbal psychotherapies for anxiety; the researchers suggest that the additional impact may be due to the physical exercise entailed in movement approaches.

Music therapy, in a meta-analytic review, has also demonstrated effectiveness. In 1986, researcher Jayne Standley reviewed 30 studies in which music therapy was used for a wide variety of conditions, including dental pain, pre-surgery, childbirth labor, and mood enhancement, among others.[17] Most of the studies showed an improvement in the individual's condition. Standley updated the study in 1992 and included the original 30 studies plus 25 new ones for a total of 55 studies.[18] For both studies, improvements were significant and comparable to other forms of psychotherapy.

Case examples using expressive arts therapy for borderline personality disorder are also encouraging. Dr. Danielle Fraenkel, Ph.D., ADTR (Academy of Dance Therapists registered), NCC (national certified counselor), LPC (licensed professional counselor), is a therapist in Rochester, New York, and is the founding director of Kinections. Former chairperson of the American Dance Therapy Association's (ADTA) credentials committee, Dr. Fraenkel has a master's degree in dance therapy and a Ph.D. in education with a specialization in counseling.

In her therapeutic approach, Dr. Fraenkel uses her body, moving with the client to create an empathic link. This relationship provides the support that is necessary for the client to feel safe. She describes the case of "Angelina," a 50-year-old client who had great difficulties with authority figures, poor boundaries, and severe depression for many years. Despite a decade of verbal therapy, many of her issues were unresolved.

But in dance/movement therapy, while Angelina continued to talk, for the most part her words emerged from the dance movement itself. She concentrated on her breath, muscle connection, and form, which helped her to discover new ways of connecting to her body and to reclaim her sense of self. After approximately 2 years of dance/movement therapy, Angelina's issues were largely resolved. She established both personal and interpersonal boundaries that resulted in major shifts in her lifestyle and in her relationships with others. Angelina reworked her developmental issues symbolically by mastering new ways to move and empower herself kinesthetically. To date, the depression has not returned.

There are two levels of credentials for dance/movement therapists. To quote the American Dance Therapy Association's Web site (www.adta.org/credenti.html):

> The Association has always distinguished between dance/movement therapists prepared to work in professional settings within a team under supervision, and those prepared for the responsibilities of working independently in private practice or providing supervision.
>
> *DTR (Dance Therapist Registered):* Therapists with this title have a master's degree and are fully qualified to work in a professional treatment system.
>
> *ADTR (Academy of Dance Therapists Registered):* Therapists with this title have met additional requirements and are fully qualified to teach, provide supervision, and engage in private practice.

For referral to a dance movement therapist, contact the ADTA (see "Dance and Movement Therapy" in appendix A).

MUSIC THERAPY

The use of music to affect mood is part of our everyday experience. "Whistling in the dark" is a time-honored way of reducing fear. Runners strap on headphones, either to get pumped up or calmed down during their daily jog. The soundtrack of a movie can elicit tension, tranquility, or romance. Music's therapeutic effects have been widely known throughout history and geography. Archeological findings originating thousands of years ago indicate that the ancient Egyptians used music as a form of therapy, and religious rituals in numerous cultures even now use music or rhythms for healing.

> *Archeological findings originating thousands of years ago indicate that the ancient Egyptians used music as a form of therapy.*

Music therapy officially became a profession in 1950, with the founding of the National Association for Music Therapy. As Bryan Hunter, past president of the NAMT explains:

As thousands of war veterans suffering physical and mental illnesses filled Veterans Affairs and other hospitals across the country, volunteer community musicians came to perform for them. The patients' physical and psychologic responses were so remarkable and consistent that hospitals began to hire musicians to play for them.[19]

Hospitals then wanted certified music therapists, so training programs were developed in the mid-1940s, and the NAMT established standards and procedures for obtaining credentials shortly thereafter. In defining music therapy, Hunter states:

Music therapy engages the client in one or more music experiences such as listening, singing, playing, improvising, writing, and moving to music in an attempt to facilitate change toward the positive end of the continuum [of health and illness]. Underlying all of music therapy practice are three important music traits. First is the element of rhythm, which sustains the temporal existence of music and holds the potential to energize and bring order, something often missing or weakened by illness or disability. Second is the nonverbal nature of music, which allows communication and responses at levels otherwise not accessible. Third is music's flexibility and adaptability, which in large part explains the diverse applications of music therapy, along with the fact that patients do not require music training to benefit from it.[20]

> *Music therapy is an appropriate modality for a number of conditions associated with borderline personality disorder, including symptoms stemming from sexual abuse, post-traumatic stress disorder, and substance abuse.*

According to the American Music Therapy Association (AMTA), music therapy is an appropriate modality for a number of conditions associated with borderline personality disorder, including symptoms stemming from sexual abuse, post-traumatic stress disorder, and substance abuse.

The AMTA Member Sourcebook reports about 5,000 music therapists in the United States. Approximately three-fourths of them practice at the bachelor's level, with the rest having higher degrees. A master's or doctoral degree is required to do music psychotherapy (as opposed to music therapy). If you have BPD, you should work with a person with a master's or doctoral degree, unless you are working with a treatment team that includes a bachelor's degree–level practitioner.

Since 1998, the Certification Board for Music Therapists (CBMT) has awarded the MT-BC (music therapist-board certified) designation to individuals who complete appropriate educational and clinical training requirements and pass a national exam; the MT-BC is the only certification available to music therapists who finished their training during 1998 or later. The American Music Therapy Association used to award three other (now extant) designations: certified music therapist (CMT), advanced certified music therapist (ACMT), and registered music therapist (RMT). Make sure that any music therapist you see has one of the four designations above. For a referral, contact the AMTA (see "Music Therapy" in appendix A).

CHAPTER 6

Alternative Approaches in Treatment

PEOPLE WITH BPD have numerous alternative medicine treatment options available today. An article in the prestigious *New England Journal of Medicine* revealed that, in 1990, Americans made 425 million visits to practitioners of unconventional medicine, which exceeded the number of visits to primary care physicians by nearly 10 percent. Out-of-pocket expenditures ($10.3 billion) for alternative or complementary treatments exceeded out-of-pocket expenditures for traditional outpatient care.[1] The American people have been embracing options such as Eastern medicine systems, wellness programs, herbs, and traditional healing programs in unprecedented numbers. Some of the most popular systems—traditional Chinese medicine, Vedic medicine, and homeopathy—will be reviewed in this chapter, with an eye to how they may help individuals with BPD.

As a behavioral scientist, I have conducted research and taught research methodology. I look for solid, valid scientific studies for all the approaches that can potentially improve physical and mental well-being. I believe, however, that to a certain extent the burden of proof lies with those who claim that well-established, widely used alternative approaches do not work. Several of these "alternative" systems have been mainstream medicine in other cultures for a very long time, with beneficial results. In other words, many of these therapies have survived the test of time and observation.

> *The burden of proof lies with those who claim that well-established, widely used alternative approaches do not work. Several of these "alternative" systems have been mainstream medicine in other cultures for a very long time.*

So, with an open mind, an explorer's attitude, and a healthy demand for supporting evidence and documented safety, let us now begin our journey into the world of alternative treatment approaches. As there are no documented alternative medicines or treatments specifically for borderline personality disorder, we will focus on possible remedies for various symptoms associated with BPD—depression, anxiety, restlessness, and impulsiveness. Also, since specific scientific studies of individuals with BPD are lacking, I interviewed specialists in each discipline, in order to get their clinical impressions.

EASTERN MEDICINE SYSTEMS

The largest Eastern medicine systems are traditional Chinese medicine (TCM), and Vedic medicine, from India. These systems are related to one another: Both focus on the "life force" ("chi" in TCM and "prana" in Vedic medicine) as being central to an individual's functioning. Both look at ways to balance the internal and external forces in one's life to create harmony. Both use herbal remedies, exercises, and meditation as interventions.

These systems have stood the test of time. Each one is thousands of years old, and has been practiced by millions, perhaps even billions of people, over the years. These systems have a markedly different view of health and illness than Western medicine, and may provide answers for some problems that cannot be provided in a Western framework.

Traditional Chinese Medicine

Traditional Chinese medicine (TCM) has been in existence for at least 2,000 years and is a radically different system from the Western allopathic medicine with which most of us grew up. In Western medicine, the body and mind are considered separate. The body is seen as a machine that can be repaired. Organ transplants and surgical repair of broken bones and torn ligaments are examples of this metaphor in action. Another Western medicine metaphor views the body as a country that can be invaded by hostile intruders. This view is related to our knowledge of bacteria, viruses, and other organisms that can disrupt our biological functioning. The Western medicine approach is that if the invaders can be fought off, the body will return to normal.

In the TCM view, a vital life force called chi (pronounced "chee," and often spelled "qi") passes through the body along a series of 14 meridians. As it flows through the meridians, chi can become blocked, causing a disruption in the person's functioning. The meridians cannot be seen, but they can be detected electrically. Most of the meridians are connected to major organs and are related to an organ's proper functioning.[2]

Two forces influence chi: yin and yang. Yin is characterized by such qualities as coldness, weakness, hollowness, and darkness. Yang, embodying the opposite of yin, represents heat, strength, solidity, and light. Beyond the focus on yin and yang, there are several different schools of

> *Traditional Chinese medicine has been in existence for at least 2,000 years and is a radically different system from the Western allopathic medicine with which most of us grew up.*

thought within TCM. One perspective focuses on the body's internal organs. Each internal organ is related to a particular emotion. The heart is associated with joy, the spleen with anxiety, the lungs with grief, the liver with anger and frustration, and the kidneys with fear or paranoia. Another approach focuses on the five elements: The body is made up of wind, water, earth, fire, and metal, all of which must be in proper balance. The season, weather, diet, and emotions affect the balance of the elements. Finally, another widely used system involves causes of disease that are divided into external and internal causes. External causes include wind, cold, summer heat, damp, dryness, and fire heat. Mental pathogens (internal causes) include overjoy, anger, anxiety, overthinking, grief, fear, and fright. Diseases can be differentiated from one another according to eight principles: exterior/interior, hot/cold, deficiency/excess, and yin/yang. What results from this conceptualization is a dynamic, interconnected system of diagnosis and ongoing evaluation.

Assessment by a Chinese medicine practitioner often involves examining the tongue and various pulses. The practitioner is checking the tongue for its color, size, coating, moisture, and the way in which it moves. Each portion of the tongue is associated with an organ in the body and a corresponding meridian. The pulses are also quite complex, as each wrist contains six pulses (each corresponding to a separate meridian) that must be analyzed in turn. The practitioner may also listen to the sound of your voice, observe the way you move, ask about your sleep patterns, and discuss your taste in food (the kinds of food you prefer and temperature at which you like to eat them). The practitioner may also investigate your urine and sweating patterns (such as sweating at night versus during the day).

> *The main interventions used in traditional Chinese medicine are acupuncture and herbs.*

Acupuncture

The main interventions used in traditional Chinese medicine are acupuncture and herbs. Acupuncture involves placing needles at particular points located along the meridians and is thought to directly affect the flow of chi. The needles come in varying lengths, and a slight electrical charge can be added. Herbs have a complex and multifaceted impact. Herbs are often described as "warming" or "cooling," related to their connection to yin versus yang forces. Herbs can impact one or more of the organs and change the balance within the body. Unlike those who use the single-herb approach, which parallels Western medicine, practitioners of Chinese medicine combine numerous herbs for an individual's treatment. This provides, according to practitioners, a more balanced and comprehensive correction to the imbalances present. TCM also emphasizes prevention and healthy living. Diet, exercise, and other practices are discussed as part of a lifestyle that promotes balance. For an entertaining and informative look at a variety of alternative interventions, see Bill Moyers's documentary, *Healing and the Mind*.[3]

Lorraine Wu, M.D., a board-certified physician in family practice, has studied TCM with leading practitioners in China and the United States. Dr. Wu, who receives numerous referrals from psychotherapists (and makes many referrals to them), reports that she has treated a number of individuals with BPD. Each treatment has been unique, as it depends on the person's unique makeup. For example, some individuals with borderline personality disorder have angry, frustrated, depressive presentations (excessive fire, insufficient kidney) while others are more fearful and anxious (excessive spleen). In general, her view is that TCM has been a helpful and important part of overall treatment. Given the common feeling among people with BPD that everything in their life is out of balance, TCM's focus on balance provides a welcome perspective.

> *Given the common feeling among people with BPD that everything in their life is out of balance, TCM's focus on balance provides a welcome perspective.*

According to Dr. Wu, TCM has been "fantastic" for her patients with post-traumatic stress disorder (PTSD). Treating PTSD must be done carefully, she notes, with a great deal of emotional support from the acupuncturist or the psychotherapist. The acupuncture often helps "break through" to underlying feelings, helping the patient feel more free and open. She states it has also helped clients with mild to moderate depression.

Dr. Wu expresses concerns about the current rush to push herbal remedies into the Western system, as if they were medications that happened to grow on plants. For example, garlic is supposed to be good for the heart and lower cholesterol, according to Western studies. In TCM, however, garlic is a heating herb. Therefore, someone who is obese, hot, and sweaty should not take garlic. She believes, when it comes to herbs, following the more complex, sophisticated Chinese system is better than attempting to map individual herbs onto syndromes (such as BPD) defined by allopathic medicine.

Despite some limitations, the available scientific evidence points to TCM as an effective modality. Acupuncture, in particular, has received a great deal of attention. A computerized search through a psychology database shows that more than 430 studies or papers on acupuncture have been completed since 1967. One study, conducted by psychologist John Allen, Ph.D., at the University of Arizona, acupuncturist Rosa Schnyer, and their colleague Sabrina Hitt, gave very encouraging findings on the use of acupuncture for depression. They randomly assigned 38 depressed participants to three different groups: a depression treatment group (acupuncture was given at the correct corresponding points to treat depression); a control condition (acupuncture was given, but at points related to another condition, not depression); and a wait-list control (no treatment was given until after the initial trial was completed). Full remission was defined as individuals no longer meeting the *DSM-IV* criteria for depression. In the treatment group, 42 percent of participants had a full remission, as opposed to 9 percent in the nonspecific treatment group, and 20 percent in the nontreatment control group.[4]

> *Despite some limitations, the available scientific evidence points to TCM as an effective modality.*

This is comparable to results one would obtain from other traditional and nontraditional treatments, such as 8 weeks of psychotherapy or meditation training. Allen and Schnyer are presently conducting a follow-up of approximately 180 individuals, in order to thoroughly test the hypothesis that acupuncture is effective for depression.

Other studies show promising results as well. Three physicians funded by the National Institutes of Health's Office of Alternative

Medicine—James Peightel, Thomas Hardie, and David Baron—describe several additional studies documenting acupuncture's effectiveness in depression and anxiety. Two of the studies found no difference between amitriptyline (a tricyclic antidepressant) and acupuncture in relieving depressive symptoms.[5]

They describe one study that followed 20 cases of "mental depression" treated with acupuncture compared with 21 control cases medicated with amitriptyline. Results, as measured by the Hamilton Depression Scale, revealed no significant differences in therapeutic effects.[6] In another study, 241 individuals suffering from depression, and who were not substance abusers, were treated with either acupuncture or amitriptyline over a 6-week period. Outcome measures showed a significant reduction in depression symptoms for both groups with no significant differences. Thus, it was concluded that acupuncture was as effective as amitriptyline in treating depression.[7]

Another study examined the use of acupuncture to reduce depression and anxiety in patients with chronic physical diseases. Of the 68 subjects, 11 suffered from anxiety, 8 from depression, and 49 from both. They were assigned to a single-blind, premeasure and postmeasure, non-controlled study design. Changes in depression and anxiety were assessed using the Hospital Anxiety and Depression scale. The study reported that 70 percent of the patients with anxiety and 90 percent of patients with depression returned to normal levels as measured by the instruments used.[8]

> The World Health Organization has recognized that acupuncture is effective for numerous medical conditions for over 20 years.

There is also evidence that acupuncture may be helpful to individuals with substance use problems. A controlled study of 54 alcoholic recidivists (relapsers) found acupuncture to bring significant reductions in expressed need for alcohol, drinking episodes, and detoxification admissions.[9]

The World Health Organization has recognized that acupuncture is effective for numerous medical conditions for over 20 years.[10]

The American Foundation of Medical Acupuncture conducted a review of world clinical literature. They compiled a list of the most frequent successful applications of acupuncture, which included depression, anxiety, and substance abuse (drugs, nicotine, food, alcohol).[11] According to an article by Patricia Culliton and Thomas Kiresuk, acupuncture, particularly when applied to the external ear, was shown to be valuable in managing substance abuse problems and reducing prescription narcotic analgesics; they report that this application has gained the respect of rehabilitation programs internationally.[12]

Dr. Vincent Brewington and associates are a bit more cautious, but still positive. Based on their review of the literature, the authors note that results from available placebo-designed studies support acupuncture's effectiveness in facilitating abstinence with alcohol, opiate, and cocaine abusers that is not due to simple placebo effect. However, they indicate that relatively few experiments have used placebo-controls, so definitive conclusions are premature. The authors cite four studies that demonstrate that acupuncture has clinical value as a detoxification treatment for opiate abuse. One study showed an additive effect of acupuncture in conjunction with methadone detoxification. The others compared acupuncture to methadone detoxification and found either comparable clinical outcomes (one study) or superior outcomes (two studies). Three studies also supported that correct site acupuncture has greater therapeutic effects than incorrect site treatment for alcoholics (two studies) and cocaine abusers (one study). The authors cited three studies that reported acupuncture to relieve psychological abstinence symptoms associated with heroin, cocaine, and alcohol abuse (such as anxiety, depression, and substance craving).[13]

Risks and side effects for medical acupuncture (acupuncture that has been adapted for medical or allied health practices in Western countries) appear to be minor. In a discussion of adverse effects, Dr. Joseph Helms notes that many patients report a sensation of well-being or relaxation following an acupuncture treatment, especially if electrical stimulation has also been used.[14] This sense of relaxation sometimes evolves into a feeling of fatigue or depression that lasts for several days. Other transient responses can be light-headedness, anxiety, agitation, and tearfulness.

Herbal Remedies

Some scientific evidence also supports the use of TCM herbal remedies. Dr. Peightel and assoicates review a number of studies that involved individuals with psychiatric conditions.[15] One study involved using the immunomodulating herb "xin shen ling." In that study, 30 individuals with chronic schizophrenia who did not respond to a variety of neuroleptic medications were given xin shen ling. The researchers found that six of seven immunologic functioning markers were significantly different from those of comparison participants. The Brief Psychosis Rating Scale (BPRS) and the Nurses' Observation Scale for Inpatient Evaluation (NOSIE) were used to assess changes in clinical symptoms before and after treatment. The results showed that BPRS and NOSIE ratings were significantly lower (better) after treatment. The clinical efficacy rate was 67 percent. The authors reported up to 3 years of follow-up in some cases, with better than expected relapse rates. Although this study used standard rating tools and tested for statistical significance, it lacked a control group and clear diagnostic and dosing details.[16]

A double-blind controlled study involving people with anxiety compared the effectiveness of suanzaoretang, an ancient Chinese remedy used for weakness, irritability, and insomnia, with the anti-anxiety medication diazepam. Ninety patients with Morbid Anxiety Inventory scores between 14 and 30 were divided into three conditions: suanzaoretang, 250 milligrams three times per day; diazepam, 2 milligrams three times per day; and placebo. Treatments were evaluated using the Morbid Anxiety Inventory, Hamilton Anxiety Scale, the Digit Symbol Substitution Test, and a 5-point Likert self-rating of functioning. Study participants were also monitored for blood chemistry values. The participants were treated for 3 weeks on a regimen of active compounds. The findings suggest that suanzaoretang is an effective anxiolytic lacking the muscular tension-relieving and insomnia-relieving qualities of diazepam. "This study is consistent

Finding a TCM Practitioner

Choosing a qualified Chinese medicine practitioner is extremely important. The American Association of Oriental Medicine (AAOM) has established national standards for practitioners wishing to become certified acupuncturists. According to Dave Molony, executive director of the AAOM, the minimum requirement for a master's in acupuncture degree is 1,750 hours, although he asserts that nearly all programs have a 2,200-hour requirement. This translates to about a 3-year training program. A doctor of Oriental medicine (D.O.M.) degree requires 4,000 hours (5 years) in addition to prerequisites of a minimum 2 years of basic science (anatomy, physiology, and so on).

There are also medical acupuncturists who are physicians trained in acupuncture, sometimes with only a very brief course (the minimum requirement is 200 hours, of which up to 150 hours can be presented on videos). Most physicians with medical acupuncture training view the patient's difficulties from a medical perspective and use acupuncture as an adjunct treatment. For example, they may treat anxiety using acupuncture. A practitioner of TCM proper views the problem differently, in terms of yin and yang, the organ systems,

with the standard expected of a drug trial. The single site and the size of the trial are all that keep this from meeting the standards required of studies examining medications for clinical use."[17]

Despite the encouraging results of TCM research, and the excitement that this approach, so radically different from Western medicine, may elicit, TCM is not a panacea. It is one more potentially helpful modality for the treatment of many conditions.

Vedic Medicine

Vedic medicine may be the most ancient system of medicine still practiced today. The oldest known texts, dating back about 5,000 and the balance of elements as described in this chapter; there is no formal category of "anxiety" in TCM.

To find a certified practitioner, you can contact the American Association of Oriental Medicine (see "Traditional Chinese Medicine" in appendix A for Web site and other contact information). You should also verify that the practitioner has a D.O.M. degree or a master's in acupuncture degree and certification as an acupuncturist.

Practicing as a traditional Chinese herbalist requires no official license, which leaves the consumer in something of a bind. Herbalists who may be highly qualified have no official credentials, whereas people with little formal training may misrepresent themselves as qualified. Inquire about an herbalist's training by asking questions such as these: How many hours or years of training do you have and from where? How much experience do you have? What books do you recommend on herbal remedies? The D.O.M. degree with certification indicates that the person is trained in Chinese herbal medicine. A practitioner with a naturopathic degree (N.D.) is likely to be trained in herbal remedies. The quality of N.D. programs varies, however, so look for a practitioner from an accredited program.

years, have their origin in Hindu beliefs and philosophy. Ayurveda, an aspect of Vedic medicine, deals with herbal healing. Currently, Vedic medicine is practiced primarily in India and in developing countries. Medical doctor and Vedic practitioner Deepak Chopra, however, is popularizing Vedic principles and beliefs in the West.

In Vedic medicine, *prana* is the name given to the life force, similar to *qi* in the Chinese system. *Pitta* is the force of heat and energy, connected to the sun and symbolized by fire. It controls digestion and other chemical reactions in the body. *Kapha* is the force of water. Linked to the moon and tides, it controls fluid metabolism in the body. *Vata* is associated with the wind (air) and relates to movement and nervous system functioning.

Usual forms of intervention for Vedic practitioners are changes in diet (including fasting), herbal medicine, yoga, and meditation. The Vedic medicine practitioner also advises on improvements in lifestyle, exercise, hygiene, and other habits.

Dr. Robert Schneider is the director of Vedic medicine at Maharishi University of Management, one of the foremost teaching institutions of this ancient art. A Western-trained medical doctor with board certification in preventative medicine, who is also thoroughly schooled in Vedic medicine, Dr. Schneider is in an excellent position to bridge the two worldviews. According to Dr. Schneider, Vedic medicine addresses four areas: mind, body, behavior, and environment.

The chief approach to the mind in Vedic medicine is meditation, especially transcendental meditation (TM). To practice TM, one should sit in a quiet room and silently repeat a single word, phrase, or sound—a mantra. Because transcendental meditation has been studied for years, the literature is too vast to review in this book. In part, TM has been popularized in the West by Harvard cardiologist Herbert Benson. To study the practice scientifically, Benson stripped TM of its traditional religious and spiritual meanings.

> *The chief approach to the mind in Vedic medicine is meditation, especially transcendental meditation (TM).*

Generally, a Hindu cleric, also called a guru, chooses a mantra for an individual, selecting it on the basis of its spiritual meaning. Benson replaced the traditional individualized mantra with a single word for all participants: the word "one." Even with this simplistic and impersonal mantra, results are impressive. Benson found improvements in blood pressure, angina, and cholesterol levels. Later, Benson reported better results by incorporating the person's spiritual beliefs (not necessarily Hindu beliefs) and making the mantra personally meaningful. For example, repeating the word "peace" or "love" can enhance the effectiveness of TM.

A large number of studies, reviewed by Murphy and Donovan, show that meditation, including TM, has positive effects.[18] Several researchers report that meditation improves mental alertness and concentration and reduces intrusions by irrelevant thoughts. Studies show improved performance on IQ tests, problem-solving tasks, and school exams in groups of people trained in meditation, when compared to non-TM control groups. A number of studies also indicate increased empathy (the sensing of another person's feelings, which is critical to interpersonal relationships) following meditation. Author Daniel Goleman, Ph.D., cites empathy as a critical component of "emotional intelligence."[19]

A number of studies have shown that TM increases the effectiveness of substance abuse programs. One meta-analysis reviewed 19 studies which showed that TM had a powerful impact on improving abstinence. Studies also show TM to be beneficial in anxiety reduction and post-traumatic stress disorder. Research further indicates that meditators demonstrate such positive effects as improved self-esteem and maturity.[20]

As in traditional Chinese medicine, Vedic medicine often employs pulse diagnosis. Many chemicals in the body—such as adrenaline, which is released into the bloodstream when we are under stress, affect pulse rate. The circulatory system receives information from the entire body. The Vedic system's complex method of taking pulses can reveal a great deal about underlying bodily states. Mind and body are interconnected in this system; mental imbalances can be caused by physical imbalances, and vice versa.

In addition to recommending yoga, the Vedic practitioner typically suggests dietary changes suited to the individual. In general, a natural diet, one rich in fruits and vegetables and free of artificial ingredients and genetically modified organisms (GMOs), is preferable. In the herbal aspect of Vedic treatment (Ayurvedic medicine), the

> *In Ayurvedic medicine, the practitioner often uses combinations of 10 to 20 herbs, sometimes more, for one person's formulation. These mixtures are synergistic—the herbs enhance each other's effectiveness.*

practitioner often uses combinations of 10 to 20 herbs, sometimes more, for one person's formulation. According to Dr. Schneider, these mixtures are synergistic—the herbs enhance each other's effectiveness and decrease or eliminate side effects. Some of the herbs used in Ayurveda are employed in modern Western medicine. For example, the prescription heart medication digoxin is derived from the digitalis plant (foxglove).

Behavioral interventions from a Vedic medicine practitioner may include advice on your daily routine, such as when to eat and sleep. Modern medicine is aware of circadian rhythms, which refer to our body's natural cycles. These cycles are related to how energetic we are at particular times of day. Circadian rhythms may explain why some people are night owls, for example, and others are early risers. Vedic medicine uses a complex system for utilizing these rhythms. In addition to daily rhythms, Vedic practitioners are aware of the influences of monthly and seasonal cycles on our functioning.

The Vedic approach to the environment has several levels. One aspect is architecture: building location, materials, and design and orientation (whether a building faces north, south, east, or west). According to Dr. Schneider, animal research shows that the brain exhibits different firing patterns when facing different directions, patterns consistent with the tenets of Vedic architecture. Recent Western studies on "sick building syndrome" demonstrate that some building materials, and the chemicals they emit, cause illnesses in sensitive individuals. Another level of environment is the community or social setting in which one lives. Changes in stress levels and states of mind in the community are related to well-being. Research shows that stress and interpersonal relationships have a powerful impact on health.

> Vedic medicine also offers treatments helping to connect mind and body. Sound and vibration therapies are similar to music therapy in the West.

Vedic medicine also offers treatments helping to connect mind and body. Sound and vibration therapies are similar to music therapy in the West. A review of the literature by Dr. Sanford Nidich and associates suggests a powerful effect of Vedic vibration techniques on both physical and mental disorders.[21]

The scientific evidence regarding Vedic medicine is strong in some areas and weak in others. Transcendental meditation, as previously discussed, has received a great deal of attention over the years, and is well-validated scientifically as a practice that improves physical and mental health. Ayurvedic herbal combinations, on the other hand, are difficult to research because they involve many herbs individualized to each person. The environmental and sound-based interventions have received some support, but further research is warranted.

CLASSICAL HOMEOPATHY

Homeopathy, developed in 1810 by German physician Dr. Samuel Hahnemann, is based on the principle that "like cures like." Dr. Hahnemann discovered that if you give a substance that causes a set of symptoms in a healthy person to someone who is suffering from those symptoms, the symptoms disappear. For example, if taking a substance causes a fever in a healthy individual, then taking that substance when you have a fever lowers it.

Homeopathy is widely utilized in numerous countries. In France, homeopathy is integrated into the national health care system and is fully reimbursed. The British Royal Family has been treated with homeopathy for generations. India has several hundred thousand homeopathic practitioners. Here in the U.S., homeopathy was once very popular and is now experiencing a renaissance. According to Todd Rowe, M.D., a group of psychiatrists in the American Psychiatric Association that practice homeopathy meet regularly at the association's annual convention.

In France, homeopathy is integrated into the national health care system and is fully reimbursed. The British Royal Family has been treated with homeopathy for generations. India has several hundred thousand homeopathic practitioners.

The traditional method of testing whether a homeopathic remedy is effective or not is called a "proving." Provings are done by giving a healthy person a substance and carefully observing the effects. Using this method, Dr. Hahnemann discovered approximately 100 remedies. Since that time, approximately 3,000 additional remedies have been developed.

When Dr. Hahnemann first began developing the remedies, the original dosages he used produced unacceptable side effects. He found that he could dilute the active ingredients by putting them in solvents, such as water, and then vigorously shaking them—a process called succussion. In this way, he was able to use smaller amounts of the active ingredients, until the quantities contained in a remedy were very small indeed. Fascinatingly, he discovered that more dilute solutions were actually more potent than the more concentrated solutions.

> *Homeopathy is different from allopathic medicine in that, like other holistic approaches, it treats the person rather than the disease.*

In some instances, solvents no longer containing the original active molecules were even more powerful as remedies. Theorists have speculated that the qualities of the solvent itself changed, which would account for some of the effects. But, to a certain extent, we do not know why the dilution effect works. Nonetheless, side effects were drastically reduced. Homeopathic remedies have almost no side effects, while conventional pharmaceutical treatments often have side effects, some of which are serious and occasionally even fatal.

Homeopathy is different from allopathic medicine in that, like other holistic approaches, it treats the person rather than the disease. The homeopathic practitioner may prescribe a "constitutional remedy," which takes into account the totality of the person. Homeopath Dana Ullman states:

> Homeopathic constitutional care refers to the homeopath's treatment of a person's totality of symptoms, past and present. A prescription of a constitutional medicine is made after a detailed analysis of the person's genetic history, personal health history, body type, and present status of all physical, emotional, and mental symptoms. This approach to homeopathic care is considerably more profound than treating a specific disease . . . by strengthening the underlying defense processes

of the organism, the correct constitutional medicine can enact a true cure, not just amelioration of symptoms or suppression of disease.[22]

For someone who presents with a mixture of what the *DSM-IV* would call anxiety, depression, anger problems, and eating disorders, a proper constitutional intervention could address all of the symptoms at once by correcting the imbalance or dysfunction that underlies them all.

Todd Rowe, M.D., is a Western-trained psychiatrist, also trained in homeopathy, with experience treating individuals with borderline personality disorder. Rowe has found homeopathy to be a very useful adjunct to psychological treatment. As in allopathic medicine, there is no "cure" for BPD. Dr. Rowe has found homeopathy helpful, however, in treating BPD's associated conditions: depression, anxiety, eating disorders, impulsiveness, and so on. Often, he receives a referral from a therapist or fellow psychiatrist when a case is "stuck," wherein the introduction of a new remedy helps get the process moving again. Dr. Rowe also uses pharmaceutical medications, if he believes they are indicated, but he uses homeopathic interventions first.

Homeopathic practitioners are likely to focus on diet and lifestyle issues, such as exercise, in addition to providing remedies. The remedies generally work through the individual. For example, a remedy may strengthen the immune system to fight an infection, rather than reduce the number of infectious organisms. Disorders are conceptualized differently, as well. In homeopathy, one does not treat depression per se, but rather the depression in the context of the person. According to Dr. Rowe, more than 100 types of depression are known within homeopathy, each one modified by the personality or other characteristics of the person. He cites, for example, angry depressions, withdrawn depressions, grief reactions, and depressions associated with feeling deflated, all of which require different treatments.

Homeopathy and Science

Modern scientists have criticized homeopathic provings because they do not control for the impact of expectations (the placebo effect).

Placebo-controlled studies of homeopathic remedies have generally been very encouraging, however. In a meta-analysis published in 1997 in the medical journal *The Lancet*, Dr. Klaus Linde and associates reviewed 89 studies covering the use of homeopathic remedies for several illnesses.[23] Overall, in randomized, double-blind studies, the

Finding a Homeopathic Practitioner

If you are seeking homeopathic treatment for BPD-related symptoms, Dr. Todd Rowe strongly suggests that you find a homeopath who has mental health training. In addition to many psychiatrists, some psychologists, social workers, and other mental health practitioners are certified in homeopathy.

The reason for going to a homeopath who is savvy about mental health is that many issues associated with borderline personality disorder may arise in the course of treatment. You may experience strong emotional reactions to your health care provider, similar to those you have in other intense relationships. If you have a problem with dichotomous thinking—categorizing people or situations in black-and-white terms—you may decide the treatment is worthless unless you experience an immediate or outstanding result. Someone with a mental health background should be able to handle these kinds of reactions. Just as it is wise to go to a psychiatrist rather than a general physician for psychiatric care, it is wise to go to a mental-health trained homeopath for your homeopathic mental-health care.

Several independent boards certify homeopaths. The Council for Homeopathic Certification requires graduation from an accredited program and passage of a rigorous exam. Open to individuals who are licensed in other fields (such as M.D.s), as well as those who are not, people who complete the process obtain certified classical homeopath (C.C.H.) designation. The American Board of Homeotherapeutics, on the other hand, is open only to medical doctors and homeopathic remedies were 2.45 times as effective as placebo. When using only the better studies, the ratio was about 1.8. The authors concluded that the notion that homeopathy's efficacy was due to a placebo effect was inconsistent with the data; in other words, homeopathy did seem to produce beneficial effects.[24] The next phase of research in this

osteopaths. Those who complete the necessary requirements obtain a D.Ht. (doctor of homeotherapeutics). Naturopathic physicians can obtain a D.H.A.N.P. from the Homeopathic Academy of Naturopathic Physicians. In addition, the National Board of Homeopathic Examiners gives several levels of certification: a D.N.B.H.E (diplomate) for physicians, osteopaths, dentists, and chiropractors; an R.N.B.H.E (registrant) for nonphysicians such as nurses, physician's assistants, and acupuncturists; and a C.P.H.T (certified practitioner) for laypeople. Finally, some states license homeopaths, which is another way to determine that the practitioner has met basic qualifications.

Contact the National Center for Homeopathy (see "Homeopathy" in appendix A) for a list of qualified homeopaths. Note that this list is limited to National Center for Homeopathy members. Many excellent homeopaths are already quite busy, so a listing would only bring excessive referrals. In *The Consumer's Guide to Homeopathy,* Dana Ullman recommends checking with health food stores, pharmacies selling homeopathic products, health professionals, alternative newspapers and magazines, the phone directory, the Internet, and your friends.[25] You should look for someone with credentials, such as a C.C.H., D.H.A.N.P., or D.Ht. Ask the practitioner whether she or he specializes in homeopathy as their primary modality. When you go to your first appointment, look for these signs that the homeopath is a good one: The initial appointment is at least an hour in length and involves extremely detailed questioning about your symptoms and extensive questioning about your psychological well-being.

field should answer the questions: How do homeopathic remedies stack up against allopathic medicine treatments? And how can homeopathic and allopathic treatments work together?

Along with the evidence of hard scientific data are the facts of clinical practice. Dana Ullman, M.P.H., argues persuasively in favor of homeopathy in *The Consumer's Guide to Homeopathy*. He notes that laboratory studies show that homeopathic remedies have biological effects, but become inactive when exposed to strong magnetic fields or excessive heat. This cannot be explained by placebo effect. He also reports that 39 percent of French family physicians, 20 percent of German physicians, and 10 percent of Italian physicians use homeopathy, and more than 40 percent of British physicians refer to homeopaths—a tangible endorsement by many physicians. Further, in the 1800s, in homeopathic hospitals that treated infectious diseases, and in mental hospitals and prisons supervised by homeopathic physicians, death rates were one-half to one-eighth the rate of those in conventional hospitals; it is hard to imagine how this could be due to placebo effects.

> *Few scientific studies focus on the use of homeopathy with mental health disorders. This does not mean its remedies do not work, only that they have not yet been proved to the best scientific standards.*

Unfortunately, few scientific studies focus on the use of homeopathy with mental health disorders. This does not mean its remedies do not work, only that they have not yet been proved to the best scientific standards. It also does not mean that provings are no evidence at all. We use provings in our everyday life. For example, the last time you drank coffee to combat low energy, you didn't need a randomized placebo-controlled design to convince you of caffeine's energizing effects.

CHAPTER 7

Nutrition and Exercise

*Your foods shall be your remedies, and your
remedies shall be your food.*

—*HIPPOCRATES*

Is there anything else you did that helped?" Carol asked.

"I changed my diet," said Alexis, "and I started to exercise."

Carol looked surprised. "How can food and exercise help someone with borderline personality disorder? We're talking about depression, anxiety, anger, low self-esteem, impulsiveness—even negative and suicidal thoughts."

"I know what you mean, but it's true," Alexis assured her. "I used to eat a lot of junk food, and I was spending my life in front of the television set. I gauged my days and evenings by what I ate and what I watched on TV. I felt lonely, bored, anxious, and depressed. I didn't know that eating poorly and not exercising were just making my BPD symptoms worse.

"Then one day, I decided there had to be more to life. I wanted to feel happy and energetic. So I began to read about how food and exercise affect our emotions and our outlook. I learned I'd been trying to self-medicate with junk food, trying to get from foods high in fat and sugar the good feelings I wasn't getting out of being alive. Lying in bed in the middle of the day or sitting on the sofa all evening wasn't helping, either. So, I got up—and stayed up—and began eating healthy and walking a little bit every day. From walking, I began running. It was like being born again, one step at a time. Now, I feel light and light-hearted, in body and in spirit."

NUTRITION

The most well-known treatments for depression, anxiety, and other symptoms of borderline personality disorder are prescribed medications and psychotherapy. Less well known is the fact that what we eat can have a profound effect on our emotional and mental health. Nutritious food is the very stuff of life, nurturing our bodies and minds with essential natural proteins, vitamins, and minerals—as well as providing our nervous system with nutrients helpful for dealing with stress, depression, mood swings, and negative life experiences. Now studies show that nutritional supplements can also help alleviate depression and other symptoms characteristic of BPD.

> Despite all the information available on nutrition, many people are, in fact, malnourished. The daily diets of many of us, while adequate in calories, are inadequate in vitamins and minerals.

Despite all the information available on nutrition, many people are, in fact, malnourished. According to the *Textbook of Nutritional Medicine* by Melvyn Werbach, M.D., nutritional deficiencies abound in the United States.[1] The daily diets of many of us, while adequate in calories, are inadequate in vitamins and minerals. For example, the average American consumes only about 60 percent of the recommended amount of folic acid, and 11 percent of Americans have deficient folate levels in their blood—a deficiency research has linked to depression.

In addition, about one-third of us consume too little vitamin B_3 (niacin). Excessive use of alcohol leads to deficiencies in vitamin B_1 (thiamine). Average intake of vitamin B_6 (pyridoxine) is 50 to 75 percent below recommended levels. Many of us are at least marginally deficient in vitamin C. Many others are deficient in vitamins A, D, E, and K. Of the minerals, iron is the world's most common deficiency, while approximately half the populations of developed countries do not get enough calcium, and less than half consume enough chromium. In addition, many people are marginally deficient in magnesium and zinc.[2]

Finally, while the American diet is notoriously high in fat, we are not getting the right kind of fats. According to Dr. Werbach: "True, certain fats are being ingested to excess. However, just as true is the fact that some of the essential fatty acids are not being ingested in adequate quantities."[3] Here we live in this land of plenty, where almost 18 percent of the population is considered to be obese, and yet we are malnourished.

While it's easy to see that vitamins, minerals, amino acids, and essential fatty acids have important implications for our general physical health, we may not be aware that they are also vital to our emotional and mental health. As with many of the other alternative treatments discussed in this book, researchers have not conducted nutritional studies specifically with individuals with borderline personality disorder. There are, however, nutritional studies on many of the psychologically distressing conditions associated with BPD. In addition, research has studied nutritional approaches for depression, anxiety, attention-deficit/hyperactivity disorder, anger, eating disorders, and substance abuse, all of which are symptoms of BPD.

Nutritional approaches can take time to produce benefits; 6 weeks is a typical period for effects to manifest, so patience is needed. On the other hand, antidepressant medications also typically take 4 to 6 weeks to kick in. Some nutritional supplements are effective in 2 weeks or less, however, and can be taken in addition to antidepressant medications to jump-start the process. The following sections examine nutritional supplements that may be helpful in alleviating symptoms associated with BPD.

Although it is safe to make general improvements in your diet, such as adding a multivitamin and mineral supplement, increasing your intake of vegetables, and increasing your consumption of omega-3 fatty acids, you should obtain expert advice when using amino acid supplements, or to find out if you have nutritional deficiencies. For advice on how to find a nutritionist or appropriate physician, see page 178.

Sugar, Caffeine, and Alcohol

It is tempting to turn to sweets when we are feeling down, and a strong cup of coffee to boost our energy. Many people have a drink to feel better. None of these approaches are sound in the long run. Sugar and caffeine tend to provide a temporary mood boost, but, ultimately, lead to further depression. According to Rita Elkins, in her book, *Depression and Natural Medicine*, anxiety, rage, apathy, and fluctuating moods are potential signs of hypoglycemia (low blood sugar, which is the "crash" we experience after a "sugar rush"). Clearly, insufficient blood sugar can exacerbate the similar symptoms already felt by individuals with BPD. Caffeine dramatically increases anxiety and sleep problems. Alcohol temporarily enhances our mood, but, ultimately is a depressant; also, studies have shown that alcohol increases anxiety.[4] Excessive alcohol use also depletes essential fatty acids and B vitamins; problems associated with deficiencies of these nutrients. So, to stabilize your mood, lay off alcohol, caffeine, and sweets.

Good Fats and Bad Fats

Americans are obsessed with reducing their fat intake. However, not all fats are equal. Essential fatty acids (omega-3) prevalent in the brain and other organs are, as their name indicates, *essential* to life. Green, leafy vegetables, fish, and flax oil are rich in omega-3s. Increasing your intake of omega-3 fatty acids tends to reduce anxiety, depression, and ADHD (attention-deficit/hyperactivity disorder). Omega-6 fatty acids, on the other hand, are found in many animal and vegetable oils. It is omega-6 fatty acids that are associated with heart disease and increased depression.

Amino Acids

Amino acids are the building blocks of proteins, which regulate vital bodily functions. For example, proteins are required in the manufacture of neurotransmitters, the chemicals critical in brain functioning. Essential amino acids are proteins our body needs but cannot make. Therefore, we must get essential amino acids from the environment through our daily diet. Without sufficient amino acids, we are unable to construct neurotransmitters. Imagine a car manufacturing plant in which brilliant engineers have designed an excellent car. The motor is in place and running smoothly, with all its parts. But without any tires, the car cannot get off the lot. Similarly, if you are missing a key amino acid, you will be unable to make the neurotransmitters you need, thus you lose a vital part in your ability to function.

Some people get a normal amount of amino acids in their diet, but their need for amino acids is higher than average. Maybe they do not absorb amino acids well, or their bodies do not use the amino acids efficiently. In such cases, having an extra amount in the form of a supplement may be helpful.

> *Some people get a normal amount of amino acids in their diet, but their need for amino acids is higher than average. Maybe they do not absorb amino acids well, or their bodies do not use the amino acids efficiently.*

Amino acids have been found to be helpful in several disorders. Depression can be reduced with tryptophan, SAMe (S-adenosylmethionine), 5-HTP (5-hydroxytryptophan), and phenylalanine. Research suggests that these supplements may be as effective as antidepressant medications, with fewer risks and fewer side effects. Alcohol cravings may also be reduced with appropriate use of amino acids. A small double-blind study showed that administration of the amino acid L-glutamine decreased desire to drink alcohol (and improved anxiety and sleep) for 9 of 10 participants. When switched to placebo, only 2 or 3 of the 10 continued to do well, strongly suggesting that glutamine exerts a

Finding a Nutritional Expert

Most physicians do not commonly make use of nutritional approaches to symptoms associated with BPD, such as depression, anxiety, and impulsivity. For this reason, the American College for Advancement in Medicine (ACAM) was developed by and for physicians to advance and promote the understanding of nutritional and preventive approaches to medicine.

Orthomolecular medicine, developed by Linus Pauling, M.D., employs nutritional approaches to healing. The Society for Orthomolecular Health Medicine and the International Society for Orthomolecular Medicine are organizations of physicians dedicated to nutritional healing.

Nutritionists can also be extremely helpful in guiding you toward a more nutritious eating plan. As most nutritional supplements do not require a prescription, a nutritionist's recommendations serve as guidance for the proper use of supplements. The International and American Associations of Clinical Nutritionists (IAACN) provide information and referrals. A CCN (certified clinical nutritionist) is certified by the Clinical Nutrition Certification Board (CNCB) to meet standards for practice.

Contact information for these organizations and their referral services is listed under "Nutrition and Nutritional Medicine" in appendix A.

positive effect.[5] Research with animals suggests that tryptophan may also decrease the desire to consume alcohol.

Vitamins and Minerals

Insufficient B vitamins increase anxiety and depression. Sufficient lithium, potassium, and zinc are also necessary to stave off depression, while magnesium and calcium reduce anxiety.[6] According to the *Text-book of Nutritional Medicine*, factors related to ADHD include deficiencies in magnesium, niacin (B_3), and thiamine (B_1). Uncontrolled human trials and laboratory studies suggest calcium, iron, copper, and zinc deficiencies contribute to ADHD. Laboratory studies provide evidence that copper, manganese, aluminum, lead, and cadmium toxicity are related to ADHD. As noted previously, there is a substantial overlap between ADHD and BPD symptoms.

There is now growing interest in treating aggression, impulsivity, and violent behavior with nutritional intervention. A placebo-controlled study in which confined adolescent delinquents received vitamin and mineral supplements showed a decrease in violent and nonviolent rule violations.[7]

According to Dr. Werbach, studies have shown that deficiencies in niacin (B_3), pantothenic acid (B_5), thiamine (B_1), vitamins B_6 and B_{12}, and vitamin C all lead to irritability. Iron deficiency, which afflicts 10 percent of American females and 3 percent of American males, is linked with aggression (although as yet only minimal data suggests that iron supplementation reverses the problem). Both human and animal studies have linked magnesium deficiency to aggression. Toxic levels of manganese, aluminum, cadmium, and lead are also associated with aggressive behavior.[8]

EXERCISE

Behavioral medicine is the field of psychology that studies behaviors affecting health. The course of most diseases, including mental health disorders, is affected by behavioral and psychological variables. Smoking is linked with several cancers, for example. Alcoholism and drug abuse damage the body's systems and organs, especially the brain and liver. The "type A" personality—a style of hostility and time-pressured behavior—is a risk factor for heart disease. More broadly, how we handle stress affects the immune system, which serves to protect us from infectious diseases and cancers. Indeed, estimates indicate that a high

Allergies and Food Sensitivities

When most of us think of allergies, what probably comes to mind is the boy whose face resembled a strawberry if he ate strawberries, or the girl who sneezed all spring. Hives and respiratory problems are common signs of allergies. However, emotional and cognitive symptoms can arise from food allergies and sensitivities as well. Allergies and sensitivities can exacerbate depression, anxiety, problems in attention and concentration, hyperactivity, and aggression.

Finding out whether you have a food sensitivity or allergy can be simple or a mystery worthy of Sherlock Holmes. In the simplest case, you discuss your problem with an allergist or nutritionist, who develops an educated hunch guided by which food allergies are the most common or by the specifics of your symptoms. Testing may be used to get more information, or you may simply be asked to eliminate certain foods from your diet. If the symptoms disappear, then you're probably on the right track—especially if the symptoms reappear when you reintroduce a food into your diet.

One study showed that 81 of 140 children with behavioral disorders—nearly two-thirds—had significant improvements after particular foods or additives were eliminated from their diet. Placebo-controlled intervention showed that the behavioral symptoms returned in three-fourths of these children after they ate the suspected foods.[9]

Ben F. Feingold, M.D., described a case of a boy, age 7, who was hyperkinetic and impulsive and engaged in many potentially dangerous behaviors, such as riding his bicycle toward oncoming cars.

percentage of all doctor visits are primarily related to lifestyle behaviors and other psychological factors. As stated in *Mind Body Health:*

> Can emotions—the way we think, the way we feel—really be responsible, at least in part, for disease? A growing body of evidence indicates that they can. Some researchers in the field believe that as many

Psychologists, psychiatrists, pediatricians, and neurologists made no headway in treating him. When salicylates (see below) were removed from his diet, his symptoms abated, and he did well at home and at school. Whenever he consumed salicylates, however, his behavioral symptoms immediately returned.[10]

The Feingold diet, which consists of avoiding all food additives and dietary salicylates, is one of the most widely used diets for ADHD. Food additives to avoid include preservatives (such as BHA and BHT), artificial flavorings (such as vanillin), food colorings (such as red 40 and yellow 5), and artificial sweeteners (such as aspartame, saccharine, and sucralose). Natural foods that contain salicylates—such as almonds, apples, cherries, cucumbers, grapes, raisins, mint, oranges, peaches, raspberries, strawberries, teas, and tomatoes—are also to be avoided. Aspirin, medications with artificial colors and flavors, and perfumes must also be avoided. (For a more comprehensive list of restrictions and guidelines for the Feingold diet, see *Why Your Child is Hyperactive* by Dr. Feingold or go to The Feingold Association Web site, www.feingold.org.)[11]

Although the Feingold diet is not a cure-all, double-blind studies show salicylate and food-additive sensitivities are relatively common in individuals with ADHD. A review by the Center for Science in the Public Interest (CSPI) found that 17 of 23 double-blind studies demonstrated that at least some children's symptoms became much worse when they consumed artificial colors or particular foods such as wheat or milk.[12]

as half of all patients who visit physicians have physical symptoms that are directly caused by emotions; others believe that the figure is as high as 90 to 95 percent.[13]

Exercise is a behavioral variable that can have a positive impact on the course of diseases and on psychological conditions, helping to stimulate circulation, ease chronic pain, and alleviate depression. Yet, exercising regularly seems to be one of the hardest things to fit into our busy schedules. In the behavioral medicine class I teach, I ask my students: "What is the best exercise?" "Swimming" is usually the first guess. True, swimming is low impact, good for the heart, and good for the muscles. But I'm looking for something else. "Walking," another student will hazard. Like swimming, walking has the virtue of being nearly risk-free and healthful for virtually all individuals. Still, I ask for more. "Bicycling?" "Rollerblading?" "Running?" "Weightlifting?" "Sex!?" they guess.

> *The best exercise is the one you will do. Motivation is usually the overlooked factor in exercise.*

The best exercise (I admit, it's a trick question!) is the one you will do. Motivation is usually the overlooked factor in exercise. With the caveats "safety first" and "everything in moderation," most exercises are healthful. We know we "should" exercise. Yet, most of us do not exercise enough, and we feel guilty about it.

One of the biggest problems with exercise for most people—not just for individuals with BPD—is all-or-none thinking. Many people fall into the trap of thinking, "I'm so out of shape, it's not worth getting started." Although I generally exercise at least three times a week, I admit thinking occasionally, while writing this book, "I'll get back in shape after the book is finished." Eventually, I found my concentration suffered so much from not exercising that I got back on my bicycle and my cross-country ski machine. Another "all-or-none" trap is for exercise to become an obsession. Many weekend athletes drive themselves relentlessly, cutting back only when they are forced to by injury, which then often makes them stop altogether.

So, what's the best way to embark on a successful exercise program? The answer is unique to each individual. The first step is to answer a few questions about yourself. Are you a "people-person" or a "lone wolf"? In other words, do you prefer exercising with others or alone? If you want to exercise with people, you may prefer gyms with aerobic classes, basketball, and swimming pools; public marathons and triathlons you can enter; or hiking clubs, such as the Sierra Club, which combine companionship with the serenity of nature—or you can take daily walks with a friend.

If you prefer exercising alone, you can enjoy walking or jogging in solitude or use electronic treadmills and cross-country ski machines at home. While exercising, try watching a movie videotape that engages your interest. Some people like moving to video-taped exercise programs. Others prefer closing their eyes and mindfully paying attention to their breath. Meanwhile, don't think in black-and-white terms about exercising. Research shows that a vigorous 30-minute workout three times per week is beneficial. And if you can't do 30 minutes, do 20. If you can't do 20 minutes, do 10. If you can't do 10, then do 5. And if you can't do 5, do 1. One minute? Yes. It adds up.

> *One of the biggest problems with exercise for most people—not just for individuals with BPD—is all-or-none thinking. Many people fall into the trap of thinking, "I'm so out of shape, it's not worth getting started."*

Try incorporating exercise into your daily routine. Rather than parking in the nearest space you can find, park at the farthest end of the lot. Get off one train stop or bus stop ahead of the closest one to your destination. A little math will help you see the impact. Let's say you add an eighth-of-mile walk—that's 220 yards—daily by parking at the back of the parking lot. You do this 5 days a week, 50 weeks per year. By the end of the year, you will have added more than 31 miles to your total exercise for the year. You will have burned more calories than you would have by running a marathon.

Another great way to squeeze in some exercise is to ride a bike for those quick errands, rather than drive the car. Running out to the store two miles away for a few items? Strap on a backpack and a helmet and ride your bike. If possible, try riding your bike to work. It saves money, reduces pollution, and keeps you fit. Be sure to praise yourself with a sincere self-compliment for every bit of exercise you do.

Aerobic Exercise

Before starting on a vigorous exercise program, first see your doctor to make sure you will not hurt yourself by engaging in the activities you choose. To get the full benefits of exercise, aerobic exercise is an essential component. *Aerobic* exercise means you have elevated your heart rate and your body is able to supply necessary oxygen to the muscles. When you go for a brisk walk, but can still talk with a friend while walking, you are exercising aerobically. *Anaerobic* exercise means your body cannot get enough oxygen to the muscles to complete the chemical reaction used to make energy, as when you sprint as far as you can. When you do anaerobic exercise, lactic acid forms and builds up in your muscles. The lactic acid produces that achy feeling you get hours after hard exercise.

If you are breathing at least a little harder than when you are at rest, and you are able to hold a conversation while exercising, then you are probably in a good aerobic zone.

How hard do you have to exercise to be moving aerobically? If you are breathing at least a little harder than when you are at rest, and you are able to hold a conversation while exercising, then you are probably in a good aerobic zone. For a more precise, scientific measurement of your aerobic level, measure your heartbeat. Your maximum heart rate, in beats per minute, should be 220 minus your age. If you are 40 years old, then, your estimated maximum heart rate is 180. You should then exercise at 60 to 85 percent of your maximum heart rate to be in the aerobic zone. Staying with the example of a 40-year-old, $180 \times .6 = 108$, and $180 \times .85 = 153$. Therefore, you should train at 108 to 153 beats per minute.

The easiest way to check your heart rate is with a heart monitor, but you can also measure your heart rate by taking your pulse on the wrist, below the thumb, or on the neck by your voice box. These pulses are relatively easy to find when you exercise, because your heart is beating harder. You must have a watch or a clock that counts seconds. Count the number of beats that occur in 6 seconds and multiply by 10 (or in 10 seconds and multiply by 6, or in 15 seconds and multiply by 4). Never use your thumb to take your pulse; your thumb has its own pulse that will interfere with getting an accurate reading.

Finding the Motivation to Exercise

One way to motivate yourself to exercise is to review how good it is for you. Regular aerobic exercise is a powerful antidepressant. In their research of studies that looked at the relationship between exercise and depression, Lynette Craft and Daniel Landers found that exercise helped alleviate depression as much as psychotherapy and medication trials did—pointing to exercise as an important adjunct to other treatments.[14]

A meta-analysis of 40 studies, conducted by Bonita Long and Rosemary van Stavel, found that exercise lowered moderate anxiety.[15] Regular aerobic exercise strengthens the heart and decreases heart disease. It also boosts the immune system, which helps combat infectious diseases and cancers. Exercise helps regulate sugar metabolism, lowers the risk of diabetes, and helps reduce a diabetic's need for insulin injections. Some people have found that exercise lessens chronic pain and improves strength, stamina, and energy.

While it is helpful to know about these benefits, if you're still not exercising, the problem is probably motivation. Knowledge alone is almost never enough to change behavior. In order to motivate yourself, you must make the information tangible, visible, and meaningful to you. A study presented at an American Psychological Association convention featured people in two different ads: One ad showed that staying in the sun was associated with skin cancer; the other showed that people who spent too much time in the sun would get wrinkles. Which ad worked better to keep people out of the sun? That's right, the wrinkles ad worked. With studies of this nature, it is often unclear why people made the choice they did. My theory is that skin cancer is relatively rare and, if caught early, a quick procedure takes care of it. You may not know anyone who has had skin cancer and, even if you do, you may never be aware of it. Skin cancer is not part of your everyday reality. But wrinkles? Everyone has seen people with wrinkles. Wrinkles are "real" to us.

Similarly, the belief that you will help prevent heart disease by exercising is, for the vast majority of us, too vague and distant in time to be of much use in motivating us. There you are, staring at the step machine, which demands effort and energy. You need a motivator that will work right now.

So, grab a notebook and a pen. Ask yourself the question: Why exercise today? To reduce depression? Write it down. To increase your energy level? Write it down. It's okay to write down "to prevent heart disease," but emphasize reasons that you will actually experience and feel, such as reduced depression or increased energy.

> *The belief that you will help prevent heart disease by exercising is, for the vast majority of us, too vague and distant in time to be of much use in motivating us. You need a motivator that will work right now.*

Pay attention to your body. Do you feel good after you exercise? Do you have more energy? Write it down. Rate your stamina on a 1 to 7 scale, with 1 being "my energy level is very low," and 7 being "I have all the energy I need" or "my energy level is great." It does not have to be a scale that will win an award from the journal *Psychological Assessment*, just something that has meaning to you. Measure your energy level every week, once per week, such as every Friday, and put it on a graph. Watching your energy level go from 3 to 4 to 5 can be a huge motivator. Charting the number of miles you walk, the number of pounds you can lift, or any other measure of progress gives you tangible and immediate feedback that is so necessary to motivation.

Making a behavioral contract with yourself can be very helpful. Every year, I have students in my behavior therapy class contract with themselves to change one of their behaviors. Many choose to increase their exercise level or lose weight. They are clever and creative and find many ways to motivate themselves. One student promised herself a weekly massage, which had the added benefit of reducing stress.

But the motivation that works above all others for most people is social support. For example, a weekly "exercise chat" with a friend, partner, or spouse can provide you with frequent encouragement. This intervention benefits by offering both the carrot and the stick. Calling and saying, "I stuck with my exercise program this week," and hearing "Way to go!" is a positive experience. Having to call and say, "I didn't meet my goal this week," is embarrassing, and most people will work hard to avoid having to say that.

Once you get into the habit of exercising, it can become self-rewarding, and external motivators aren't as necessary. This self-reward comes in various forms, including the release of endorphins, your body's own morphine. Endorphins are responsible for the phenomenon called "runner's high." People often report feeling a deep sense of euphoria, peace, and well-being after about 20 minutes of running. The rhythmic nature of running itself powerfully contributes to this. Once you experience this positive sensation, you are more likely to stay with your exercise program.

> *Once you get into the habit of exercising, it can become self-rewarding, and external motivators aren't as necessary.*

For individuals with BPD who are also survivors of physical or sexual abuse, however, it is possible that this pleasurable sensation from exercise may paradoxically induce ambivalent or negative emotions. For such survivors, the endorphins generated by exercise may be mistakenly linked with sexual feelings—sexual feelings that, in turn, may carry feelings of shame or guilt. In addition to talking with a psychotherapist, it is important that you learn to be compassionate with yourself and give yourself permission to enjoy the lighthearted feeling that can accompany exercising.

In addition to talking with your counselor, movement therapies such as dance or yoga (covered in chapter 5) offer an opportunity to work through such feelings and issues. Learning to appreciate yourself and allowing yourself to enjoy wholesome, positive sensations and pleasure is critical to your ultimate recovery from borderline personality disorder—and to your happiness.

CHAPTER 8

Self-Help

"Y OU SEEM SO calm," Carol told Alexis. "Even when I first came over tonight in a panic, I could feel your calmness, and it helped me calm down."

"I'm glad," said Alexis. "I focused on my breath. I became fully present in the moment. I became aware of the connection between us, and the boundary between us."

Carol felt a sarcastic comment coming on, like "How Zen of you," but squelched it. Why did she always fend off good feelings with negativity? Another emotion came over her—a yearning for this same calmness. "What do you mean by 'fully present'?"

"It's part of mindfulness practice," Alexis began. "I learned mindfulness in my dialectical behavioral therapy program, as a treatment for borderline personality disorder. I meditate on my own now, and I take a yoga class. By sitting and paying attention to my thoughts and feelings, I can make a choice about what I need to do in that moment."

"So how did you stay calm when I first came in?" Carol asked. "If you'd come over to my house crying and panicky, I probably would've gotten upset, too."

"At first, I felt your panic and your pain. I concentrated on breathing my own air, which helped me focus on our separateness and to feel my inner strength and calm. I wanted to take care of you, but I recognized that if I made it my job to absorb your pain, then I would be just as upset as you were because I would be stuck with the same sense of distress. Instead, I kept breathing and feeling our distinctness. By doing so, I could be here, fully present, available for you to talk to. Maybe you need your pain right now. Sometimes, if you learn from it, pain can be a temporary gift to guide you to healing and wholeness."

"Can you teach me how to do this?" asked Carol.

"I'll give you the number of my DBT program. That's the way to start."

Carol felt rejected by Alexis's answer. "Can't you just teach me, Alexis? You know me so well."

Alexis answered calmly, "That wouldn't be good for you or for me, Carol. The place to start is the DBT program. When you've finished the mindfulness program, you can join my weekly meditation group. In the meantime, we can still talk on the phone and visit each other. I'm your friend, Carol. You need someone else to be your therapist and your mindfulness teacher."

Carol's panic at feeling rejected subsided. The calmness in her friend's voice and demeanor was contagious.

Alexis reassured her, "It will feel good to be with other people who understand. I'll get you that phone number."

THE SPIRIT OF SELF-HELP

This chapter is a guide to the many ways in which you can help yourself overcome some of the symptoms of borderline personality disorder. These self-help practices can be used to get you started on your path to health and well-being. They can also be used as an accompaniment to treatment, supplementing essential psychotherapy and antidepressant medication. What follows are proven stress management techniques, along with methods for changing your customary ways of thinking.

Safety First

The first rule of treatment is "safety first." If you feel suicidal, the best course of action is to go to the nearest hospital emergency room immediately. There, you will be evaluated and possibly admitted to a psychiatric unit. You will be kept safe until you can handle life again on your own. No matter how depressed or hopeless you feel right now, it is most likely that you will soon feel at least somewhat better. Time and medications administered at the hospital bring most people around in less than a week.

> *The first rule of treatment is "safety first." If you feel suicidal, the best course of action is to go to the nearest hospital emergency room immediately.*

The same rule of "safety first" applies if you feel you are about to lose control of your impulses and hurt someone else. Venting anger by physically attacking another person has serious repercussions: It is illegal and it can lead to criminal prosecution. Even physical fights in which no serious injuries occur can permanently damage relationships and lead to guilt and regret. Therefore, if you feel you could hurt someone else, leave the situation. If the feelings persist, go to the emergency room and say you are having uncontrollable urges to hurt someone.

View this chapter as a way of "putting it all together." You don't have to implement all of these suggestions at once. Start by changing one small thing, beginning with the easiest choice. For example, choose an apple rather than ice cream as a snack. Once a day, make a positive dietary change. Join an online support group. Change is best when it occurs slowly, so that you have time to absorb it into your life. Making a revolutionary change, such as cutting all sweets out of your diet, leads to feelings of deprivation, followed by relapse. Trying to change all of your coping behaviors at once is likely to leave you feeling overwhelmed. Another suggestion, if cutting applies to you, is this: Instead of cutting yourself, try holding an ice cube to your wrist. Think of this approach as letting fresh air into your life, by opening one window at a time.

You can implement change in two ways: One is to implement the easiest changes first, as noted above; the other is to implement the most important changes first. These two paths do not always lead to the same choice, in which case you can make a decision. In general, it's best to start with balancing your emotions. According to Marsha Linehan, Ph.D., borderline personality disorder is fundamentally a problem with emotion regulation. She draws an analogy between your sensitivity and your having a sunburn. If you have a sunburn at the beach, the first thing to do is to put up a protective umbrella to shield you from the sun's harmful rays. Likewise, emotion regulation skills, such as relaxation and meditation, can act as a protective shield from painful stimuli you may encounter.

STRESS REDUCTION BASICS

This chapter offers a self-help guide to finding a more emotionally peaceful place within you. Along this path are 12 fundamentals of healthy stress reduction. These fundamentals, which include living mindfully and de-escalating extreme emotions, point the way to an increased ability to overcome or side-step the bumps along life's road. The fundamentals of healthy stress reduction are:

1. Live mindfully.

2. Balance your lifestyle with rest, exercise, nutrients, and activities.

3. Balance your relationships with communication, empathy, and boundary setting.

4. De-escalate extreme emotions, such as anger, depression, and anxiety with calming responses.

5. Engage in stress reduction techniques, such as humor, relaxation training, yoga, prayer, or meditation.

6. Engage in spiritually satisfying experiences regularly; nurture your soul.

7. Avoid excessive use of substances, such as alcohol, drugs, or food.

8. Join a support group.

9. Know your rights.

10. Cope with any stigma you may feel about having borderline personality disorder.

11. Replace self-destructive and impulsive behavior, such as self-sabotage, self-injury, suicide attempts, and other impulsive acts, with positive and self-nurturing behavior.

12. Orchestrate therapists, doctors, helpers, and healers into a team that meets your needs.

These skills are important to everyone, but especially to individuals with BPD. If you have BPD, it is a safe bet that you either have not learned stress management skills sufficiently, or that you are not applying them adequately; you will need a combination of education, repetition, and motivation to succeed in lowering your stress level. Hopefully, this chapter will provide education and some motivation—then it is up to you to practice, practice, practice. Find a few techniques that bring you peace, joy, or relief, and stick with them. Find settings that will encourage you. For many of my clients, these stress management skills are among their favorite aspects of psychotherapy.

1. Live Mindfully

"If the practitioner knows his own mind clearly he will obtain results with little effort," says Zen master Thuong Chieu. "But if he does not know anything about his own mind, all of his effort will be wasted."[1]

In her dialectical behavior therapy program, Dr. Marsha Linehan starts with "core mindfulness skills." What is mindfulness, and why is it so important? An example will illustrate:

A belligerent samurai, an old Japanese tale goes, once challenged a Zen master to explain the concept of heaven and hell. But the monk replied with scorn, "You're nothing but a lout—I can't waste my time with the likes of you!"

His very honor attacked, the samurai flew into a rage, and, pulling his sword from its scabbard, yelled, "I could kill you for your impertinence."

"That," the monk calmly replied, "is hell."

Startled at seeing the truth in what the master pointed out about the fury that had him in its grip, the samurai calmed down, sheathed his sword, and bowed, thanking the monk for his insight.

"And that," said the monk, "is heaven."

The sudden awakening of the samurai to his own agitated state illustrates the crucial difference between being caught up in a feeling and becoming aware that you are being swept up by it. Socrates' injunction "Know thyself" speaks to this keystone of emotional intelligence: awareness of one's own feelings, as they occur.[2]

> *I tell my students that mindfulness is like learning to ride a bicycle. You do not learn to ride a bicycle by going down a steep, rocky, stump-strewn path on your first ride.*

Mindfulness refers to being fully present in the moment, fully aware of one's thoughts, feelings, and circumstances. The idea of mindfulness is well developed in the Buddhist *vipassana* meditation tradition, which is approximately 2,500 years old. By meditating—being fully present in the moment with minimal distractions—one is able to clear away distractions and see the process of one's own thoughts more clearly. Dr. Jon Kabat-Zinn describes meditation as a "laboratory" in which we see our thoughts unfold. When we then see these same thoughts and feelings occurring in the real world, we are more prepared to deal with them.

I tell my student meditators that mindfulness is like learning to ride a bicycle. You do not learn to ride a bicycle by going down a steep, rocky, stump-strewn path on your first ride. You start with training wheels on a smooth, flat, car-free road. Mindfulness is best begun by sitting in silence or by such movements as yoga, tai chi, or walking. The test, however, is applying mindfulness to your daily life in the real world. Buddhist monk Thich Nhat Hanh says this in *The Miracle of Mindfulness:* "Every day and every hour, one should practice mindfulness. That's easy to say, but to carry it out in practice is not."[3]

One of my meditation class participants, "Dr. A," is a busy hospital physician. One of her unit nurses, Laura, often got extremely worked up during stressful medical situations. Through meditation practice, Dr. A realized that her own reality and Laura's reality were separate and that Laura's assessment that something was urgent or an emergency did not mean it really was. In a moment of clarity, Dr. A saw that when Laura got worked up, it started a cascade of stress, in which Dr. A got worked up, and she, herself, then spread the stress like a contagion to others on the unit. From then on, instead of playing out this habitual script in the usual way, Dr. A attended to her breathing. She became centered and calm. Rather than reacting, mindlessly following her first impulse, Dr. A responded by taking Laura step-by-step through a rational, rather than an emotional, assessment of the situation. This strategy led both the doctor and the nurse to address the situation with a sense of focus and calm.

The samurai tale illustrates mindfulness, the difference between feeling angry and being aware you feel angry. In teaching mindfulness to my students, I say: "There is a difference between watching the rushing waters of a river from the embankment and trying to swim in the river." We can gain insight from taking note of rushing emotions, without diving in and drowning in them. Mindfulness is transcendence. By rising above and transcending emotions, we gain a clearer perception of the situation and ourselves, leading to a more accurate vision of reality. Instead of viewing events as simply happening to us, we can see the role of each person, including ourselves, in events. Mindfulness is a skill best learned through daily practice.

> *Mindfulness is a full awareness of the present moment, accompanied by a feeling of being "centered" and "grounded."*

Mindfulness is a full awareness of the present moment, accompanied by a feeling of being "centered" and "grounded." In a moment of mindfulness, all is in flow, and the universe seems simple. It is as if the clutter has been swept away, allowing you to see unimpeded. Living in the moment has tangible benefits. As Joe, a former mindfulness student, said, "When I look at just this moment, it's never that bad." Joe often felt overwhelmed by the demands of running his own business. But by staying present in the moment, he felt clear and focused and could see daily demands as manageable. Instead of feeling rattled by events, Joe learned to take events in stride.

> *Although "living in the moment" may seem similar to being impulsive, it is actually its opposite.*

Although "living in the moment" may seem similar to being impulsive, it is actually its opposite. Impulsivity involves reflexive action. For example, remember Jane from chapter 1? In a state of anxiety, she actually jumped out of a moving car. If Jane had been schooled in mindfulness, she would have "sat" with the anxiety and observed the anxious thoughts and feelings, as they coursed through her mind, like debris floating down a river past her. She could have focused on her breathing as a mental and psychological anchor that steadied her. In this way, Jane would have been able to sit calmly through the remainder of the ride, without injuring herself or others.

Paths to Mindfulness

There are several ways to become mindful. One way is to practice meditation. Before discussing various methods of meditation, let's dispel some of the myths about meditation. The biggest myth is that meditation is a direct path to peace and tranquility and that such serenity occurs quickly. Many of my meditation students express frustration that they are "not doing it right" or "can't get into it." Meditation is a learned skill, presumably as difficult as learning to play a musical instrument, yet no one would expect to sit down at a piano after taking a few lessons and perform a concerto. Nonetheless, many people have expectations of instant "success" with meditation. It is important to let go of expectations and judgments, including judgments about how "well" one is meditating.

Tranquility from meditation emerges from the practice of it. A person who takes a monorail to a mountaintop no doubt experiences the same breathtaking view as one who climbed the mountain. If the goal is to become an experienced mountaineer, however, the climb is the point. To become more balanced in everyday life, it is best to encounter the same struggles in your meditation practice that you encounter in real life. For example, if you have difficulty coping with boredom—a problem for many American meditators and an even bigger problem for meditators with BPD—the way in which you transcend boredom during your meditation is the way you can transcend boredom in daily life.

One of the paradoxes of meditation is that progress is best made in the absence of striving. Striving for the goals of tranquility, inner peace, or even relaxation hinders the ability to meditate properly. In order to meditate, just follow the most mundane of instructions. If you are doing a breath-watching meditation and you are paying attention to your breath, then you are doing it right. If you are doing a thought-watching meditation and you are paying attention to your thoughts—without "forcing" your thoughts in any particular direction—then you are doing it right, even if you are feeling anxious, frustrated, or angry because of a situation in your life. Roll out the welcome mat for those feelings. Rather than saying to yourself, "I must be doing this wrong because I'm not relaxed," ask yourself what this experience means to you. Allow the experience to be your teacher, your mentor, and your own private Zen master.

> *One of the paradoxes of meditation is that progress is best made in the absence of striving. Striving for the goals of tranquility, inner peace, or even relaxation hinders the ability to meditate properly.*

Among the excellent books and tapes available on mindfulness meditation is Jon Kabat-Zinn's *Full Catastrophe Living*. A guide in mindfulness practice, it is directed toward using meditation to treat pain and illnesses. The otherwise physically healthy individual with borderline personality disorder can benefit from this approach. The author's more poetic and readable *Wherever You Go, There You Are* is a great guide for beginning meditation. Both of Kabat-Zinn's books have corresponding cassette tapes, available on order forms in the back of each book. The Center for Mindfulness, which Kabat-Zinn directed for years and which carries on the work of promoting mindfulness, lists trainers and programs on its Web site (see "Meditation and Mindfulness" in appendix B).

Other excellent books on meditation include Lawrence LeShan's *How to Meditate*, Jack Kornfield's *A Path with a Heart*, and Thich Nhat Hanh's *The Miracle of Mindfulness*.

2. Balance Your Lifestyle

Nurture yourself with rest, exercise, nutrients, and activities. These resources are building blocks upon which you can construct a healthy, balanced lifestyle.

Eat a Healthful, Balanced Diet

As we saw in chapter 5, diet affects your mental and physical well-being. Eating a diet rich in vegetables, whole grains, beans, and fruits, with smaller amounts of meat, fish, poultry, and cheese, and minimal sugar and fat, will help you feel healthy and strong. Eating organically grown foods minimizes your exposure to chemicals and maximizes nutrients and flavor. Take a daily multivitamin/mineral supplement, especially if you have depression. Take omega-3 supplements of flax oil and fish oil, especially if you have ADHD symptoms.

A good basic book about general nutrition is *Nutrition for Dummies*. But if you have borderline personality disorder, you may have

---

Balancing Your Lifestyle
- Eat a healthy, balanced diet
- Engage in regular exercise
- Get plenty of rest
- Manage your activities wisely

special nutritional needs or deficits. A consultation with a nutritionist is recommended. Melvyn Werbach's *Textbook of Nutritional Medicine* discusses such BPD symptoms as depression, anxiety, and ADHD. You may want to talk over this information with your doctor or nutritionist. If you have ADHD, then *The LCP Solution*, by B. Jacqueline Stordy and Malcolm J. Nicholl, is a key resource.[4]

Engage in Regular Exercise

> *Focus on the euphoria of exercise. Let go. Enjoy the moment. Enjoy the feeling of air filling your lungs, the rhythm of your body.*

For most people, the recommended amount of exercise is 20 to 30 minutes, three to five times a week. Exercise lifts depression, reduces anxiety, encourages sleep, improves concentration, reduces weight, improves cardiovascular health, alleviates body aches, and reduces risk of disease. Whether you utilize aerobic exercise, strength training, or walking, you can exercise alone, with friends, or in a group. Exercise helps balance mind, body, and spirit.

As was stressed in chapter 7, the best exercise is the one that you will do. Find an exercise you like and stick with it. Focus on the euphoria of exercise. Let go. Enjoy the moment. Enjoy the feeling of air filling your lungs, the rhythm of your body, and the feeling in your muscles. Let go of future strivings and be fully present, right here, right now.

Then enjoy a delicious and healthy post-workout meal. Food takes on a particular pleasure when you're hungry from physical activity, as opposed to food you eat out of stress or boredom. As my grandfather used to say, "Hunger is the best sauce."

Get Plenty of Rest

The average American does not get enough sleep. In addition, alcohol, drugs, depression, and even our families can interfere with sleep. Alcohol interferes with REM sleep, the phase during which we dream, leaving us sleep-deprived. Depression and anxiety can also make us sleepless. A National Sleep Foundation poll showed that families with children under 18 got less sleep per night than people without children. If your child has a sleep problem, then you have a sleep problem. *Healthy Sleep Habits, Happy Child*, by Marc Weissbluth, M.D., provides behavioral programs for helping your child sleep.

Pay attention to your body. Lack of sleep leads to low productivity and accidents. Driving while sleepy can be as dangerous as driving under the influence of drugs or alcohol. For individuals with borderline personality disorder, who are already prone to depression and trouble regulating emotions, lack of sleep can negatively affect the quality of your life.

Forgoing the cultural pressures to cut back on sleep can be profoundly difficult. There are enjoyable television shows to watch late at night. There are friends to call on the phone and plans to make. Remind yourself that daily life will be more satisfying if you are properly rested.

Manage Your Activities Wisely

Schedule enough activities so that you feel engaged and energized, but avoid scheduling so many activities that you become overwhelmed. What drives us to overcommit? Our culture offers so many things to do. We are constantly barraged with advertising and social messages encouraging us to do more, buy more, and work more. If you are overburdened and overscheduled, reduce your exposure to advertising and social pressure by reducing television time. You also may need to make some life choices, such as reducing some activities and decreasing your workload. Avoid making big changes on impulse. Talk about possible positive changes with a counselor or trusted friend.

> *Schedule enough activities so that you feel engaged and energized, but avoid scheduling so many activities that you become overwhelmed.*

On the flip side, avoid scheduling so few activities that you become bored. In a way, this is phrased backwards because people who are bored and depressed tend to schedule fewer activities. If you are underactive, make a list of pleasurable activities. Eliminate from the list anything harmful, such as drug abuse. If you cannot think of anything, remember happy times you've had. Make a list of anything that's ever given you pleasure. If you still cannot think of anything, then you should seek professional help. You may have anhedonia, which literally means "absence of pleasure." Anhedonia is a powerful sign of clinical depression.

Once you have completed your list of pleasurable activities, pick an easy one to accomplish and make it happen. For example, if your list includes "take a walk in the park," then make time to go for a walk in the park. Set a specific time and treat it like an important appointment. If you want to see a friend, then make it a date. How many times have you said, "Let's get together sometime," and it never happens? If you want an activity to happen, be specific about when and where you will do it.

Good books on time-management include Alan Lakein's *How to Get Control of Your Time and Your Life*, Richard Carlson's *Don't Sweat the Small Stuff*, and Stephen Covey's *The 7 Habits of Highly Effective People* and *First Things First*.

3. Balance Your Relationships

Our relationships are among the most important aspects of our lives, but most of us are never directly taught how to improve them.

We learn by watching others and by trial and error. If you were exposed to people with poor social skills, especially early in life, you may have picked up some bad relationship habits. A good way to pick up positive relationship skills is to spend time with happy couples whose relationships you admire. Learning their positive relationship skills can greatly enhance your own relationships. Communication, empathy, and setting of boundaries exemplify good relationship skills.

> *Our relationships are among the most important aspects of our lives, but most of us are never directly taught how to improve them.*

Communication

Communication is one of the most difficult, most sophisticated tasks in which we humans engage. When I first started teaching stress management at a government institution, employees appreciated learning new skills and their morale was reasonably good. The government, however, began making cutbacks. Morale deteriorated over time. Employees grumbled: "Administration is messing up our lives, and now they're sending us to stress management to try and fix it! Why don't they just do something about the stress they're creating in the first place!" It was the same class. We were the same instructors. What had changed was the context. The previous feeling of trust was strained. The message I know that administration was trying to communicate—"We value you and want you to be happy"—was now interpreted as: "We blame you. We deny our responsibility to create a good working environment. If you're feeling stressed out, it's your problem; deal with it." Given the complications involved in communication, it's not surprising it often breaks down.

To add complexity: We cannot *not* communicate. If you are in proximity to another person, you are communicating. Communication is more than just words. In addition to what we say, how we say it can make or break relationships—so can what we do and how we carry ourselves. Not saying something can be just as powerful a communication as saying something.

Communication 101: Being Assertive

Assertiveness means expressing your true feelings, wants, or desires while bridging the middle ground between being too passive, too aggressive, or passive-aggressive. Common examples of these approaches abound in everyday commerce. Let's say you ordered a medium-done steak in a restaurant, but it arrives well-done. A passive response would be to force a smile and say to the waiter, "It's delicious." A too-aggressive response is easy enough to imagine: "What is this (expletive)!" A passive-aggressive response would be to sulk, making everyone at the table miserable. In contrast, an assertive response would be to request politely that your original order be filled.

Being appropriately assertive in relationships is trickier. Let's say someone hurt your feelings by forgetting your birthday. A passive response would be to feel sorry for yourself. An aggressive response? Sarcasm or hostility expressed verbally or behaviorally. A passive-aggressive response means hostile action against someone by not doing something, such as giving the person the "silent treatment" and not communicating when they try to apologize.

Assertiveness is based on a few fundamental principles. One is healthy entitlement. You have certain basic rights, and you should be prepared to enact them. Psychologist Manuel Smith, Ph.D., calls it your fundamental assertive right: "You have the right to judge your own behavior, thoughts and emotions, and to take the responsibility for their initiation and consequences upon yourself."[5]

Exercising your fundamental assertive right, however, entails being aware of your needs, moods, thoughts, and feelings, and taking responsibility for expressing them in a constructive manner. The mindfulness section of this chapter can be extremely helpful in that regard. Psychologists Robert Alberti and Michael Emmons, in their classic book *Your Perfect Right*, note the function, or goal, of assertive behavior: "Assertive behavior promotes equality in human relationships, enabling us to act in our own best interests, to stand up for ourselves without undue anxiety, to express one's feelings comfortably, to exercise personal rights, without denying the rights of others."[6] Assertiveness means being clear and straightforward.

> *E*xercising your fundamental assertive right entails being aware of your needs, moods, thoughts, and feelings, and taking responsibility for expressing them in a constructive manner.

Communication 201: Close Relationships

Communication in close relationships can be complex. Intricate patterns of communicating evolve over time. Since so many phrases are ambiguous, one of our best guides is knowing the person. When your loving husband says, "I think you're dynamite," he probably means he thinks you're terrific, not that you have a hot temper. Even in close relationships—perhaps *especially* in close relations—miscommunications occur. For people with borderline personality disorder, close relationships often produce more miscommunications than other people may experience because intimacy stirs up invalidating experiences from the past. For example, a woman with BPD may assume, unconsciously or automatically, that her husband is being critical or demeaning in the same way that someone in her past was.

The best way to address communication problems of this sort is with a sentence formula I learned from Jon M. Gottman's *A Couple's Guide to Communication:*

When you say or do X to me,

in situation Y,

I feel Z.

For example, "When you forget to say anything to me on my birthday, I feel hurt," or "When you don't pay attention to me at the party, I feel furious." By saying "I feel" rather than "You make me feel," you provoke less defensiveness. You are owning your part of the interaction. You are not implying, "You are a terrible person for making me feel bad." You are saying, "I feel bad." The implied message is: "Since you care about me, my feeling bad is something we need to work on. Since I am a worthwhile person, it is not okay for you to say things I experience as hurtful. This is a problem we need to resolve."

For people with BPD, close relationships often produce more miscommunications than other people may experience because intimacy stirs up invalidating experiences from the past.

Your feelings are what they are, and they are okay. They are your radar, your most sensitive indicators of your thought processes, your ways of viewing the world, your values, and your involvement in a relationship. When we don't express our feelings verbally, we must either suppress them or act them out. One reason very young children have more tantrums than adults do is that they lack alternative ways of expressing their feelings. When you say to a 2-year-old, "You may not have a cookie," she experiences rage and shows it by screaming, flailing her arms and legs, and generally creating an unpleasant scene. She is developmentally too immature to say, "When you do not give me a cookie before dinner, I feel angry and disappointed." When you can "reason" with the child by saying, "Dinner first, then a cookie," tantrums become less frequent. Similarly, with adults, if we can say, "I feel angry and disappointed," we are less likely to act it out by screaming. Talking things out, when possible, is almost always the best solution, as it carries little downside and tends to pave the way for better conflict resolution next time around.

> *Talking things out, when possible, is almost always the best solution, as it carries little downside and tends to pave the way for better conflict resolution next time around.*

Giving criticism is also an art. Sometimes, in order for a relationship to work, we need to tell others we don't like how they are doing things. But how we say it affects how well our message is received. In any communication, especially when you criticize, start out by empathizing. Imagine what it would feel like to be the other person. How will it feel for him to hear what you are about to say? How would you feel? If he disappointed you, perhaps you can give him credit for his efforts. Start your message with something positive, if you can.

Compare these two statements:

"I hate it when you're late. I don't even want to go now!"

"I'm sure you were trying to get everything perfect for our date. When you're late, though, I feel tense and pressured. It's more important to me that you're on time."

Or these:

"Stop leaving your junk around the house!"

"I know you're busy now, and it's hard to make time to clean up. If you could find one place to leave your stuff until you have time to put it away, I'd really appreciate it."

By recognizing that the person has good intentions or is under pressure, you can go a long way toward making a criticism easier to swallow and enhancing your chances of gaining compliance. Please do not misconstrue this as saying things you don't mean in order to get the other person to do what you want. Any "empathizing" that is not genuine is likely to backfire and make things worse.

Empathy

If I had to pick just one tool to help me get through life, it would be empathy. Empathy means truly understanding another person. It's not sympathy or pity, which is feeling sorry for someone. It's not problem solving. Empathy answers the question: "How does that person feel?" How do we empathize better with others? Begin with the question: "How would I feel in that situation?" But this is just a starting point. The key to empathy is not guessing, imagining, or figuring. It's listening. Listen to what the person has to say. Then listen some more.

> *Empathizing does not mean you have to like or approve of what someone said or did; it means you have to understand what happened from their point of view.*

The hardest time to empathize is when you are feeling hurt by someone. This may be when showing empathy is most important, however. Empathizing does not mean you have to like or approve of what someone said or did; it means you have to understand what happened from their point of view. Imagine you are feeling sad and blue, so you call a friend. On this night, she says, "I'm sorry. I can't talk to you tonight." You probably feel hurt and abandoned. The empathic thing to say would be: "Is everything all right?" Helping someone can be very healing. She might say: "I'm okay, but I need some time to myself tonight." That may be harder for you to handle, but stay empathetic. Haven't you ever needed or wanted to be alone? But be sure to paraphrase back what the person says in order to make sure you have it straight.

Many people with borderline personality disorder are extremely empathic, particularly those who've experienced abuse. According to Daniel Goleman, Ph.D., in his book *Emotional Intelligence:*

> While emotional neglect seems to dull empathy, there is a paradoxi-
> cal result from intense, sustained emotional abuse, including cruel,
> sadistic threats, humiliations, and plain meanness. Children who en-

dure such abuse can become hyperalert to the emotions of those around them, in what amounts to post-traumatic vigilance to cues that have signaled threat. Such an obsessive preoccupation with the feelings of others is typical of psychologically abused children who in adulthood suffer the mercurial, intense emotional ups and downs that are sometimes diagnosed as "borderline personality disorder." Many such people are gifted at sensing what others around them are feeling, and it is quite common for them to report having suffered emotional abuse in childhood.[7]

> *The hardest time to empathize is when you are feeling hurt by someone, but that may be when empathy is most important.*

This level of empathy is a gift because empathy is one of life's most important skills. The difficulty for some people with the gift of extreme empathy is feeling engulfed. Knowing how another person feels and what another person wants becomes a command to fulfill those wants and needs. It's important not to let relationships overwhelm your own wants and needs under the pressure to fulfill another person. For victims of abuse, survival itself may have depended on responding to another person's needs; this response may still be embedded in their psyches though the threat to their survival is no longer present. If you have this pattern, it is important to work on setting boundaries with others.

Setting Boundaries

Setting boundaries is a common difficulty for people with borderline personality disorder. Clients with BPD often come in for a therapy session, share compelling personal information, and then never return. They violated their own boundaries by opening up too quickly and, as a result, experienced feelings they could not handle, such as vulnerability, fear, or shame. They then felt the need to reestablish boundaries by creating the physical distance of not continuing therapy. This same response may be seen in personal relationships, which is why boundary-setting is so important. One guideline is to recognize you have the right to say "no." The decision to do or say anything is yours. You have a right to listen to other people's problems without making them your problems.

Another form of boundary-setting is recognizing you have a right to privacy. You do not have to tell others intimate things about yourself. Many people believe it is essential to share everything with your psychotherapist. In reality, what you need to share varies a great deal, depending on the therapeutic approach being taken, and the difficulty you are trying to address. Allow the relationship with the therapist to develop and unfold over time.

For people with identity diffusion, a symptom of borderline personality disorder, setting boundaries can be difficult. It is hard to separate what is "me" from what is "not me" if my identity is constantly shifting. A boundary that makes sense one day does not make sense the next. Work on knowing yourself and your true feelings. Use meditation, creative arts therapy, psychotherapy, and other techniques. Boundary-setting and identity development can happen in tandem, where progress in one supports progress in the other. *Boundaries: Where You End and I Begin*, by Anne Katherine, is an excellent resource. Another book on the subject, *Boundaries: When to Say Yes, When to Say No to Take Control of Your Life*, by Henry Cloud and John Townsend, is based on Christian values and received a strong review in *Authoritative Guide to Self-Help Resources in Mental Health*, by John Norcross and his associates.[8]

> *For people with identity diffusion, a symptom of BPD, setting boundaries can be difficult. It is hard to separate what is "me" from what is "not me" if my identity is constantly shifting.*

4. De-Escalate Extreme Emotions

Emotions are essential to our functioning. Joy, fear, anger, love, sadness, and anxiety are part of being human. When emotions get out of balance, however, they can be troublesome. Individuals with BPD are prone to experiencing emotions in the extreme. Learning to balance your emotions will greatly enhance your satisfaction with life.

Most people want, naturally, to reduce their anxiety and depression. Anxiety and depression feel terrible. Anger, however, is different. For better or for worse, anger often feels good in the short term, with a sense of release once you "let it out." People often do what you want in order to get you to calm down, so you feel powerful. Some people feel a self-righteous sense of pride, believing the other person "deserved" the outburst, and seeing their anger as just retribution or a moral duty. These temporary "rewards" lead to increased use of anger. Others view anger as a completely irrational emotion that overtakes them and which they can do nothing about. It is important to identify the reasons you want to reduce your anger.

What is the problem with anger, then? Anger, especially if it leads to hostility or violence, can cause problems in relationships, cost you your job, or create legal problems. Often, once the blowup is over, people experience remorse, guilt, and other negative emotions. Finally, research has shown that excessive expression of anger has a strong link with heart disease.

For many people, changing their angry behavior is not easy and requires a great deal of motivation. List the reasons you want to reduce your angry outbursts. Keep your list with you in your wallet or purse and refer to it often. Anger is an emotion that overtakes us in an instant. Usually, the anger itself does not get us into trouble. It is the action that follows the anger—the acting-out based on the angry feeling—that causes problems for us.

Counting to 10 before taking any action is one way to reduce acting in the heat of the moment. Thinking about the consequences of your actions, and asking yourself the question, "Is it worth it?" is a natural antidote to impulsiveness. Another technique on how to challenge your thoughts, which will work for anger, depression, and anxiety, is called the three-column technique.

Using the three-column technique is as easy as ABC.[9] The "A"—Antecedent—column lists the situation that occurred prior to your getting angry (or depressed or anxious). The "C"—Consequence—column lists what happened as a consequence of the situation. It refers to your feelings—angry, upset, frustrated, and so on. The "B"—Belief—column lists your thoughts when you feel that way. Start by listing the Antecedent and Consequence (what happened, and how you felt):

Antecedent	Consequence
Cut off by driver	Angry
Broke up with girlfriend	Depressed

Now fill in the Belief column:

Antecedent	Belief	Consequence
Cut off by driver	That jerk could have gotten me killed! He should watch where he's going! I'll teach him a lesson!	Angry
Broke up with girlfriend	No one will ever love me again. I'm a failure with women. I'm no good.	Depressed

Once you see the beliefs, start to challenge them. Could it be that the driver just made a mistake? Have you ever cut anyone off, accidentally? Were you injured? Was your pride? Is that worth retaliating? With regards to the break-up, have you ever broken up with anyone before? Did you feel bad forever? Did you find someone else who cared about you? Even if you have not had a good relationship yet, does that mean you never will? Aren't you taking steps to improve yourself? (After all—you are reading a self-improvement book!) Even if, worst case, you are a failure with women, does that mean you are no good? Have you never performed any acts of kindness? Have you never done anything worthwhile? After they are challenged, you may find the thoughts coming into better balance and perspective:

Antecedent	Belief	Consequence
Cut off by driver	Thank goodness I was not hurt. Breathe. Stay calm. Perhaps that person was going to the hospital, or made a mistake.	Relieved, calm, forgiving
Broke up with girlfriend	It is a shame that this relationship did not work out. I will learn more about myself, to avoid making the same mistakes. I will learn more about what to look for in a partner, so that I can pick someone who is a better match for me.	Sadness, hopefulness

Books on how to challenge your thoughts to improve how you feel include David Burns's *Feeling Good: The New Mood Therapy* and its companion volume, *The Feeling Good Handbook*, as well as Christine Padesky's *Mind Over Mood*, based on a cognitive-behavioral approach.

5. Engage in Stress Reduction Techniques

Relaxation, yoga, prayer, and meditation can have profoundly positive effects on our overall mood, adjustment, and feelings. Likewise, humor and laughter benefit our mood and our health. Laughing stimulates the release of endorphins, the brain chemicals that produce euphoria and reduce pain. As Norman Cousins discovered during his recovery from illness, 10 minutes of good, hard laughter daily can significantly aid healing. Often, when we feel depressed, very little seems funny and we don't want to make the effort to seek out opportunities to laugh.

In my clinical experience, television sitcoms, while helpful for an easy laugh, are not funny enough to help most clients. In this case, feeling amused or chuckling is not sufficient. Only paroxysms of laughter will do. Videos can help. Classics such as Marx Brothers' movies, physical humor as in Woody Allen's *Sleeper,* Bill Cosby routines, stand-up comedy routines, and so on, can produce the kind of grabbing-your-sides, gasping-for-air laughter that works as a tonic on outlook and mood. This level of hilarity is so vigorous and invigorating that it can have the therapeutic effect of physical exercise.[10]

> *Humor and laughter benefit our mood and our health. Laughing stimulates the release of endorphins, the brain chemicals that produce euphoria and reduce pain.*

Beyond laughter, humor is part of a philosophy of life. According to C. W. Metcalf, in his educational video "Humor, Risk, and Change," humor means taking our problems seriously—and ourselves lightly. He describes a pilot who lost navigational control while flying. He steered the plane by alternately firing the engines. Approaching the airport, he asked the tower which runway he should use. The tower had cleared all the runways, and he could use any one he wanted. The pilot, responsible for his own life and the lives of his passengers, quipped, "Oh, great. Not only do I have to fly the plane, I have to pick the runway, too!" Rather than getting tight, he allowed himself to get loose. Although he took the situation seriously, he used humor to lighten the moment. When we clamp down and get overly serious or frightened, our thinking becomes narrow and restricted. Humor can help us to loosen up enough to stay free, creative, and focused. The plane landed safely.

In another example, Metcalf draws a circle on a blackboard, stating, "This is the center of the known universe." A foot away from the figure, he writes an "X" and says, "This is you. Notice you are not the center of the known universe."

It often feels to us that our situation is unique. Our troubles seem so large that there appears to be no way around them. They occupy the entire field of our vision. The introduction of humor steers us away from this mistaken view and helps put our troubles in perspective. Seeing that we are not the center of the universe gives us permission to be ordinary human beings, without the melodrama. At its best, humor shows us how alike we are. Certainly, there is hurtful humor. Sarcasm, belittlement, and making fun of others are kinds of veiled hostility. This type of humor has little healing value for the perpetrator or viewers and is harmful to the victim.

> *Seeing that we are not the center of the universe gives us permission to be ordinary human beings, without the melodrama.*

A more healing variety is "me, too" humor. While performing, a comedian with newborn twins took out his keys and jingled them, asking the audience, "You like that?" The audience chuckled. "Good," he said, "because that's the only joke I've written in 6 months." The audience roared. Who could not relate to how exhausting and overwhelming it is to have young children, so that you can't get anything done? Another comedian, with very active toddlers, spoke about trying to pick them up. "They all learn this same judo move." He undulated his body, slithering in a downward motion with his arms straight over his head, and the audience roared with understanding laughter. "Where do they learn this? Is there some toddler training program they all go to that parents don't know about?"

Good humor connects. It helps us to feel okay about our modest role in the universe. It helps us recognize the overwhelming forces we all have to cope with. We try to have an impact and are thwarted. We do everything wrong, yet we can still think of ourselves as successful. Our plans are dashed, yet things often work out for the best. Likewise, our plans can go perfectly—and result in a complete mess. Such is life. You can laugh or cry. Laughing is much more fun. Sit down with Allen Klein's book, *The Healing Power of Humor* (see "Humor" in appendix B) and you'll see that this is so.

6. Nurture Your Soul

Engaging in spiritually satisfying experiences regularly nurtures your soul, which can help soothe the emotional ups and downs of BPD. Spirituality can be defined in many ways. For some, it refers to religious ideas, such as a relationship with God, or specific activities, such as prayer. For others, spirituality refers to a feeling, such as peace or well-being. Still others view spiritual experience as uniting with the divine or becoming one with something greater than oneself. Just as spirituality has many definitions, many paths—including prayer, meditation, and communing with nature—lead to spirituality.

In the hustle-bustle of life, we can easily defer the pursuit of spiritual well-being to the demands of job, bills, and other obligations. Taking time to be fully present "to smell the flowers," however, gives life depth and richness.

Buddhist monk Thich Nhat Hanh describes a scene in which he as his traveling companion Jim sat under a tree eating a tangerine:

> He began to talk about what we would be doing in the future. Whenever we thought about a project that seemed attractive or inspiring, Jim became so immersed in it that he literally forgot about what he was doing in the present. He popped a section of tangerine in his mouth and, before he had begun chewing it, had another slice ready to pop into his mouth. He was hardly aware that he was eating the tangerine. All I had to say was, "You ought to eat the tangerine section you've already taken." Jim was startled into realizing what he was doing.[11]

By being in two places at once, Jim was not engaged in experiencing his own life; he was cut off from his own experience. Hanh compares it to not having lived in those moments. When you are eating a tangerine, eat a tangerine. When you are doing the dishes, do the dishes. When you are dining with your friends, dine with your friends. How often are our bodies in one place and our minds elsewhere? How often do you see people nowadays dining with friends yet speaking to someone else on a cell phone? To try to do both at once is futile. You may have to "multitask" at work, but you don't have to in your personal life.

A spiritual approach can lead to transcendence of current circumstances. No matter what your background is, prayer is an ancient practice that attends to a fundamental human need to connect with something greater than ourselves, to connect to the divine, to connect to the eternal. Catherine Maurice, in *Let Me Hear Your Voice*, beautifully describes her experience with prayer. Maurice, who was filled with despair after her 2-year-old daughter was diagnosed with autism, tells about facing anti-spiritual sentiments:

> How difficult it is for a woman like me—intellectually oriented, impatient, competitive, overly sensitive to criticism or disapproval—to write about prayer. In some circles I have frequented, there is such intolerance of traditional religious forms and rituals, such scorn for those who, in desperate childish wishfulness, need to posit the great Santa-in-the-Sky, the eternal Daddy who fixes everything, including evil, including death.[12]

She then goes on to describe her experience with prayer:

> But now, in the face of this crisis, I did not rationally decide to turn to prayer: I threw myself into prayer. I held on to prayer as though it were one floating spark in a black tempestuous sea. My prayer was pure petition. I was far from any worshipful, contemplative love, far from any serene joy before the Almighty. My prayer was frantic, sobbing, desperate begging. "Lord, make it not be. Give me back my baby girl. Give her back to me. Don't let this happen. Stop it. Give her back!"[13]

Later, she prayed again:

> There was a candle and an icon on my dresser. I lit the candle and gazed into its warm soft glow . . . I sat in that small circle of light and tried to feel the presence of God. "Lord, I need your help, so

badly. . . ." All along, I had been asking for reality to be changed: "Please make the diagnosis be wrong, please make her not be autistic. . . ." This night was different. I had to ask for something else. "Lord, send me . . . fill me with . . . Your strength . . . Your peace . . . Give me Your strength and Your peace, and I will be able to go on." But there was one more thing I needed to say, one hard and terrible thing. Gazing into the light, I raised my clasped hands and bowed my head, willing myself to trust in His love. Then I whispered the words that my heart hated, my soul decreed, "Thy will be done." And I was flooded, instantly, impossibly, with comfort. I knew the stillness of a child who, trembling alone in the dark, suddenly feels herself enfolded in loving arms. I was rocked with love, soothed by peace.[14]

There is an old saying: There are no atheists in the foxhole. In our hour of need, many of us reach out. And many of us feel comfort. People who have faith and who surrender themselves to prayer can do remarkably well in trying circumstances. I am reminded of two clients with whom I worked when I was on a hospital hospice team. Hospice care indicates that the patients who are dying have chosen comfort measures to ease the pain of their disease, when treatment to try to cure the disease is no longer considered viable. One client was angry, sullen, and withdrawn. Not ready to die, he cursed his fate. The other client seemed radiantly filled with peace. He was able to connect to his family until the last moment. He believed he was going to a better place. Both patients had cancer. Both patients had pain. Both were about the same age. One patient had faith, however, and the other did not.

Books that I have found most useful to myself and my clients for spiritual guidance and inspiration include Thich Nhat Hanh's *The Miracle of Mindfulness*, Jon Kabat-Zinn's *Wherever You Go, There You Are* and *Full Catastrophe Living*, Richard Carlson's *Don't Sweat the Small Stuff*, and Laibl Wolf's *Practical Kabbalah*. Traditional religious institutions can be places of love and healing; clergy can best direct you to readings in your religious faith. Retreats, such as meditation weekends at places like the Omega Institute in Rhinebeck, New York, can also provide respite, healing, and insight.

7. Avoid Excessive Use of Substances

Some individuals with borderline personality disorder have concurrent problems with substance abuse, such as overuse of alcohol, drugs, or food. Many people start drinking or taking drugs as teenagers, in an attempt to fit in. Others are attempting to "self-medicate" away feelings of depression and anxiety. Still others are trying to fill a void, a feeling of emptiness. Some people abuse drugs or alcohol for the rush. The motivation may vary, but all of these individuals are putting themselves at risk for addiction.

Once substance use crosses the line to addiction, whatever original problem you were seeking to alleviate invariably pales by comparison to the problems created by addiction. Addiction to alcohol often promotes a downward spiral and destroys relationships. Usually, employment is the last to go (the motivation being to get money to buy alcohol), but ultimately jobs are swept away by the tidal wave of addiction. Those who use illegal drugs are in worse shape, from contact with exploitive or dangerous dealers to committing crimes to get money for drugs to arrests and prison. Illnesses, such as liver disease and brain damage, often follow alcohol abuse, while use of illegal drugs is associated with brain damage and the spread of potentially fatal communicable diseases (such as AIDS).

If you are taking drugs or alcohol, you may not be a good judge of whether or not you have a problem. Denial runs deep.

If you are taking drugs or alcohol, you may not be a good judge of whether or not you have a problem. Denial runs deep. I've known clients who drank wine coolers or beer the way other people drink water yet denied they had a drinking problem. Common rationalizations include, "I know others who drink just as much." Translation: They know alcoholics not yet in recovery. "It doesn't interfere with my life." Significant others beg to differ.

Many people do stop substance abuse on their own. The conventional wisdom is that total abstinence is best. Stopping drinking and drugging is similar to changing other behaviors, however. A combination of high motivation and good support produces the best outcome. Why do you want to stop using? Are you afraid of harming or losing your children? Destroying an important relationship? Losing your job? Winding up in jail? Although fear is one motivator, hope is a better one. Picture yourself living a positive, drug-free existence. Many experts in the field agree that one of the best antidotes to substance abuse—perhaps the best—is having a positive life you don't want to sidetrack with a detour into drugs or alcohol.

One approach to recovery from addiction is joining a recovery group such as Alcoholics Anonymous (AA). AA and many other groups are based on "12-step" philosophies. In current AA parlance, the word "God" is often replaced with "higher power" to broaden its appeal, because a basic principle of the program is that to recover you need to acknowledge a spiritual power. Participants are required to attend daily meetings at first; the frequency is later reduced. You also get a sponsor, someone you can call 24 hours a day to help you resist the urge to drink. AA has local chapters worldwide. Other support dealing with addictive behaviors includes: Narcotics Anonymous (NA), Overeaters Anonymous (OA), and Gamblers Anonymous (GA). There are also groups for families, such as Al-Anon (for friends and families of alcoholics) and Alateen (recovery program for teenagers).

The unmistakably religious character of the 12 steps is a turn-off to some people, either because they are atheists or because they do not have the kind of relationship with God that AA promotes. AA is also based on a medical model of addiction, which views alcoholism as a disease.

Rational Recovery (RR) offers an alternative view. RR sees addiction as a normal process that is governed by the same process as appetite. Addicts use drugs because of the overwhelming pleasure they produce. In this model, the brain is divided into the "animal brain," which regulates such cravings as sexual urges and hunger, and the neocortex, which is "you"—the higher self possessing language, motor control, and control over actions. Rational Recovery does not have ongoing support groups; in fact, it opposes support groups on several grounds, one being that support groups bring potential users together. RR is a brief program (eight 90-minute sessions) that teaches people to alter their "self-talk" in order to achieve total abstinence ("I will never drink again," for example). In addition to reporting effectiveness with alcohol and drug addiction, Rational Recovery reports success with overeating and other addictive behavior. Jack Trimpey's *The Small Book* and *Rational Recovery: The New Cure for Substance Addiction* are two good sources for learning more about RR.

LifeRing Secular Recovery (LSR) rejects the religious aspects of Alcoholics Anonymous, but maintains the use of support groups. LSR is based on sobriety, secularity, and self-help. LSR contends that sobriety is the appropriate goal for addicts, rather than controlled drinking/using. Secularity indicates that people of any faith or no faith are welcome; religion or faith is not an explicit part of the program. Self-help indicates that the groups consist of people with similar problems attending meetings that are not led or monitored by professionals. LSR's *The Handbook of Secular Recovery*, which you can download from the Internet (see "Substance Abuse/Dependence" in appendix B), provides an overview of the program, vignettes from participants, and practical tips for getting started.

8. Join a Support Group

Support groups can be particularly helpful for individuals with borderline personality disorder. A support group lets you know you are not alone with your particular problem. At first, however, individual therapy is most helpful to the majority of people with BPD. A support group can later be added to supplement therapy or for long-term maintenance and further growth after essential gains have been made in therapy. Your therapist may recommend a good support group, or you may find a support group in your area through TARA APD (Treatment and Research Advancements Association for Personality Disorder).

There are also several online support groups. While professionals don't participate in these "sanctuary" sites, moderators are vigilant about keeping the sites safe and positive. The anonymity of the Web can provide support while avoiding the vulnerability BPD individuals may feel in the presence of other people or a professional.

Support groups can be particularly helpful for individuals with borderline personality disorder. A support group lets you know you are not alone with your particular problem.

Soul's Self-Help Central, a caring and informative self-help Web site with a variety of information on many subjects, offers a strong focus on BPD and its many issues. On the award-winning site, webmaster A. J. Mahari shares her own struggle with BPD and her recovery from its symptoms. The site has a spiritual tone, with poetry and personal stories of individuals who have the disorder or who are in recovery. The site (www.soulselfhelp.on.ca) has great book lists and excellent links to other BPD sites.

MH Sanctuary, owned and operated by Patty Pheil, M.S.W., is an excellent Web site for people seeking information on BPD. In addition to its BPD Sanctuary, the site offers information on self-injury, co-dependence, grief, anorexia, bulimia, alcoholism, chemical dependency, domestic violence, depression, anxiety, panic attacks, post-traumatic stress disorder, survivors of suicide, children of people with BPD, families of people with mental health disorders, teenagers with depression or anxiety, narcissistic personality disorder, and dissociative identity (multiple personality) disorder. The Borderline Sanctuary site (www.mhsanctuary.com/borderline/index.html) offers listings for individuals with BPD and for their families, along with listings of doctors and therapists who specialize in BPD. Pheil, who packs her online newsletter (*BPD Sanctuary*) with up-to-date information, also offers therapy by phone and over the Web. The site also lists groups specifically for professionals to share information. MH Sanctuary has won several awards.

BPD Central (www.bpdcentral.com), started by Randi Kreger, provides information for family members of people with BPD. A quote from the Web site reads: "Loving a borderline can be tough. You need support and information. But it's difficult for others to understand the confusion, anger, self-blame, frustration, and grief you may feel. Finding practical information about interacting with a borderline is also a challenge." The Web site's premise, "loving a borderline can be tough," may be a difficult message for people with BPD to hear, especially early in their journey to wellness. Thus, if you have BPD, you may want to enter this site only if you are trying to deal with a significant other who also has the disorder.

9. Know Your Rights

Did you know that mental illness is considered a form of disability? As a disability, it is covered by the provisions of the 1990 Americans with Disabilities Act (ADA). The ADA includes a workplace clause, which requires your company to make "reasonable accommodations"—such as restroom handrails for those in wheelchairs and Braille information in elevators for the blind—for individuals with disabilities. A potential reasonable accommodation for a person with BPD might be flexible work hours in order to attend psychotherapy sessions. Other institutions, such as educational settings, are also required to make reasonable accommodations.

If your disability leads to impairment in a major life activity, you may be eligible for accommodations under the law. According to Barbara Uniek of the Great Lakes ADA Center in Chicago, Illinois, people with BPD may be eligible for flexible scheduling or a secluded workspace. Accommodations are not based on diagnosis, but on the specific impairment. For example, if you have difficulty concentrating, either due to a symptom of BPD or medications, you may receive an accommodation such as a secluded workspace. You can contact one of the 10 national ADA centers at (800) 949-4232, which automatically connects you to the center for your region.

While you must demonstrate need in order to receive an accommodation, your confidentiality should be safeguarded. For example, a student who wants an accommodation must provide an accommodation letter to the school's designated disability accommodation official as documentation. Students need not share the nature of their disability with professors, only their accommodation letter, which does not disclose the nature of the disability. While serving as the accommodation officer at my school for several years, one of the most common accommodations I wrote was to allow students an extra week to complete assignments because of such conditions as depression, ADHD, a writing disorder, dyslexia, and arthritis. Accommodations may not be for the condition itself, but to address the special needs arising from medication side effects. For example, someone who takes sedating medications may be permitted to tape record classes; someone who has dry mouth from a medication needs to suck on ice chips or drink water during class.

> *If your disability leads to impairment in a major life activity, you may be eligible for accommodations under the law. People with BPD may be eligible for flexible scheduling or a secluded workspace.*

"Reasonable" accommodations, however, means you do not have a right to an accommodation in an "essential job function." For example, a blind person cannot work as a pilot because vision is an essential part of flying safely. The ADA also states that accommodations should not create an "undue burden" on the employer. If a small company with modest profits were asked to make accommodations costing $100,000, it could prove the accommodation is an "undue burden." Most accommodations, however, are either free (turning in papers late) or reasonably low-cost.

10. Cope with Stigma

Stigma means a mark of dishonor or disgrace. Unfortunately, in our culture, people with emotional disorders or mental illnesses are stigmatized. According to authors Jan Fawcett, Bernard Golden, and Nancy Rosenfeld in *New Hope for People with Bipolar Disorder*, their excellent review of the stigma faced by people with bipolar disorder, the factors that create and perpetuate stigma are fear, ignorance, and shame. Fear is related to inappropriate portrayals in the media. Although people with mental illness evidence equal or even lower rates of violence than the general population, television and films tend to portray them as being more violent and dangerous. Ignorance about mental illness leads some people to judge mental illness as a moral failing or a lack of willpower, rather than a complex interaction of biological and psychosocial forces. Fawcett, Golden, and Rosenfeld state: "It is no surprise that the stigma of mental illness has been very strong in Western culture, because our society places a high value on self-control, free will, and individual responsibility. It is not difficult to see how these values, coupled with ignorance, have led to the public view of mental illness as a sign of character weakness."[15]

> *Ignorance about mental illness leads some people to judge mental illness as a moral failing or a lack of willpower, rather than a complex interaction of biological and psychosocial forces.*

As we know from previous chapters in this book, borderline personality disorder is not a lack of willpower or other character weakness, but involves biological factors (such as differences in the serotonin system in impulsive individuals), social factors (such as the breakdown of stabilizing psychosocial forces), and psychological factors (such as the use of black-and-white thinking). Many people also mistakenly think that emotional disorders or mental illnesses are permanent and untreatable; scientific research has dispelled this notion. Perhaps even more common is the belief that a mental illness is not a big deal; for example, some people equate depression with their own feelings of sadness on a bad day. We know that emotional disorders and mental illness are much more than that.

Shame, another factor in creating stigma, refers to not living up to one's own standards and feeling bad about it. Shame leads to isolation, depression, and anxiety; the individual often tries to "pass" as not having emotional problems and then fears being "discovered."

Research shows that many people fear the stigma of mental illness, which may lead to job discrimination, rejection by others, and other forms of exclusion from society, more than they fear the mental illness itself.[16]

Even more distressing is the stigma that individuals with BPD report receiving at the hands of mental health care providers. It is abhorrent to consider that you could go to a mental health practitioner for help and then feel stigmatized by that person. As this is a potentially explosive issue, it is vital to present a balanced perspective here.

When delivered by mental health care providers, stigma takes on a special meaning. If a therapist says to a roomful of therapists, "I have nine borderline clients in my caseload right now," it's likely they will groan, "Oh, no!" Some therapists limit the number of people with BPD that they will accept as clients. Understandably, people with BPD may consider this arbitrary and unfair. Part of the problem is that, until recently, therapists often hesitated or refused to inform clients with BPD of their diagnosis, reportedly out of concern of stigmatizing the client. But this concern doesn't really ring true. It is the client's decision whether to tell others or not. So why not tell the client? The real reason for the withholding of the diagnosis may have to do with some therapists' own negative feelings toward treating clients with BPD.

Research shows that many people fear the stigma of mental illness, which may lead to job discrimination, rejection by others, and other forms of exclusion from society, more than they fear the mental illness itself.

It is helpful to explore the roots of this negativity within the therapeutic community. According to John Gunderson, M.D., when a therapist is not specifically trained and prepared to deal with borderline personality disorder, the therapy often goes very badly. As a result, such therapists experience negative emotions—guilt, feelings of incompetence, fear, anxiety that the client will harm himself, and perhaps even anger over the client's cruel accusations said in a moment of rage. In this context, the therapist untrained in treating BPD may come to dislike having clients with the disorder. Until recently, few good treatments for BPD were available. Today, many therapists are still not trained in cutting-edge advances and effective treatment methods for borderline personality disorder. My own experience with clients with BPD changed dramatically and positively when I started to share the diagnosis with them and to take aim at the symptoms.

> *When a therapist is not specifically trained and prepared to deal with borderline personality disorder, the therapy often goes very badly.*

The belief that clients with BPD are "difficult" to treat, in terms of time and energy, is generally true in my opinion. For this reason, therapists in outpatient private practice are wise to limit the number of people with BPD in their practice. But, consider that this choice may be a good thing for their BPD clients as well. Anger or resentment on the part of clients is rooted in mistaken notions about the disorder and its treatment. These notions include various myths:

Myth 1: BPD is no harder to treat than any other disorder, and so limiting one's practice is discriminatory and arbitrary.

Myth 2: Therapists are special (read superhuman) and should not be emotionally drained by their work.

Myth 3: All therapists should know how to treat all problems.

None of these statements is true. Therapists who treat clients with BPD need to be respected for responsibly practicing their profession, and setting their boundaries to their own comfort level.

On the other hand, none of the previous explanations make it acceptable for therapists to stigmatize clients. There are ongoing efforts to educate therapists and others about BPD. Dr. Marsha Linehan has been a powerful force in de-stigmatizing BPD within the therapeutic community. Valerie Porr's TARA APD organization is working to educate the government and the public about BPD. Still, the battle against stigma toward BPD is ongoing. Each of us must combat it in every way we can with information, education, and compassion.

To overcome this kind of prejudice, Fawcett, Golden, and Rosenfeld recommend practicing C.A.R.E.: Compassion, Advocacy, Recognition, and Education. Compassion lies at the root of overcoming stigma through the suspension of judgment and the exercise of empathy. Advocacy means speaking out to government officials and to the public, to fight for the rights of people with emotional disorders, mental illness, and disabilities. Recognition means putting a human face on the condition. When a well-known person or a celebrity comes forward and talks about having borderline personality disorder, public awareness and compassion are likely to soar. Finally, education is the answer to ignorance. The more people know about BPD, the sooner mistaken notions and stereotypes will fall by the wayside.

11. Find Ways to Avoid Self-Destructive and Impulsive Behavior

Self-injury, suicide attempts, and other self-damaging acts are the scourge of people with BPD. Often, the key to recovery is breaking the cycle of these impulsive, self-destructive acts. Despite the obvious disadvantages to engaging in these behaviors, the person who does them has compelling reasons to commit these acts. The person who makes a suicide attempt feels absolutely desperate. The person who cuts herself experiences immediate relief. Breaking the cycle of these behaviors, then, gets back to the fundamental issue: How do you avoid acting on impulse? How do you resist the urge to get immediate relief?

As with changing other behaviors, the key is often to get to the point of thinking about long-term consequences. The techniques we covered for anger management are helpful: Make a choice to defer action, even if for a few seconds. Think about long-term consequences. And challenge all-or-none thinking and other cognitive errors. In this way, you might try reducing the damage from self-injury by using an ice cube rather than a sharp implement to induce pain. An ice cube held against the wrist produces a painful, throbbing, pounding sensation that many self-mutilators find sufficient. The goal of feeling something and gaining relief is achieved. The ice cube is not so cold that it causes long-term damage, however. Again, consider the long-term consequences of your decisions and your actions.

In addition, create for yourself a more satisfying life in general. Appreciating your life is a great antidote—perhaps the best antidote—to suicidal thoughts and feelings. Eating healthfully, exercising, improving communication skills, developing your spiritual life, and engaging in stress-reducing activities represent proven paths to wellness. Therapists and other teachers can be wise guides in this process. Having patience with yourself and with others is important. Steven Levenkron's sensitively written *Cutting: Understanding and Overcoming Self-Mutilation* is a great self-help resource. Armando Favazza's *Bodies Under Siege* is a more academic, cross-cultural look at the phenomenon. The Self-Injury Web site (www.palace.net/~llama/psych/injury .html) includes information, personal stories, a support group, and valuable links to other Web sites. Focus Adolescent Services (www .focusas.com/Resources.html) also has a great deal of information.

> *The key to breaking the cycle of self-destructive behavior is often to get to the point of thinking about long-term consequences.*

12. Orchestrate a Healing Team

The late Ed Roberts was one of my personal heroes. A high quadriplegic, Ed could not move below the level of the neck. He required a ventilator to help him breathe. He was entirely dependent on technology and on other people to help him meet his most basic needs, including eating, breathing, and getting around. Yet Ed was one of the most independent people on the planet. "Special Ed," as he was affectionately known, was a great leader of the disability rights movement. He was instrumental in founding and implementing the independent living movement that brought people with disabilities out of nursing homes and into their own apartments and houses. Once told by his vocational rehabilitation counselor that he was too disabled to work, Roberts went on to become a rehabilitation counselor. He was ultimately appointed by then-Governor Jerry Brown to be the director of rehabilitation for the State of California.

Ed Roberts used to say that the meaning of independence has nothing to do with the ability to move about or to do things for or by yourself. Independence, he said, is about the locus of power. If you are the one calling the shots, then you are independent. If you are under the control of another person, then you are not independent. When he lived in a nursing home, staff determined what happened and when it happened. But when he lived in his own home and could hire attendants, Roberts was able to control the action. If an attendant did not meet his needs, he could fire him and get another. This is power and independence.

Similarly, one way of viewing your "self-help" program is to properly orchestrate your health care providers—your therapists, doctors, helpers, and healers—into a team that meets your needs. The traditional medical model views the doctor as an omniscient authority who takes care of you by telling you what to do. A different model is to think of your health care providers as expert consultants. You do not want to have to go out and get a degree in nutrition, psychology, or psychiatry. Instead, you hire people to provide you with information and advice; it is your choice whether to act on their recommendations or not. You have options. We health care providers are the ones playing the violins, cellos, and harps, but you are the conductor. You are the one who is charged with bringing all the instruments together into a harmonious symphony.

> *We health care providers are the ones playing the violins, cellos, and harps, but you are the conductor, bringing all the instruments together into a harmonious symphony.*

CHAPTER 9

Family Perspective of Borderline Personality Disorder

by Valerie Porr, M.A.

Valerie Porr, M.A., is the founder of the Treatment and Research Advancements Association for Personality Disorder (TARA APD), the largest national nonprofit education and advocacy organization representing consumers, families, and providers affected by BPD. TARA APD has operated a national Helpline (1-888-4-TARA APD) since its inception in 1995; currently sponsors support groups in New York City, Pittsburgh, Philadelphia, San Francisco, San Diego, Washington D.C., and Northwest Canada; and offers an 8-week course, "Family Education and DBT Coping Skills Workshop, Creating a Therapeutic Family Environment," that focuses on helping BPD families learn coping skills based on dialectical behavior therapy (DBT).

HOW DOES BPD behavior appear to a family member or spouse? Imagine walking down the street alongside someone you love. Suddenly he starts acting as if you had stomped on his foot, deliberately causing him injury. The change in his behavior toward you would be understandable as a reaction had you deliberately injured his foot;

however, you did no such thing. Perhaps you bumped into him while walking along, a bump so minor you didn't even notice it. You are therefore clueless when there is a sudden, quixotic behavioral shift and you are now the recipient of hurtful behavior and insults.

Families, friends, and loved ones are in the unique position of bearing the brunt of erratic behaviors that they neither cause nor comprehend. To make matters worse, they generally have little or no information available to help them decipher the actions that wreak havoc upon their lives. Without help or support, families struggle to understand and deal with loved ones whose moods may swing from one extreme to another without any apparent provoking event to explain the shift, or who seem to overreact to incidents that, to the family, seem to be of minor importance. Impulsivity is another equally confusing BPD characteristic that often leads to risky behaviors, dangerous for the people with BPD and others. Family members are further bewildered by the problems people with BPD have with memory. They seem to recall painful experiences from the past with the emotional intensity as if the incidents had just occurred; their emotional wounds do not seem to heal nor does the emotional pain abate with the passage of time. It is as though they are doomed to carry a toxic sack of memories. The person with BPD may be perpetually angry with family members, unable to forgive past perceived slights or events.

> *Families, friends, and loved ones are in the unique position of bearing the brunt of erratic behaviors that they neither cause nor comprehend.*

Coping with this combination of BPD characteristics leaves families feeling confused, frustrated, and helpless. They experience a profound sense of failure when the situation in their homes goes from difficult to more difficult to virtually impossible to manage, despite their efforts to improve or control it.

Frustrated with their failure to alleviate the situation, families often turn to other family members and friends for support. Despite a somewhat more objective view, these people lack the understanding of BPD required to give advice that might bring about positive change. This situation is further complicated by the tendency of people with BPD to describe themselves as "perpetual victims," holding families and spouses personally responsible for events that either never occurred or occurred in a completely different manner than described. In spite of being personally blamed for most of these events, family members remain dismayed over the degree of psychic pain they sense their loved one experiencing. They feel helpless to alleviate this suffering, are concerned for the person's safety, and worry about the present and future quality of their loved one's life. Well-meaning support people may counsel families to "get tough" and to stop "indulging" the person with BPD. These dilemmas leave the family on a lonely roller-coaster ride, hurtling from anger and frustration to despair and hopelessness.

Thus, families can become part of the problem, either cringing in the fear of causing another outburst or disruptive incident, or chasing the person with BPD away. Others become so angry and critical of their loved one that they cannot contain their exasperation. Still others become total enablers. Given the circumstances, any of these responses is certainly understandable. Family members witness their loved one being highly functional in one situation but dysfunctional in another. How can the child have graduated from college, yet now qualify for disability payments? Families retain the memories of a bright, happy, often talented and high-functioning child who seems to have disappeared into the body of this person who may look and sound like their child, but behaves as no one they now want to know.

WHAT FAMILIES OBSERVE

Long before they learn the diagnosis, family members may observe indicators of BPD, such as these:

Impulsivity. Although family members may be aware that their loved one exhibits impulsive behaviors, many do not know that this key component of BPD is biologically based. Impulsivity puts the lives of people with BPD into a constant "knee-jerk" mode. Something happens and they simply react, without monitoring, without a rheostat to control the intensity of their responses. They do not know how to slow down, cope with, or control their reactions. It's little wonder that people with BPD are known to shoplift, spend money excessively, gamble, become sex addicts, and participate in aggressive incidents leading to arrest. They may perpetrate domestic violence or road rage or become stalkers. Families often believe their loved ones should be able to control this behavior but are merely being willful. Unfortunately, they may then judge, criticize, or demand that the person with BPD change or immediately stop the offending behavior. Dialectical behavior therapy (DBT) offers an answer to this dilemma. It teaches the person with BPD coping skills, such as "mindfulness." This includes exercises in deep breathing and other methods designed to slow down responses, to create a space between the "knee" and the "jerk" of the impulsive response. Learning these skills can bring some behavior control to the person with BPD.

> *Although family members may be aware that their loved one exhibits impulsive behaviors, many do not know that this key component of BPD is biologically based.*

Mood Dysregulation. Families can see that their loved ones switch moods with alarming frequency. Mood dysregulation, a major BPD symptom, is also thought to be biologically and/or genetically based. Understanding these mood dysregulations can help families decipher the erratic behaviors they observe. A young woman with BPD who volunteered at the TARA APD offices revealed that her mood changed as many as 27 times in one day! The distress caused by having absolutely no control over their moods accounts for some of the pain experienced by people with BPD.

Anxiety. Many families describe behaviors caused by anxiety, often beginning in early childhood. While this is a chronic problem for the person with BPD, most professionals and researchers are not aware of its early onset. Klonopin and BuSpar, medications used for anxiety, are frequently prescribed for people with BPD. Research is showing a linkage between anxiety, impulsivity, and mood disorder. People with BPD often suffer with all three.

Exquisite Sensitivity. More than any other BPD symptom description, the term "exquisite sensitivity" resonates with family experience when raising a child who is eventually diagnosed with BPD. Parents often describe these children as expressing extreme sensitivity from infancy onward. The children often express this as experiencing acute sensitivity to textures to the point that many articles of clothing are unwearable because they are too "itchy," or as simply not liking how certain clothing (even just a clothing label) feels against their skin.

These children are super-sensitive to sound, sometimes perceiving normal conversation as "screaming" or a comfortable music level as "blaring." Many complain that the taste of various foods is too strong, light hurts their eyes, or various odors are particularly offensive. They are also sensitive to the emotional nuances of other people and their responses. Parents, out of ignorance or misunderstanding, often invalidate these sensitivities. Family members are seldom aware that people with BPD are not making up these reactions, but are truly supersensitive to their environment.

Many people with BPD cannot sleep at night. This, too, may start in infancy. It is almost as if their circadian rhythm is dysregulated. This may account for the frantic calls that many make in the wee hours of the morning that loved ones find so exasperating.

Unusual Reactions to Pain. Parents also tell us that children who later developed BPD often had unusual reactions to pain. Some, with a very low pain threshold, can be described as supersensitive to pain. These are the children who cry excessively when they get hurt or get an injection. Others, on the other hand, have an extremely high pain threshold, feeling almost no pain. These are the children who never cry when they get injections. Many people with BPD self-injure by cutting or burning themselves. They claim they feel relief, rather than pain, when they self-injure.

Cognitive Distortion. Families almost unanimously describe the difficulties they have, and have always had, in communicating with their loved one with BPD. Statements meant to be interpreted logically seem to be processed through an emotional filter. Words seem to be processed in the wrong part of the brain. A simple request, such as "Pass the vegetables, please," is distorted and can elicit a retort such as "I'm not the maid," or "Why don't you want me to eat?" It is almost as if BPD is a language disorder or is "emotional dyslexia." People with BPD need someone to hear them, someone who can speak their language, someone who can enter into their world and articulate their unverbalized behavior or emotions. This may explain why validation, a key component of DBT, is so effective in communicating, decreasing volatile reactions, and developing trust with people who have BPD.

HOW FAMILIES ARE AFFECTED

When seeking support or advice from a friend, family member, or professional, families of those with BPD will describe the explosive, rageful, abusive, or hurtful behavior they have experienced. Instead of receiving the support they need, they often encounter a "What are you talking about?" or "raised-eyebrow" response. Others can't imagine that the "sweet" or "nice" person they know is capable of expressing intense rage or hurling venomous insults and accusations. The ability of those who have BPD to suddenly switch behaviors is illustrated by a psychiatrist's description of a medical doctor he was treating for BPD. During a counseling session, his client was in the midst of a rage attack when she was beeped by her office. She answered the call in a perfectly calm tone, gave appropriate directions for the care of her patient, hung up, and went back to raging.

It is not too difficult to understand how the frustration of living with someone with BPD can have a ripple effect on family members. Families live in a psychic war zone that takes a toll both mentally and physically. Many family members could easily meet criteria for post-traumatic stress disorder, or, more aptly, "persistent" traumatic stress disorder. When struggling to cope with BPD without any explanatory educational material or peer support, family members often report developing stress-related disorders. These may range from high blood pressure, heart attacks and stroke, migraines, abuse of prescription medication, eating disorders, depression, anxiety, sleep disorders, and work problems ranging from distraction, lost work days, and poor job performance to actual job loss. Many concerned family members will deplete savings, retirement benefits, or trust funds; mortgage their homes; or travel anywhere in an attempt to obtain appropriate effective treatment for their loved one. Many marriages do not survive the stress created by coping with a loved one with BPD.

Often, people with BPD accuse family members of abuse. They can be so convincing that the accused person may be ostracized by other family members and friends, lose custody of children, or be criminally charged. In the hierarchy of blaming parents for mental illness, parents of people with BPD now rank number one, overtaking their predecessors: the "schizophrenogenic" mothers purported to cause schizophrenia and "ice-box" or "refrigerator" mothers who were told that their cold, nonbonding behavior caused their child's autism. This is due in part to professional misunderstanding of the BPD diagnosis and the public's ignorance of the symptoms, severity, and concurrent degree of disability of this chronic mental illness.

HOW FAMILIES COPE

Many families, not having an understanding of the dysregulation and pain their loved one is enduring, keep doing what they have been doing, even though it has not been effective. Not knowing how to cope or being too frightened of doing the wrong thing, they often maintain the status quo and make no changes. This means perpetuating angry scenes, blaming and judging, sustaining alienation, distrust, emotional storms, frustration, and chronic feelings of being helpless or overwhelmed. Or they continue behavior that fosters framing people with BPD as "helpless victims" who cannot take care of themselves, make major decisions, or solve problems; in short, they become enablers, taking complete care of the person with BPD. This type of family is usually convinced that their loved one cannot improve.

During adolescence especially, many families lose the ability to cope with their children as the impulsive acting out reaches the level of dangerousness. The families find themselves totally ill-equipped to exercise any control of the at-risk adolescents. Desperate to achieve some level of safety, parents become frantic. They seek out therapists, tough-love groups, 12-step programs, or mental health organizations. The advice they receive is generally inappropriate and tantamount to pouring kerosene on an already vigorously burning fire. These families need support and structured help, including coping skills.

Some families choose to abandon ship. They give up by completely severing their relationship with a loved one with BPD, such as spouses who choose to divorce. However, the by-product of such decisions is often guilt, hopelessness, grief, and shame. While families may no longer face stormy incidents on a daily basis, emotional pain and loss become their constant companions. Although the person with BPD may be absent, an empty chair remains at the family dinner table. Guilt, blame, perpetual grieving, a sense of failure, and a profound sadness are now uninvited guests at every family event. For some families and spouses, severing the relationship may be the only decision they can make. Although not an easy choice, it is understandable. Family members are only human and they, too, are doing the best they can.

FAMILIES' EXPERIENCES WITH THE MENTAL HEALTH SYSTEM

When all their efforts to help a loved one with BPD reach a dead end or proverbial "brick wall" and attempts to live with the situation fail, families often seek the assistance of a mental health professional. Instead of finding the needed help and support, many BPD families and spouses report that they often encounter blame and stigma. Families are shut out by the constraints of "confidentiality" imposed by some clinicians. Rarely are families given an adequate explanation for the baffling symptoms, or offered information on treatment options and prognosis. Insensitive therapists often stigmatize BPD families by assuming the family has abused their child and is therefore responsible for the illness. Families are often left in psychic isolation, struggling to balance their concerns over the obvious suffering and risky behavior of the person with BPD with their own need to protect themselves from destructive BPD behaviors.

Furthermore, professionals who lack understanding of the biological foundation for the impulsivity and emotional dysregulation characteristic of those with BPD sometimes offer families inappropriate advice, such as "You have a right to a life," and "You need to create personal boundaries and set limits." Such advice serves to frame the person with BPD as the "enemy" from whom family members must protect themselves, thus reinforcing family anger and possibly extinguishing whatever feelings of empathy may yet remain. Although well-intentioned, establishing such boundaries often disregards the jeopardy they may create because the person with BPD will usually misinterpret the boundaries as punishment or blame. This may explain why "tough love" can be a more dangerous than effective technique for people with BPD.

When their method of treatment doesn't seem to help their patients, therapists can feel as out of control and overwhelmed as do families. The patients are often dropped from treatment for exhibiting the very behavior that brought them into therapy in the first place. The clinician often blames this on the "manipulative" patient or the "treatment-resistant" patient rather than admit that treatment is not alleviating this person's pain. If the "therapeutic alliance" is abruptly dissolved, the person with BPD can be left even more devastated by yet another abandonment. Conversely, people with BPD often maintain a long-term relationship with a therapist despite lack of improvement in their condition, because they fear abandonment and change.

> *Families are often left in psychic isolation, struggling to balance their concerns over the obvious suffering and risky behavior of the person with BPD with their own need to protect themselves from destructive BPD behaviors.*

WHAT FAMILIES NEED

To cope effectively with a loved one with BPD, families need much more than the current mental health system provides. For example:

Families need straight talk. Families need an explanation of the diagnosis that includes a description of the neurobiology underlying BPD and how it impacts the behaviors they find so confusing and frustrating. They need a realistic evaluation of prognosis.

Families need psychoeducation. Unfortunately, at present, understanding the cause of BPD is like trying to complete a jigsaw puzzle when pieces are missing and no picture of the finished puzzle is available. People with BPD and their families need a viable, overall hypothesis as to what engine is driving the disorder and how the various systems interact or account for BPD behaviors.

Families need support. No family should be expected to cope with a person with BPD in isolation. They need support and services only a structured mental health system can and should provide, as well as the shared humanity and support of other families and spouses facing similar pain and problems. Their frustration and self-blame can be transformed when they realize they are not the only ones facing these problems. A key component of DBT is a clinical team approach to treatment. Family members also need a team. TARA APD provides such support and services, teaching family members how to apply DBT skills within the family.

> *No family should be expected to cope with a person with BPD in isolation. They need support and services only a structured mental health system can and should provide, as well as the shared humanity and support of other families and spouses facing similar pain and problems.*

Families need to be heard. Clinicians and researchers would benefit by talking to family members. They would learn about the developmental signposts exhibited by many children who eventually develop BPD. TARA APD has been collecting data and anecdotes from parents across the country for the past 6 years. It is our hope that family observations and experiences regarding childhood diseases, accidents, sleep patterns, allergies, and sensitivities will spawn innovative research into the "second hits" that may combine with genetic or biological vulnerability and contribute to the development of BPD.

Families need to grieve. An often overlooked aspect of coping with mentally ill family members is the need to grieve for the loss of what they could have been had they not become ill and for the loss of the families' hopes and dreams. Although people with BPD may look the same physically, they are no longer the people the families once knew. Friends and other family members do not generally acknowledge this loss, leaving the family with invalidated grief. Sharing their pain with others who face the same problems is both helpful and healing.

CREATING A THERAPEUTIC FAMILY ENVIRONMENT

Treatment can be more effective if families are able to create a therapeutic family environment that reinforces the skills essential to dialectical behavior therapy (DBT) and validates the emotional reactions of those with BPD. This allows family members to feel less helpless and out of control and more inclined to empathy. This requires the following changes:

Families must radically accept the illness. Families must first radically accept the existence of BPD as a severe, persistent, chronic mental illness with wide-ranging mercurial symptoms. Although this is not the life the family had in mind for their beloved child, it has become their child's reality. Acceptance is more easily accomplished with a clear understanding of BPD and how its symptoms are expressed in their loved one's life. Acceptance also allows for empathizing with the pain and disability that results from this illness. With acceptance, new goals can be established and expectations can be modified. One mother, for example, found empathizing with her child's chronic psychic pain easier when she imagined the word *pain* written across her daughter's forehead and pictured tears rolling down her daughter's face.

Families need to accept that their loved ones are not manipulating them but are desperately attempting to cope with intense psychic pain. Although coping is the intent of many of their behaviors, people with BPD, unfortunately, often choose methods that are maladaptive, self-destructive, or harmful to others. Families then feel manipulated and angry. But impulsive people cannot manipulate. Simply understanding this brings relief and can begin to replace the anger in the home with empathy.

> *Families need to accept that their loved ones are not manipulating them but are desperately attempting to cope with intense psychic pain.*

Families need to reframe their expectations. By not radically accepting the ramifications of BPD on behavior, families will generally make unrealistic demands on their loved ones that lead to conflict and increased stress in already difficult relationships. "If he'd only get a job!" "Why doesn't she get an apartment?" "Why isn't she married like her friends?" Family members unwittingly create enormous distress by focusing on problems or situations that actually have little relevance to the bigger picture of this chronic mental illness or to the long-range management of BPD.

For example, one mother was agonizing over her fear that her daughter would lose her job at Sears. In the grand scheme of the daughter's life, this job had little relevance. Her illness, almost by definition, made it likely that she would not keep this job. Therefore, the mother's worrying and creating stress about the job, boyfriend, or condition of her daughter's room only served to exacerbate their already fragile relationship. By accepting that her daughter is doing the best she can at the moment and picking only battles to fight that are really important, the mother would, in the long run, help decrease stress and improve their relationship.

Typically, as the behaviors of a person with BPD escalate, the family tries harder and harder to control either the situation or the person. Using arbitrary, aversive control such as rules, boundaries, or limits to effect change generally does not work. Neither will giving advice, offering to solve the person's problems, blaming, judging, or criticizing. Positive change strategies incorporating validation, cheer-leading, reminding the person of prior success in problem solving, and asking "What skills could you have used to solve this problem?" are much more effective. The foundation for change is the radical acceptance of BPD, acceptance of the symptoms of the illness, of how they are played out in the person's life, and of the degree of pain and disability the person lives with due to this illness.

The changes that will create improvement are minuscule, changes by which the person learns to handle individual situations, one at a time. This is called "shaping." By understanding how change is created and applying learning theories, families can "head off" blowups. Families must realize that change can occur, but it will only be in "baby steps." It's important that families refrain from saying things such as "Get a job," "Snap out of it," "Calm down," "It's no big deal," or "Why are you getting so upset?" It's also helpful to avoid starting sentences with judgmental words such as "you" and to steer clear of criticism and blame.

Families need to validate the feelings of their loved ones. Just as sign language is a special language for communicating with a deaf person, "validation" is a special language for communicating emotionally. People with BPD often seem deaf to logical thinking. Processing information as emotions renders them unable to use logic to solve problems and frustrates them when others offer logical explanations as interpretations of events. This experience is heightened whenever

> *The foundation for change is the radical acceptance of BPD, acceptance of the symptoms of the illness, of how they are played out in the person's life, and of the degree of pain and disability the person lives with due to this illness.*

they are upset or emotionally aroused. Validation affirms that we accept and verbally acknowledge another person's emotions and feelings as his or her very own experience of the world. Validation is the language that lets families in, that allows them to be heard, and allows people with BPD to decipher the requests the families are making.

To validate the person with BPD, family members need to actively listen by focusing on the person, making eye contact, and reflecting that they actually hear and accept what is being said. It is crucial for families and spouses of people with BPD to understand that validation is *not* understanding, praising, consoling, agreeing with, or sympathizing; nor is it fixing things. In order to validate, families do not need to know *why* something happened; they do not need to approve or disapprove of the behavior, agree or disagree with the person's interpretation of events or action taken. Whereas praise speaks to what action a person takes, validation speaks only to hearing what the person is feeling. Validation is not about behavior but is about feelings.

> *Families can change their frustration and anger to empathy and action when they begin to advocate for system change.*

For example, rather than expressing his own fear, disappointment, or anger that his son may have lost another job, a father would instead validate his son's feelings by reflecting, "I can see you are really sad and embarrassed about losing this job."

Families must become advocates for change. Families can change their frustration and anger to empathy and action when they begin to advocate for system change. Only by increasing research funding, making appropriate, evidence-based treatment such as DBT available in all communities, and including families in the therapeutic process can we ensure that our loved ones with BPD will indeed have hope for better lives.

HOPE FOR ALLEVIATING THE PAIN OF BPD

Recovery from BPD, however, requires the participation of the people who are ill; no one can do it for them. Families cannot expect magic from a therapist, no matter how good he or she may be. People with BPD must agree to participate in their own therapy—attend all sessions, do the homework, and master the skills—before change can occur. Although families cannot take responsibility, they can facilitate change by being supportive of the therapy and the changes their loved ones are trying to make. Families can endorse, validate, and cheerlead positive efforts being made. They can monitor medication for side effects or noncompliance.

Finding the key to communication may help to decrease the number and intensity of volatile incidents in the home. The increase in trust that can result from improved communication may eventually allow people with BPD to accept treatment recommendations from family members. When people with BPD work as a team with their families, they can learn to cope with their illness and have lives worth living.

CHAPTER 10

Future Directions

WE HAVE COME a long way in the treatment of borderline personality disorder. About 25 years ago, treatment was considered nearly hopeless. Today, specialized treatments offer new hope. An estimated 75 percent of people with BPD who undergo just over 2 years of appropriate treatment have sufficiently reduced symptoms to the point that they no longer meet the criteria for the disorder.[1] This chapter outlines some of the advances being made in ongoing research projects, early intervention, and other hopeful avenues such as advocacy and support groups.

ADVANCES IN ESTABLISHED APPROACHES

Several ongoing research projects are evaluating currently used psychotherapies such as dialectical behavior therapy, family therapy, and cognitive-behavioral therapy. Researchers are also conducting studies of medications and neurobiology that are likely to lead to advances in our understanding and treatment of BPD.

Biological Advancements

Research into the biology of BPD is continuing. University of Chicago psychiatrist and researcher Emil Coccaro, M.D., is conducting one particularly promising study to examine the role of serotonin in impulsive aggression and suicidal behavior. In addition to taking measurements of brain structures and functions, Dr. Coccaro is including a clinical medication trial looking at the effectiveness of fluoxetine (the generic name for Prozac) to improve symptoms. Another focus of the study is a trial of combined fluoxetine and cognitive-behavioral therapy with men who abuse their spouses.[2]

Paul H. Soloff, M.D., of the University of Pittsburgh, is currently conducting a study entitled "Psychobiology of Suicidal Behavior in BPD." The study examines the clinical, psychosocial, and biological risk factors for suicidal behavior in individuals with borderline personality disorder. Those with BPD are compared to depressed patients and "normal" controls on measures of serotonin functioning, history of childhood abuse, and other suicide risk factors (concurrent depression, alcohol and drug abuse or dependence, impulsiveness and aggressiveness, interpersonal stressors, low social support, and lack of psychiatric treatment). The study employs PET scan imaging to determine the role of serotonin in BPD and suicidal behavior.[3] The participants will be followed for 1 year, with annual follow-ups thereafter, in order to discover which factors are the best predictors of suicide.

Researcher J. John Mann, M.D., at the Conte Center for the Neuroscience of Mental Disorders (CCNMD), is conducting a related series of studies entitled "The Neurobiology of Suicidal Behavior."[4] As previously noted, serotonin is involved in impulsivity, aggression, and anxiety, all of which underlie suicidal behavior. One CCNMD project involves animal studies of the genes that regulate serotonin function and the related behaviors. A second project will investigate serotonin neurons in the brain stem, amygdala, and prefrontal cortex of suicide victims and people with depression, looking at the role of genetic factors in serotonin functioning.

In another ongoing study, CCNMD researchers are looking at potential risk factors for suicide, so that we can better identify individuals who are likely to make an attempt; such information will allow us to perform controlled treatment studies, which currently are al-most nonexistent. Two additional studies are looking at families, as-sessing how suicidality, aggression and impulsivity, serotonin-related genes, and psychopathology are passed from adults with major de-pression to their children and from parents with disorders to adoles-cents. The biological and behavioral components the studies are examining—impulsivity, suicidal behavior, serotonin, the amygdala, and the prefrontal cortex—have all been implicated in borderline per-sonality disorder.

Research in Dialectical Behavior Therapy

Nearly half a dozen studies of dialectical behavior therapy (DBT) funded by the National Institutes of Health are presently under way. The treatment's founder, Marsha Linehan, Ph.D., is leading three of them. In conjunction with the University of Miami, Dr. Linehan is looking at the treatment of individuals with BPD who are abusing substances. She is randomly assigning individuals with BPD and sub-stance abuse to DBT or treatment-as-usual in the community. The goal is to determine whether there are reductions in substance abuse, suicidal behaviors, therapy-interfering behaviors, other dysfunctional behaviors that reduce the quality of life and negative affect, and im-provement in general functioning and interpersonal skills. In a second study at the University of Washington, Dr. Linehan is continuing her research with people with BPD who have parasuicidal behavior, using stricter control conditions (such as making sure that everyone in the control group has some form of psychotherapy). She hopes to deter-mine conclusively whether DBT provides something unique, or if the positive findings in DBT can be accounted for by other, more general factors in psychotherapy (such as years of therapist experience, num-ber of hours of treatment, or just the availability of affordable treat-ment). Finally, Dr. Linehan's third grant-funded project is aimed at consolidating present knowledge and training a cadre of DBT spe-cialists via a program at the University of Washington.[5]

Barbara Stanley, Ph.D., is doing a study at the New York State Psychiatric Institute, entitled "Treating Suicidal Behavior and Self-Mutilation in BPD."[6] This randomized controlled clinical trial is investigating the combination of DBT and SSRI medication (fluoxetine) versus other conditions. Specifically, Dr. Stanley is looking at four possible combinations of therapy, fluoxetine, and placebo: DBT plus placebo; DBT plus fluoxetine; fluoxetine plus clinical management; and placebo plus clinical management. The study sample will be 180 people with BPD, who will be randomly assigned to treatment for 12 months, and will then be followed up 12 months after treatment ends (a total of 24 months). The study, which began in 2000, is expected to take 5 years, since several sets of patients will need to be run in order to have a large enough sample.

Sarah Chisholm-Stockard, Ph.D., of the University of Wisconsin, is investigating the effectiveness of DBT for individuals with BPD and depression.[7] The main outcomes under investigation are reducing depression and parasuicidal behavior. As part of the study, Dr. Chisholm-Stockard will also be looking at factors that determine who drops out of treatment and why.

Research in Psychodynamic Psychotherapy

An exciting randomized clinical trial (controlled study) is currently under way at Cornell University–New York Hospital, Westchester Division, comparing the effects on BPD of Otto Kernberg's psychodynamic approach (transference-focused psychotherapy, or TFP) and Dr. Linehan's DBT.[8] It will be fascinating to see what emerges from this study. To date, although there is a large body of clinical literature on the use of psychodynamic psychotherapy for BPD (mostly theory and case studies), extremely few are clinical trials. Therefore, this study is essential in determining the impact of TFP. I am hopeful that this project will also help individuals with BPD and those who refer them to treatment to make better-informed decisions about what type of therapy to try first.

Research in Schema Therapy

Studies on modifications of standard treatments specific to personality disorder will also likely yield useful information. One promising modification is Jeffrey Young's schema therapy, a form of cognitive behavioral therapy. Clinical trials comparing schema therapy for personality disorders to treatment as usual are in progress. I am optimistic about the outcomes of these trials, as CBT has generally been an effective therapeutic strategy.

Advances in Client-Centered/ Humanistic Psychotherapy

As discussed previously, the limited research on client-centered/humanistic psychotherapy indicates that it seems to alleviate much of the emotional angst that can accompany BPD. Since client-centered therapists often do not focus on diagnosis, however, there is not much in the literature on borderline personality disorder from client-centered and humanistic therapists. Dr. Margaret Warner's "Fragile Process" theory holds promise as a way to get client-centered/humanistic therapists more involved in the treatment of individuals with BPD and bring effective treatments to the people who need them.[9]

> *Limited research on client-centered/humanistic psychotherapy indicates that it seems to alleviate much of the emotional angst that can accompany BPD.*

Research in Family Therapy

Family interventions for BPD, though to some degree still in their infancy, also offer great promise. Recent findings show outcomes are improved when families are involved.[10] One ongoing study, mentioned in chapter 3 (see page 99), is University of Miami researcher and clinician Dr. Daniel Santisteban's project entitled "Developing Family Therapy for BPD Drug Abusing Youths."

His therapeutic approach, called borderline adolescent family therapy (BAFT), combines Dr. Salvador Minuchin's structural family therapy with DBT skills training modules. Phase I of the project, which has already been completed, was to develop a treatment manual and videotape series to create a unified treatment approach. Phase II, currently under way, is to assign clients randomly to either BAFT or a referral to a community agency, and to look at outcomes (changes in drug use, borderline behaviors, conduct problems, and skills development) and theory regarding why the therapy works (such as changes in family patterns of interactions and therapeutic alliance with the therapist). The researchers will also examine predictors of who does well versus who does not do well with these interventions.

> *Family interventions for BPD, though to some degree still in their infancy, offer great promise.*

Perry Hoffman, Ph.D., of the Weill Medical College of Cornell University, is conducting research on family systems and BPD. The study has two parts. One is to see how family factors, such as the absence of parental pathology, high emotional involvement, low perception of burden, high patient validation, effective familial problem-solving, low negative affective style, and knowledge about the disorder, will predict one-year patient outcome as measured by: frequency and severity of suicidal behaviors, number of re-hospitalizations, and behaviors that limit the quality of life (including depression, alienation in family relationships, generalized hopelessness, level of loneliness, and reasons for living).[11] The second part of the study is to add a family therapy component to a DBT program and see if and how it improves outcomes (on the same measures). This 5-year NIH-funded research started in 1999.

ADVANCES IN EARLY DETECTION AND INTERVENTION

Dr. Linehan notes that, although we have come a long way in the treatment of borderline personality disorder, we have not come far enough.[12] Until every person can achieve satisfactory recovery from

BPD in a reasonable amount of time, our work is not over. Actually, until we can prevent the disorder from occurring at all, we have much more to do. Further research is needed to find better ways to treat this condition. We also need to make better use of existing interventions. The total research effort required for this multifaceted disorder is enormous.

Throughout this book, we have seen a diversity of therapeutic treatments, from traditional psychotherapy to creative arts therapy, some of which have not yet been scientifically studied. Ultimately, all therapies need to undergo the rigors of scientific scrutiny for us to understand their individual effects, as well as their combined benefits.

Meanwhile, we need to "catch" the disorder earlier, before borderline behaviors become entrenched, when BPD is more readily treatable. Early intervention and prevention hold tremendous possibilities. One approach that appears to offer great potential in treating borderline personality disorder in its earliest stages is the floor time model.

> *Although we have come a long way in the treatment of borderline personality disorder, we have not come far enough. Until every person can achieve satisfactory recovery from BPD in a reasonable amount of time, our work is not over.*

The Floor Time Model

The DIR (developmental, individual-difference, relationship-based) model, also known as the floor time model, was first described by psychiatrist and world-renowned developmental specialist Stanley Greenspan, M.D., in 1989, and has since developed into a mature and effective discipline. The DIR model has been used as an approach to autism and related disorders, but it is a comprehensive system for children of all kinds.

Not long ago, autism was considered almost entirely untreatable, and those who had it spent their lives receiving custodial care in institutions. Despite it being a biologically based disorder, autism has responded well to behavioral and psychosocial interventions. As the

brain has a great deal of plasticity when a child is very young, significant neurological changes can occur. As a metaphor, imagine a house
under construction. When the electrical wiring is first put in, it may
be relatively easy to do some rerouting and
rewiring to make the system work properly.
Later, once the walls are in place, it may be very
difficult to make changes in many areas. The
nervous system is similar. At a young age, different brain functions can be taken over by other
areas, and different pathways can be rerouted to
get to key areas; later on, it is much more difficult for this to occur. Unlike the wiring in a
house, however, at some point it may not be possible within the brain
to make the kinds of "wiring" (neurological) changes necessary to
fully correct a deficit or disorder. Therefore, the sooner one inter-
venes, the better.

> *As the brain has a great deal of plasticity when a child is very young, significant neurological changes can occur.*

In order to examine the effects of his interventions, Dr.
Greenspan conducted a chart review of 200 of his patients. All of the
subjects had autistic spectrum disorders; 75 percent of the sample had
autism, and the remainder had the closely related diagnosis pervasive
developmental disorder. The results of the review? According to Dr.
Greenspan:

> After a minimum of 2 years of a comprehensive, relationship and de-
> velopmentally based intervention program, 58 percent evidenced very
> good outcomes. These children became trusting and intimately related
> to parents, showed joyful and pleasurable affect, and, most impres-
> sively, had the capacity for learning abstract thinking and interactive,
> spontaneous communication at a preverbal and verbal level.[13]

In fact, a small subset of the children who showed the very best
recoveries were indistinguishable from children who had never had
developmental problems. Dr. Greenspan points out, however, that
this was not a representative population of children with autism; they
were the children who came to his practice. It could be that they were

more motivated, or had other distinguishing characteristics. There-fore the percentages, such as the 58 percent who had very good out-comes, should be taken to mean only that some children with autistic spectrum disorder have the potential for making very good progress. On the other hand, children with less severe problems are easier to work with and require less intense interventions to become emotion-ally and cognitively balanced. This means that there is great hope for the child who has features that may someday lead to borderline personality disorder (what I will call a "pre-borderline" child). I am hopeful that early intervention will eliminate vast numbers of person-ality disorders from ever developing.

Dr. Greenspan anchors his approach to sensory systems, which have clear biological underpinnings. These include processing tactile (touch), auditory/verbal, visual/spatial, motor planning/sequencing, and taste/smell stimuli. Individuals differ with regard to how well they modulate, or regulate, each of these modalities. Sensory modulation involves all of the sensory modalities: tactile, auditory, visual, vestibu-lar (relates to balance), proprioceptive (body awareness, especially re-garding location in space), olfactory (smell), taste, and pain reception. For each modality, the individual can be overre-active (hypersensitive) or underreactive (hyposen-sitive) in each domain.

Children who are at risk of developing BPD are more impulsive and experience enormous mood swings relative to other young children. Dr. Greenspan labels these problems in regula-tion, especially affect (emotional) regulation. In addition, the child who has a tendency toward BPD has difficulties with visual/spatial process-ing. What is exciting about Dr. Greenspan's approach is that these patterns, which affect dys-regulation and visual/spatial processing, can be identified and treated not only in childhood, but even in infancy. There are specific, ef-fective strategies used to help the child to regulate. Just as Marsha

> What is exciting about Dr. Green-span's approach is that patterns that affect dys-regulation and visual/ spatial processing can be identified and treated not only in childhood, but even in infancy.

Linehan had noted that the invalidating environment leads to emotional difficulties, Dr. Greenspan has observed that validation (empathy) leads to healing.

DIR intervention with children is called "floor time." Floor time means just what it sounds like: getting on the floor with the child and playing together. Floor time is a very special type of play, however. During floor time, you are helping the child move up the developmental ladder and balance all of the sensory modalities. Other key interventions include engaging the child at his level, and challenging him to be creative, inquisitive, and playful.

It is easy to miss problems with emotional regulation. People often view the child's resulting behavior as willfulness or being spoiled, rather than as a largely biologically determined way of processing information. Floor time works out emotional regulation.

> *Through floor time, the parent can approach the child in many different ways to determine which brings about the desired response.*

Through floor time, the parent can approach the child in many different ways to determine which brings about the desired response. Of course, the desired response changes with age; early in life, the task is for the parent and child to form a mutual engagement and attachment. If this does not occur easily and naturally, experimenting with different tones of voice, looking at the infant in different ways, and using different kinds of touch will help the parent see whether the child is hyper- or hypo-reactive in any of the sensory domains.

The floor time approach suggests a soothing approach to the hypersensitive child (who may be at risk for BPD later on in life). For example, if your child is playing with a doll, you can pick up another doll and slowly approach, saying "He-e-ere I-I-I co-o-ome," allowing the child plenty of time to move or turn away. The child who is hypersensitive to touch often responds better to certain kinds of touch than other kinds. For example, the child who cannot tolerate light touch may respond well to deep pressure. With patience and persistence, you will learn about the child's predilections, and the child will build a broader range of responses and become better able to tolerate stimulation.

With older children, the use of language and symbols are essential tools to modulate emotion. Using symbolic play, such as having figures act out emotions, can help the child become more flexible and understand emotions better. Back-and-forth communication, directly expressing and processing feelings, can also be vital to learning emotional regulation skills. Later on, the parent and child will engage in mutual interactions that are increasingly complex.

Anyone can learn to use floor time, but it is my impression that it cannot be learned from a book. Dr. Greenspan has released a video that has 20 hours of instruction. Therapists from many disciplines have been trained in the floor time approach, including psychologists, occupational therapists, physical therapists, nurses, and speech/language pathologists. These individuals can be hired as therapists for your child. Insurance often covers all or part of the cost; there are also government programs, with labels such as

> *Therapists from many disciplines have been trained in the floor time approach, including psychologists, occupational therapists, physical therapists, nurses, and speech/language pathologists. These individuals can be hired as therapists for your child.*

"early intervention," that may cover all of the costs if your child is qualified for services. The therapists often come to your home. Also, the therapist can supervise you as you engage in floor time with your child, so that you can learn how to do it. It feels like play—it is truly fun and rewarding. Unlike just playing, however, floor time allows you to cope effectively with and resolve those unexpected outbursts and other problems, so that the joy of interacting with your child deepens and becomes more fulfilling.

If you want to learn more about the floor time approach or to reinforce what you are learning under a therapist's guidance, Dr. Greenspan has numerous excellent books. *The Child with Special Needs* details the

DIR model and gives explicit examples of how to identify problems and use floor time. *First Feelings* and *The Irreducible Needs of Children* are excellent books on child development. In my interview with him, Dr. Greenspan also recommended *The Growth of the Mind*, *The Challenging Child*, and *Building Healthy Minds* (see appendix B for the full references).

If you believe that your child is hypersensitive or "difficult" in any way, it would be wise to contact a floor-time specialist, no matter how young your child is. Interventions can now be done with infants just a few months old. As with medical conditions, the sooner you catch it, the more easily you can remediate it. Referrals are available through the Interdisciplinary Council on Developmental & Learning Disorders (ICDL; see appendix B for contact information).

> *If you believe that your child is hypersensitive or "difficult" in any way, it would be wise to contact a floor-time specialist, no matter how young your child is. Interventions can now be done with infants just a few months old.*

Developmentally Based Psychotherapy is Dr. Greenspan's book for professional psychotherapists about working with older children and adults using the principles of the DIR model. Although floor time is a well-established treatment modality for children with affect regulation problems, no scientific studies have been done yet with developmentally based psychotherapy for people with borderline personality disorder. The book was written in 1997, and it is my impression that the therapy is not yet widespread as a form of treatment for adults. For instance, there is no formal network of therapists who use this model. Due to its close alignment with biological processes and developmental theory, it strikes me as a very promising form of treatment, so I include it as a potentially useful new treatment to watch for in the future.

ADVANCES IN ALTERNATIVE MEDICINE

There are also exciting developments in alternative medicine. A scientific base of information is building, pointing to treatments for specific conditions. The general public and the medical profession are becoming better acquainted with alternative healing modalities. With increased treatment options, you will be more likely to find an approach that works for you.

Specific scientific studies involving individuals with borderline personality disorder and alternative treatments have yet to be undertaken. Studies of the efficacy for BPD of medical systems such as traditional Chinese medicine, Vedic medicine, homeopathy, and other modalities would be useful, but some approaches are not well suited to scientific verification. As stated previously, however, their healing abilities have stood the test of time, having been used as a primary medicine in other cultures for centuries, and in some cases for thousands of years.

ADVANCES IN SELF-HELP AND ADVOCACY

Another exciting area is the self-help movement for individuals with BPD and their loved ones. Family support networks, advocacy groups, and online support communities, such as those developed by TARA APD, provide safe havens for people to express their feelings and to share information. These groups will most likely increase in popularity as they expand services and education. Such support networks reassure families of people with BPD that they are not alone.

Along these lines, I would like to close with a clarion call for advocacy. Millions of people have borderline personality disorder, yet the condition and its far-reaching effects are under-recognized. The government underfunds research on theory and treatment, the media hardly know BPD exists, and the general public has not heard of it. This is simply not acceptable.

The government underfunds research on theory and treatment, the media hardly know BPD exists, and the general public has not heard of it. This is simply not acceptable.

Perhaps the greatest virtue of the United States is our shared belief in people's rights. Our Declaration of Independence states, "We

A "Manhattan Project" for BPD

A hopeful development in BPD research is the establishment in 1999 of a private Swiss foundation called the Borderline Personality Disorder Research Foundation (BPDRF). The foundation has brought together a number of the world's leading scientists and clinicians to study BPD. The mission statement on their Web site (www.borderlineresearch.org) reads:

> Framed as the "Manhattan Project" for understanding and treating BPD, the Borderline Personality Disorder Research Foundation has organized an international, multidisciplinary, and renowned group of scientists. The BPDRF is currently coordinating research at six universities to draw on each other's strengths in developing an integrated research paradigm to study BPD. These Universities have joined to become a cross-site and multidisciplinary Consortium under the scientific leadership of Eric R. Kandel, M.D., of Columbia University. The Consortium has been organized into six core scientific areas: 1) genetics and epidemiology, 2) animal models, 3) neuroimaging, 4) psychobiology, 5) diagnosis, and 6) treatment.[14]

The BPDRF has a multimillion-dollar budget for scientific studies. Its scientific advisory board includes leading figures whose research is reviewed in this book, including John Gunderson, M.D., and Larry J. Siever, M.D. I look forward to seeing the results of this most promising collaboration.

hold these truths to be self-evident, that all men are created equal, that they are endowed by their Creator with certain unalienable rights. . . ." Our Constitution begins with the Bill of Rights. Among these rights should be the expectation of being able to live free from stigma. In order for this expectation to be realized, mental health conditions must be researched and illuminated.

On the political front, efforts at increasing funding to research treatment of borderline personality disorder are taking off. Valerie Porr, of TARA APD, recently met with Senator Dick Gephardt and Representative Patrick Kennedy to discuss increasing NIMH funding. Congress is seriously considering a "Patients' Bill of Rights," which is designed to reduce the ability of insurance companies to limit access to care. This is extremely important to individuals with chronic conditions such as BPD.

Consider this an invitation to join in the effort to increase awareness of BPD and to encourage our leaders to direct more funding to the efforts to find effective treatments. Whether you have borderline personality disorder or you know someone who does, join with others who are battling the stigma of mental illness in general (in an organization such as NAMI), and borderline personality disorder in particular (in an organization such as TARA APD). Sometimes it may feel as if you are all alone when you or someone you care about has a mental illness, but this is not so. More than 50 million people in the United States have mental illnesses or disabilities. Together, that large a group can have a huge impact. Join with others to work to strengthen the Americans with Disabilities Act, which has recently been limited in its scope by narrow interpretations by the courts. Write to your government representatives, members of the House of Representatives and Senate on both the state and federal levels, in support of laws that protect individuals with mental illnesses, mandate insurance companies to include coverage of personality disorders, and increase research funding for borderline personality disorder.

Perhaps most important, talk to people about the disorder. Talk to friends you can trust. If a well-known person with the disorder were to come forward about living with BPD, he or she would move mountains.

> *Whether you have borderline personality disorder or you know someone who does, join with others who are battling the stigma of mental illness in general, and borderline personality disorder in particular.*

When people who have felt helpless and powerless join with others, they discover new strengths. By working together, we may someday create a world in which all people with borderline personality disorder and their families will not only be accepted into the compassionate fabric of society, but will also be fully empowered to lead lives of hope, dignity, and health.

Appendix A: Referral Resources

CHINESE MEDICINE

See "Traditional Chinese Medicine"

COUNSELING

**National Board of Professional
Counselors (NBPC)**
3 Terrace Way, Suite D
Greensboro, NC 27403
Phone: (336) 547-0607

E-mail: nbcc@nbcc.org
Web site: www.nbcc.org

Web site has an interactive referral
service to counselors.

DANCE AND MOVEMENT THERAPY

**American Dance Therapy
Association (ADTA)**
2000 Century Plaza, Suite 108
10632 Little Patuxent Parkway
Columbia, MD 21044
Phone: (410) 997-4040

Fax: (410) 997-4048
E-mail: info@adta.org
Web site: www.adta.org

Provides referrals and information
on credentials.

DIALECTICAL BEHAVIOR THERAPY

**Behavioral Technology
Transfer Group**
4556 University Way N.E., Suite 221
Seattle, WA 98105
Phone: (206) 675-8588
Fax: (206) 675-8590

E-mail: information
@behavioraltech.com
Web site: www.behavioraltech.com

Provides information about where
to get dialectical behavior therapy.
An invaluable resource.

HOMEOPATHY

**American Board of
Homeotherapeutics**
617 W. Main Street.,
   4th Floor
Charlottesville, VA 22903
Phone: (804) 295-0362
Fax: (804) 295-0798

Open to medical doctors (MDs)
and osteopathic physicians (DOs);
awards DHt-Diplomate in
homeotherapeutics.

**Council for Homeopathic
Certification**
P.O. Box 460190
San Francisco, CA 94146
Phone: (415) 789-7677
Fax: (415) 695-8220

Open to all professions; awards
CCH-certified in classical
homeopathy.

**Homeopathic Academy of
Naturopathic Physicians**
12132 S.E. Foster Place
Portland, OR 97266
Phone: (503) 761-3298
Fax: (503) 762-1929
E-mail: swolf@teleport.com
Web site: www.healthy.net
   /HANP

Open to naturopathic physi-
cians (NDs); awards DHANP—
Diplomate of the Homeopathic
Academy of Naturopathic
Physicians.

**National Board of
Homeopathic Examiners**
P.O. Box 15749 PMB 832
Boise, ID 83715
Phone: (208) 426-0847
Fax: (208) 426-0848

Open to all professions; awards
DNBHE—Diplomate of the
National Board of Homeopathic
Examiners.

**National Center
for Homeopathy**
801 N. Fairfax Street, Suite 306
Alexandria, VA 22314
Phone: (703) 548-7790
Fax: (703) 548-7792
E-mail: info@homeopathic.org
Web site: www.homeopathic.org

MARITAL/FAMILY THERAPY

The American Association for Marriage and Family Therapy (AAMFT)
1133 15th Street, N.W., Suite 300
Washington, DC 20005
Phone: (202) 452-0109
Fax: (202) 223-2329
Web site: www.aamft.org

According to their Web site, "The American Association for Marriage and Family Therapy (AAMFT) is the professional association for the field of marriage and family therapy. We represent the professional interests of more than 23,000 marriage and family therapists throughout the United States, Canada and abroad." Web site has a therapist locator.

MUSIC THERAPY

American Music Therapy Association (AMTA)
8455 Colesville Road, Suite 1000
Silver Spring, MD 20910
Phone: (301) 589-3300
Fax: (301) 589-5175
E-mail: info@musictherapy.org
Web site: www.namt.com
Call or e-mail for a referral.

Certification Board for Music Therapists
506 E. Lancaster Avenue, Suite 102
Downingtown, PA 19335
Phone: (800) 765-2268
E-mail: info@cbmt.org
Web site: www.cbmt.com

NUTRITION AND NUTRITIONAL MEDICINE

The American College for Advancement in Medicine (ACAM)
23121 Verdugo Drive, Suite 204
Laguna Hills, CA 92653
Phone: (800) 532-3688
Fax: (949) 455-9679
E-mail: acam@acam.org
Web site: www.acam.org

From the Web site: "Founded in 1973, the American College for Advancement in Medicine (ACAM) is a not-for-profit medical society dedicated to educating physicians and other health care professionals on the latest findings and emerging procedures in preventive/ nutritional medicine. ACAM's goals are to improve skills, knowledge and diagnostic procedures as they relate to complementary and alternative medicine; to support research; and to develop awareness of alternative methods of medical treatment." Site includes a "Doctor Search" to help you to find an ACAM physician from a database of over 1,000 MDs and DOs.

American Association of Nutritional Consultants

302 E. Wiona Avenue
Warsaw, IN 46580
Phone: (888) 828-2262
Fax: (219) 267-2614
E-mail: wilma@aanc.net
Web site: www.aanc.net

Offers free referrals to over 1,500 members, online or by phone. All clinicians have passed exams to be certified nutritional consultants. The online directory is at www .healthkeepers.net; click on "Practitioner Referrals."

International and American Associations of Clinical Nutritionists

16775 Addison Road, Suite 100
Addison, TX 75001
Phone: (972) 407-9089
Fax: (972) 250-0233
Web site: www.iaacn.org

Call for referrals.

International Society for Orthomolecular Medicine (ISOM)

16 Florence Avenue
Toronto, Ontario, Canada M2N 1E9
Phone: (416) 733-2117
Fax: (416) 733-2352
Web site: www.orthomed.org/isom /isom.htm?1

Orthomolecular physicians use natural substances (such as nutrients) to prevent and treat disorders. The Web site has numerous resources, including a list of research and treatment institutes throughout the world, Web resources, and links.

Society for Orthomolecular Health Medicine (OHM)

2698 Pacific Avenue
San Francisco, CA 94115
Phone: (415) 922-6462
Fax: (415) 346-4991.
E-mail: sohma@aol.com

PSYCHIATRY

The American Psychiatric Association
1400 K Street N.W.
Washington, DC 20005
Phone: (888) 357-7924
Fax: (202) 682-6850

E-mail: apa@psych.org
Web site: www.psych.org

Represents over 40,000 psychiatrists. Provides referrals through their public affairs division.

PSYCHOLOGY

The American Psychological Association
750 First Street, N.E.
Washington, DC 20002
Phone: (800) 374-2721 or
    202-336-5510
TDD/TTY: (202) 336-6123
Web site: www.apa.org

For referrals, call (800) 964-2000.

Association for Humanistic Psychology
45 Franklin Street, Suite 315
San Francisco, CA 94102
Phone: (415) 864-8850
Fax: (415) 864-8853
E-mail: ahpoffice@aol.com
Web site: ahpweb.org

Offers free referrals to 300 clinical practitioners who believe in humanistic/whole person approaches to healing. Referrals are online under the Humanistic Professional Directory.

SOCIAL WORK

National Association of Social Workers
750 First Street N.E., Suite 700
Washington, DC 20002
Phone: (800) 638-8799 or
    (202) 408-8600
Web site: www.naswdc.org

The National Association of Social Workers (NASW) is the world's largest membership organization of professional social workers (over 150,000 members). You can search for a practitioner online at www.naswdc.org/register/disclaimer.htm, which takes you to a disclaimer, which then has a button to click to begin your search.

TRADITIONAL CHINESE MEDICINE

American Association of Oriental Medicine
433 Front Street
Catasauqua, PA 18032
Phone: (888) 500-7999 or
   (610) 266-1433
Fax: (610) 264-2768
E-mail: aaom1@aol.com
Web site: www.aaom.org

Provides free referrals (available online) to over 1,000 acupuncturist members who have completed training, passed a national certification exam, and are state licensed.

National Acupuncture & Oriental Medicine Alliance
14637 Starr Road, S.E.
Olalla, WA 98359
Phone: (253) 851-6896
Fax: (253) 851-6883
Web site: http://acuall.org

Offers free referrals to over 8,000 acupuncturists who are either state licensed or national board certified. Online referrals available.

TRANSFERENCE FOCUSED PSYCHOTHERAPY

The Personality Disorders Institute
Cornel Psychotherapy Program
The New York Presbyterian
   Hospital–Westchester Division
21 Bloomingdale Road
White Plains, NY 10605

Phone: (914) 997-5940
E-mail: info@borderlinedisorders
   .com
Web site: www.borderlinedisorders
   .com/public.htm

VEDIC MEDICINE

College of Maharishi Vedic Medicine
Maharishi University of
   Management
Fairfield, IA 52557
Phone: (800) 369-6480 or
   (641) 472-1110
Fax: (641) 472-1179
Web site: www.mum.edu/CMVM
   /index.html

Maharishi College of Vedic Medicine
2721 Arizona Street, N.E.
Albuquerque, NM 87110
Phone: (888) 895-2614
Fax: (505) 830-0538
E-mail: mcvmnm@aol.com
Web site: www.mapi.com

Referrals available online. International organization. Offers free referrals to Vedic medicine practitioners.

YOGA

American Yoga Association
P.O. Box 19986
Sarasota, FL 34276
Phone: (941) 927-4977
Fax: (941) 921-9844
E-mail: info@americanyoga
  association.org
Web site: www.americanyoga
  association.org

International Association of Yoga Therapists (IAYT)
2400A Country Center Drive
Santa Rosa, CA 95403
Phone: (707) 566-9000
Fax: (707) 566-9185
E-mail: mail@iayt.org
Web site: www.iayt.org

Offers free referrals to over 1,000 IAYT members who provide yoga therapy. Has detailed information on their yoga education and certifications.

Appendix B: Self-Help Books, Videos, and Web Sites

ABUSE/TRAUMA

BOOKS

The Courage to Heal by Ellen Bass and Laura Davis (New York, Harper Perennial, 1992). Primarily for women who were sexually abused as children, this excellent resource received 5 stars (top rating) from the *Authoritative Guide to Self-Help Resources in Mental Health*. There is a companion volume, *The Courage to Heal Workbook* (Laura Davis, 1990), which provides step-by-step exercises.

Victims No Longer: Men Recovering from Incest and Other Sexual Child Abuse by Michael Lew (New York: Harper & Row, 1990). Most books on abuse focus on women; this one is specifically for men, and does an excellent job.

ORGANIZATIONS/WEB SITES

David Baldwin's Trauma Information Page
Web site: www.trauma-pages.com/index.phtml

Comprehensive, with dozens, perhaps hundreds, of links.

Soul's Self-Help Central
Web site: www.soulselfhelp.on.ca

Has a "sexual abuse" button on the left side of the Web page. Information, support, connections between abuse and obesity; an excellent site with a "warm" feel.

ART THERAPY

BOOKS

The Creative Connection: Expressive Arts as Healing by N. Rogers (Palo Alto, CA: Science & Behavior Books, 1993). A beautifully written book about expressing your feelings through art and finding inner strength and balance.

ORGANIZATIONS/WEB SITES

The National Coalition of Arts Therapies Associations
c/o ADTA
8455 Colesville Road, Suite 1000
Silver Spring, MD 20910
Phone: (714) 751-0103
Web site: www.ncata.com

Web site has convenient links to the major organizations for art therapy, dance therapy, drama therapy, music therapy, psychodrama, and poetry therapy.

ADVOCACY

ORGANIZATIONS/WEB SITES

National Alliance for the Mentally Ill (NAMI)
Colonial Place Three
2107 Wilson Blvd., Suite 300
Arlington, VA 22201
Phone: (703) 524-7600
NAMI HelpLine: (800) 950-6264
Web site: www.nami.org

From the mission statement on the Web site: "The National Alliance for the Mentally Ill (NAMI) is a nonprofit, grassroots, self-help, support and advocacy organization of consumers, families, and friends of people with severe mental illnesses, such as schizophrenia, major depression, bipolar disorder, obsessive-compulsive disorder, and anxiety disorders. Founded in 1979, NAMI has more than 210,000 members who seek equitable services for people with severe mental illnesses, which are known to be physical brain disorders." I disagree that mental illnesses are "physical brain disorders" (we've shown in this book that the data support an approximate 50/50 contribution from biology and environment), and they (NAMI) do not seem to be particularly strong on personality disorders. Nonetheless, NAMI is a good organization, fighting for a good cause. The only way to get them to push harder on personality disorders is to let them know how important it is for them to do so.

The Treatment and Research Advancements Association for Personality Disorder (TARA APD)

23 Greene Street
New York, NY 10013
Phone: (212) 966-6514
Web site: www.tara4bpd.org

The premier BPD advocacy group in the United States. A not-for-profit corporation founded in 1995 in order to fight stigma, educate, and encourage research for personality disorders, especially borderline. They have support groups in many locations throughout the country.

ANGER

BOOKS

The Anger Control Workbook by M. McKay and P. Rogers, (Oakland: New Harbinger, 2000). This excellent book contains a step-by-step guide for overcoming anger.

The Dance of Anger by H. Lerner (New York: Harper Row, 1985). According to the *Authoritative Guide to Self-Help Resources in Mental Health*, "This excellent guide is a careful, compassionate exploration of women's anger and an insightful guide for turning anger into a constructive force that can reshape women's lives." A superb resource.

ORGANIZATIONS/WEB SITES

Controlling Anger—Before It Controls You

Web site: www.apa.org/pubinfo/anger.html

A good overview of anger from the American Psychological Association.

ANXIETY

BOOKS

The Anxiety and Phobia Workbook by Edmund J. Bourne (Oakland, CA: New Harbinger, 1995). A practical book with specific skills to overcome anxiety. Excellent.

Mastery of Your Anxiety and Panic II by David H. Barlow and Michelle G. Craske, (Albany, NY: Graywind, 1994). This excellent guide received 5 stars from the *Authoritative Guide to Self-Help Resources in Mental Health*.

ORGANIZATIONS /WEB SITES

Panic Anxiety Education Management Services, Anxiety/Panic Hub
Web site: www.paems.com.au/index.html

Extremely comprehensive; includes information on treatment, research, an online treatment program, chat, and definitions of the different anxiety disorders.

ATTENTION-DEFICIT/HYPERACTIVITY DISORDER (ADHD)

BOOKS

Answers to Distraction by Edward M. Hallowell and John J. Ratey (New York: Bantam Books, 1996).

Driven to Distraction: Recognizing and Coping with Attention Deficit Disorder from Childhood Through Adulthood by Edward M. Hallowell and John J. Ratey (New York: Simon & Schuster, 1995).

Answers to Distraction and *Driven to Distraction* and were written by two physicians who have ADHD, and who are specialists in the field. These are outstanding guides to conventional treatment.

Ritalin-Free Kids: Safe and Effective Homeopathic Medicine for ADHD and Other Behavioral and Learning Problems by Judyth Reichenberg-Ullman and Robert Ullman, (Roseville, CA: Prima Health, 2000). *Ritalin-Free Kids* discusses the use of homeopathy for ADHD; the authors report excellent results with few side effects. An important alternative to medications.

The LCP Solution: The Remarkable Nutritional Treatment for ADHD, Dyslexia, and Dyspraxia by B. Jacqueline Stordy and Malcolm J. Nicholls, (New York: Ballantine Books, 2000). Discusses the use of nutrition to reduce the symptoms of ADHD. They report excellent results with no side effects; an important alternative to medications.

BORDERLINE PERSONALITY DISORDER

BOOKS

The Angry Heart: Overcoming Borderline and Addictive Disorders by J. Santoro and R. Cohen (Oakland: New Harbinger, 1997). Provides step-by-step guidelines in how to overcome BPD based on Santoro's perspective on the disorder.

Eclipses: Behind the Borderline Personality Disorder by M. F. Thornton, (Madison, AL: Monte Sano, 1998). *Eclipses* is Melissa Ford Thornton's account of her and other patients' experiences with dialectical behavior therapy. A balanced, effective, and often moving book—important in that it is written from the perspective of the client.

I Hate You—Don't Leave Me: Understanding the Borderline Personality by J. Kreisman and H. Straus (New York: Avon, 1989). The original book on BPD for the general public. Very informative and loaded with case examples. At this point it is a bit dated—for example, it does not make reference to cognitive-behavioral therapy, which is now a major school of thought. Nonetheless, a very fine book.

Let Me Make It Good: A Chronicle of My Life with Borderline Personality Disorder by Jane Wanklin (Buffalo, NY: Mosaic Press, 1997). This book is at times raw and uneven. There are a few technical errors in the book as well, such as where names are mixed up. At times, it is plodding and repetitive. For all its flaws, however, it is among the most "real" books I've ever read regarding a person with a mental health disorder. I would say that Jane's case was on the severe side, and that not everyone with BPD will undergo such intense experiences. Her story is ultimately positive and life-affirming.

Lost in the Mirror: An Inside Look at Borderline Personality Disorder, 2nd ed. by Richard A. Moskovitz (Dallas, TX: Taylor Trade Pub., 2001). A compassionate and informative guide.

Skills Training Manual for Treating Borderline Personality Disorder by Marsha M. Linehan (New York: The Guilford Press, 1993). Linehan has the most thoroughly developed skills training system for borderline personality disorder available. This guide includes skills that are on handouts, including easy-to-remember phrases to help bring the information to mind when you need it.

Stop Walking on Eggshells: Taking Your Life Back When Someone You Care About Has Borderline Personality Disorder by P. T. Mason and R. Kreger, (Oakland: New Harbinger, 1998). This book is written from the perspective of the partners of people with borderline personality disorder. It helps them to deal with the pain, guilt, and anger the disorder has caused. People with BPD should be in at least partial recovery before reading this book.

FILMS/VIDEOS

Girl, Interrupted (Columbia Pictures, 1999). The real-life story of Susanna Kaysen, who was hospitalized for borderline personality disorder. A moving story, which shows both the strengths and vulnerabilities of a person with BPD. Rated R for strong language and content related to drugs, sex, and suicide.

ORGANIZATIONS/WEB SITES

Behavioral Research and Therapy Clinics

Web site: http://brtc.psych.washington.edu

Gives information about Dr. Marsha Linehan's Behavioral Research and Therapy Clinics at the University of Washington. Has excellent information about dialectical behavior therapy.

BPD Central

Web site: www.bpdcentral.com

According to the Web site, "A collection of resources for people who care about someone with borderline personality disorder." Includes a great deal of information. The support group, "WelcomeToOz," is for individuals who have a significant other with BPD. To subscribe to WelcomeToOz, go to http://yahoogroups.com/group/WelcomeToOz. There are special subgroups for siblings, parents, adult children of parents with BPD, men, Christians, and gay/lesbian individuals.

Mental Health Sanctuary

Web site: www.mhsanctuary.com

This site is run by Patty Pheil, M.S.W. In addition to borderline personality disorder, it has sites for over 30 other physical and mental health disorders. Extremely informative. Has links to therapy referrals.

Personality Disorders Institute

Web site: www.borderlinedisorders.com/public.htm

This site has an overview of BPD, from the Personality Disorders Institute, Cornell Psychotherapy Program, New York Presbyterian Hospital, Westchester Division.

Soul's Self-Help Central

Web site: www.soulselfhelp.on.ca

An excellent Web site, with support groups and a great deal of information. Has approximately a dozen additional mental health issues (for example: PTSD, bipolar, and sexual abuse).

COMMUNICATION AND ASSERTIVENESS

BOOKS

Boundaries: Where You End and I Begin by A. Katherine (New York: Fireside, 1991). As the title indicates, this (excellent) book is about boundaries—a topic of critical importance to many people with BPD.

A Couple's Guide to Communication by J. Gottman, C. Notarius, J. Gonso, and H. Markman (Champaign, IL: Research Press, 1976). Although over 25 years old, this may still be the best book on communication I have ever seen. The book provides specific techniques on how to improve communications with others, and wise lessons on appropriate attitudes to hold when we communicate.

When I Say No I Feel Guilty by M. J. Smith (New York: Bantam, 1975). Smith provides specific techniques on how to be assertive, and numerous memorable examples of assertive behavior. Although written more than 25 years ago, it is still fresh and relevant.

Your Perfect Right by R. E. Alberti and M. L. Emmons (San Luis Obispo, CA: Impact Publishers, 1997). Provides an excellent path to becoming more assertive.

DEPRESSION AND SUICIDE

BOOKS

The Feeling Good Handbook, rev. ed. by D. Burns (New York: Plume, 1999). A companion volume that provides workbook-like materials to jump-start your program.

Feeling Good: The New Mood Therapy, rev. ed. by D. Burns (New York: Avon, 1999). A wonderful book that uses a cognitive-behavioral approach to overcome not only depression but also anxiety, anger, and other troubling emotions.

Mind over Mood: How to Change How You Feel by Changing the Way You Think by D. Greenberger and C. Padesky (New York: Guilford, 1995). An excellent book, based on cognitive-behavioral principles.

ORGANIZATIONS/WEB SITES

American Suicide Foundation
1045 Park Avenue, Suite 3C
New York, NY 10028
Phone: (800) 273-4042 or (212) 210-1111

Provides referrals nationally to support groups for suicide survivors.

Metanoia
Web site: www.metanoia.org/suicide
"If You Are Thinking about Suicide . . . Read This First," by Martha Ainsworth. An excellent site, with empathic, compassionate advice for someone who is suicidal. Includes links and hotline numbers.

National Depressive and Manic Depressive Association
730 North Franklin
Chicago, IL 60610

Phone: (800) 826-3632

Web site: www.ndmda.org

Provides education, support, and advocacy for individuals with depression or manic depression.

Suicide and Suicide Prevention

Web site: www.psycom.net/depression.central.suicide.html

Contains dozens of links and resources. Extremely comprehensive.

Wing of Madness

Web site: www.wingofmadness.com

This site was started to provide information about depression, and has evolved into a community. Includes links, support, and a great deal of information. The site received five stars (top rating) from the *Authoritative Guide to Self-Help Resources in Mental Health*.

EATING DISORDERS

BOOKS

Fat Is a Feminist Issue: The Anti-Diet Guide to Permanent Weight Loss by S. Orbach (New York: Berkley Publishing Group, 1978). Discusses the pressures on girls and women to be thin, and the meaning of weight to women in general.

The Golden Cage: The Enigma of Anorexia Nervosa by H. Bruch (Cambridge, MA: Harvard University Press, 2001). This is a sensitively written book that gives insights into the meaning of anorexia.

ORGANIZATIONS/WEB SITES

American Anorexia/Bulimia Association, Inc. (AABA)

165 W. 46th Street, Suite 1108

New York , NY 10036

Phone: (212) 575-6200

National Eating Disorders Association (NEDA)
603 Stewart Street, Suite 803
Seattle, WA 98101
Phone: (206) 382-3587
Web site: www.nationaleatingdisorders.org

NEDA represents the merger of two formerly separate advocacy organizations: AABA and EDAP. Their Web site is excellent; information is provided in an upbeat, positive fashion. Includes information about eating disorders, support groups, and referrals. There is also a "watchdog" program to pressure advertisers who promote idealization of thinness to reconsider their approach, and to reward advertisers who promote self-esteem enhancing images.

Something Fishy
Web site: www.something-fishy.org

An outstanding site; includes vast amounts of information regarding eating disorders. The site contains poetry and shared experiences of individuals with eating disorders, and links to bulletin boards, chat groups, and psychotherapy resources. Top-rated eating-disorders Web site in the *Authoritative Guide to Self-Help Resources in Mental Health*, earning 5 stars (highest possible rating).

EXERCISE

BOOKS

Exercising Your Way to Better Mental Health: Combat Stress, Fight Depression, and Improve Your Overall Mood and Self-Concept with These Simple Exercises by Larry M. Leith (Morgantown, WV: Fitness Information Technology, 1998). Summarizes the scientific literature on exercise and mental health, and provides guidelines for setting up and maintaining your exercise program.

EXISTENTIALISM/MEANING OF LIFE

BOOKS

Man's Search for Meaning by Victor Frankl (New York: Simon & Schuster, 1959). This honest, revealing book chronicles psychiatrist Victor Frankl's grueling experiences in the Nazi death camps, and his inspiring philosophy that emerged from them. He talks about the search for meaning in life, which is central to all of us.

HOLISTIC HEALTH/ALTERNATIVE & COMPLEMENTARY MEDICINE (SEE ALSO MEDITATION AND YOGA)

BOOKS

The Alternative Medicine Sourcebook: A Realistic Evaluation of Alternative Healing Methods by S. Bratman (Los Angeles: Lowell House, 1997). This is an overview by a physician who refers to alternative health practitioners, and who has used herbal remedies himself. Bratman attempts to separate the "wheat from the chaff" in the alternative/complementary medicine area. Generally a good and balanced review.

Clinician's Complete Reference to Complementary & Alternative Medicine by D.W. Novy (St. Louis, MO: Mosby, 2000). Novy's edited volume is a compilation of contributions from outstanding experts and covers some 50 alternative practices including meditation, yoga, dance/movement therapy, hypnotherapy, Ayurveda, homeopathy, and traditional Chinese medicine. Each chapter provides an overview, scientific information, and contact information regarding referrals and credentialing. An excellent resource.

The Consumer's Guide to Homeopathy: The Definitive Resource for Understanding Homeopathic Medicine and Making It Work for You by Dana Ullman (New York: G. P. Putnam's Sons, 1995). A clearly written text explaining the theory and practice of homeopathy, and how it can help you.

Dragon Rises, Red Bird Flies: Psychology, Energy & Chinese Medicine by Leon Hammer (Barrytown, NY: Station Hill, 1991). Dr. Hammer is a psychiatrist and Chinese medicine practitioner. This book provides a clear description of the five elements, and the connection between TCM and psychology. Foreword by Ted Kaptchuk.

Encyclopedia of Nutritional Supplements by M. T. Murray (Roseville, CA: Prima Publishing, 1996). Contains seven parts: introduction, vitamins, minerals, essential fatty acids, "accessory nutrients" (such as flavonoids), glandular products (such as liver extracts), and a guide to specific conditions (everything from acne to varicose veins). Very readable and comprehensive.

Healing and the Mind by Bill Moyers (New York: Doubleday, 1993) and Bill Moyers, *Healing and the Mind* (video) (New York: D. Grubin Productions, 1993). This five-part series was originally aired on public television. Moyers interviews both patients and providers in this fascinating documentary. The series includes a 30-minute segment that demonstrates Jon Kabat-Zinn's Mindfulness-Based Stress Reduction program. The series is available in many public libraries.

The Web That Has No Weaver: Understanding Chinese Medicine by T. J. Kaptchuk (Chicago: Contemporary Books, 2000). A comprehensive and highly readable overview of traditional Chinese medicine. Foreword by Andrew Weil, M.D.

ORGANIZATIONS/WEB SITES

AlternativeMedicine.com
Web site: www.alternativemedicine.com

Claims to be the Internet's largest alternative medicine database—and it probably is. Contains vast amounts of information, including practitioner "yellow pages" to direct you to local clinicians, and links to numerous alternative medicine organizations.

Alternative Medicine Foundation
5411 W. Cedar Lane, Suite 205-A
Bethesda, MD 20814
Phone: (301) 581-0016
Web site: www.amfoundation.org

A nonprofit organization that, according to the Web site, is dedicated to "Providing consumers and professionals with responsible, evidence-based information on the integration of alternative and conventional medicine."

Healthworld Online
Web site: www.healthy.net

Contains information and networking on a wide array of alternative medicine approaches.

The National Center for Complementary and Alternative Medicine (NCCAM)
NCCAM Clearinghouse
P.O. Box 7923
Gaithersburg, MD 20898
Phone: (888) 644-6226
International: (301) 519-3153
Web site: http://nccam.nih.gov

According to their Web site, NCCAM, "at the National Institutes of Health (NIH) is dedicated to exploring complementary and alternative healing practices in the context of rigorous science; training CAM researchers; and disseminating authoritative information."

HUMOR

BOOKS

The Healing Power of Humor: Techniques for Getting Through Loss, Setbacks, Upsets, Disappointments, Difficulties, Trials, Tribulations, and All That Not-So-Funny Stuff by Allen Klein (Los Angeles: J. P. Tarcher, 1989). This book covers the use of humor to help to overcome stress and other difficulties in life. Poignant, funny, entertaining, and serious—all at the same time. A gem.

MEDICATIONS

BOOKS

Complete Guide to Prescription and Nonprescription Drugs 2002 by H. W. Griffith and S. W. Moore (New York: Berkley Publishing Group, 2002).

Essential Guide to Prescription Drugs 2002 by J. W. Long and J. J. Rybacki (New York: HarperCollins, 2002).

Essential Psychopharmacology: Neuroscientific Basis and Clinical Applications by Stephen M. Stahl (New York: Cambridge University Press, 1996). Describes mechanisms of action of medications; not a practical guide to the use of specific medications.

Physicians Desk Reference's PDR Family Guide to Prescription Drugs (New York: Three Rivers Press, 2001).

ORGANIZATIONS/WEB SITES

RxList

Web site: www.rxlist.com

Provides important information about thousands of medications; easy to use. Received the maximum rating (4 stars, excellent) from John Grohol's *The Insider's Guide to Mental Health Resources Online* (New York: Guilford, 2002).

U.S. Food and Drug Administration

5600 Fishers Lane
Rockville, MD 20857
Phone: (888) 463-6332
Web site: www.fda.gov

Provides information, especially about the safety of foods and medications.

MEDITATION AND MINDFULNESS

BOOKS

Don't Sweat the Small Stuff, And It's All Small Stuff: Simple Ways to Keep the Little Things from Taking over Your Life by Richard Carlson (Thorndike, ME: G.K. Hall, 1998). This terrific little book is about living in the moment and getting your priorities in order. Filled with wisdom.

Full Catastrophe Living: Using the Wisdom of Your Body and Mind to Face Stress, Pain, and Illness by J. Kabat-Zinn (New York: Delta, 1990). In *Full Catastrophe Living*, Kabat-Zinn illustrates the Mindfulness-Based Stress Reduction program that he developed at the University of Massachusetts Medical Center. It includes a step-by-step guide on how to start the program on your own, and ordering information for Kabat-Zinn's meditation tapes. This book focuses mostly on physical health issues, such as pain and disease. Kabat-Zinn may be the most important voice in bringing mindfulness to the Western world.

How to Meditate by L. LeShan (Boston: Back Bay Books, 1999). As the title indicates, this is a practical guide to various forms of meditation.

The Miracle of Mindfulness by Thich Nhat Hanh (Boston: Beacon Press, 1975). This brief, poetic gem of a book is packed with wisdom about how to live mindfully, in the here-and-now.

Practical Kabbalah: A Guide to Jewish Wisdom for Everyday Life by L. Wolf (New York: Three Rivers Press, 1999). This wonderful book has specific meditation exercises and words of wisdom from the Jewish mystical tradition.

Wherever You Go, There You Are: Mindfulness Meditation in Everyday Life by J. Kabat-Zinn (New York: Hyperion, 1994). Filled with wisdom, this book is a powerful antidote to the mindlessness of our hustle-bustle world. It includes specific meditation exercises. You can order a tape set (information is in the back of the book) to make getting started easier. A quick read, and a great place to start finding out about mindfulness. Wonderful!

ORGANIZATIONS/WEB SITES

Center for Mindfulness in Medicine, Health Care, and Society
University of Massachusetts Medical School
55 Lake Avenue North
Worcester, MA 01655
Phone: (508) 856-2656
Web site: www.umassmed.edu/cfm/

To quote the Web site, "The Center for Mindfulness in Medicine, Health Care, and Society is dedicated to furthering the practice and integration of mindfulness in the lives of individuals, institutions, and society through a wide range of clinical, research, education, and outreach initiatives in the public and private sector. . . . The Center for Mindfulness was founded in 1995 and is supported by philanthropy, foundation grants, and program revenues. The CFM is part of the Department of Medicine, Division of Preventive and Behavioral Medicine, at the University of Massachusetts Medical School." The Web site includes a list of mindfulness programs that you can take throughout the country.

NUTRITION

BOOKS

The American Dietetic Association's Complete Food & Nutrition Guide by R. L. Duyff (Minneapolis, MN: Chronimed Publishing, 1996). This 600+ page volume is packed with useful information about proper nutrition and diet, avoiding food-borne illnesses, how to shop, dining out, food for children, how to eat while pregnant, and nutrition for older adults, athletes, and vegetarians.

The LCP Solution: The Remarkable Nutritional Treatment for ADHD, Dyslexia, and Dyspraxia by B. J. Stordy and M. J. Nicholls (New York: Ballantine Books, 2000). This book provides scientifically based recommendations on how to use essential fatty acids to treat learning disorders, including ADHD. Includes details of how to use supplements, and in what quantities, to achieve results.

Nutrition for Dummies, 2nd ed. by C. A. Rinzler (Foster City, CA: IDG, 1999). Part of the yellow-clad "for Dummies" series that now permeates our culture, it does what it intends to do: provides the most important, mainstream nutritional information in an easy-to-read format.

Textbook of Nutritional Medicine by Melvyn R. Werbach with Jeffrey Moss (Tarzana, CA: Third Line, 1999). This text, which appears to be designed as a text for medical students and/or physicians, is understandable for the layperson. It has chapters on dozens of diseases, including numerous mental health disorders (anxiety, depression, ADHD). Dr. Werbach, a psychiatrist who developed an interest in nutritional aspects of treating disorders, has created an authoritative text covering vast amounts of scientific research. It provides specific information about which nutrients to use for which disorders.

ORGANIZATIONS/WEB SITES

AlternativeMedicine.com
Web site: www.alternativemedicine.com

Contains sections on orthomolecular medicine and nutritional supplements.

Healthworld Online
Web site: www.healthy.net

Contains an excellent nutrition center.

U.S. Food and Drug Administration
5600 Fishers Lane
Rockville, MD 20857
Phone: (888) 463-6332
Web site: www.fda.gov

Provides information, especially about the safety of foods and medications.

PARENTING/EARLY DETECTION

BOOKS

Building Healthy Minds: The Six Experiences That Create Intelligence and Emotional Growth in Babies and Young Children by Stanley I. Greenspan with Nancy Breslau Lewis (Cambridge, MA: Perseus Books, 1999).

The Challenging Child: Understanding, Raising, and Enjoying the Five "Difficult" Types of Children by Stanley I. Greenspan with Jacqueline Salmon (Reading, MA: Addison-Wesley, 1995).

The Child with Special Needs: Encouraging Intellectual and Emotional Growth by S. Greenspan and S. Wieder, with R. Simons, (Reading, MA: Perseus, 1998). An excellent companion if you are doing floor time with your children.

First Feelings: Milestones in the Emotional Development of Your Baby and Child by Stanley I. Greenspan and Nancy Thorndike Greenspan (New York: Viking, 1985).

The Growth of the Mind: And the Endangered Origins of Intelligence by Stanley I. Greenspan with Beryl Lieff Benderly (Reading, MA: Perseus, 1998).

The Irreducible Needs of Children: What Every Child Must Have to Grow, Learn, and Flourish by T. Berry Brazelton and Stanley I. Greenspan (Cambridge, MA: Perseus, 2000). Written by two of our generation's leading experts in child development, this is an excellent primer on parenting.

ORGANIZATIONS/WEB SITES

The Interdisciplinary Council on Developmental & Learning Disorders
4938 Hampden Lane, Suite 800
Bethesda, MD 20814

Phone: (301) 656-2667

Web site: www.icdl.com

Includes a parent network and useful links. ICDL can provide referrals for "floor time" therapists.

POST-TRAUMATIC STRESS DISORDER (PTSD) (SEE ALSO "ANXIETY" AND "ABUSE/TRAUMA")

ORGANIZATIONS/WEB SITES

National Center for PTSD

Executive Division

VA Medical Center, 116D

White River Junction, VT 05009

Phone: (802) 296-5132

Web site: www.ncptsd.org

Packed with information from the government's PTSD site.

Soul's Self-Help Central

Web site: www.soulselfhelp.on.ca

Has a "PTSD" button on the left side of the Web page.

RESEARCH ON BORDERLINE PERSONALITY DISORDER

ORGANIZATIONS/WEB SITES

Borderline Personality Disorder Research Foundation (BPDRF)

Eric A. Fertuck, Ph.D., Administrative Coordinator

The Rockefeller University

1230 York Avenue, Box 36

New York, NY 10021

Phone: (212) 327-7344

Web site: www.borderlineresearch.org

A private foundation that conducts research on borderline personality disorder.

National Institutes of Health (NIH)

Web site: www.nih.gov

Describes past and current research funded by NIH.

SELF-HELP

BOOKS

Authoritative Guide to Self-Help Resources in Mental Health by J. C. Norcross, J. W. Santrock, L. F. Campbell, T. P. Smith, R. Sommer, and E. L. Zuckerman, (New York: Guilford, 2000). This incredible review is based on a survey of mental health practitioners, and evaluates books, videos, and Web sites. Each item is rated on a scale of 1 to 5 stars. In my book, the *Authoritative Guide* rates 5 stars!

SELF-INJURY

BOOKS

Bodies Under Siege: Self-Mutilation and Body Modification in Culture and Psychiatry by A. Favazza (Baltimore, MD: Johns Hopkins University, 1996). An academic, cross-cultural look at the phenomenon of self-injury.

Cutting: Understanding and Overcoming Self-Mutilation by S. Levenkron (New York: Norton, 1998). This sensitively written book is a great self-help resource.

ORGANIZATIONS/WEB SITES

Focus Adolescent Services

Web site: www.focusas.com/Resources.html

An excellent adolescent site. It includes information, book reviews, links for treatment options, and referrals on a wide array of topics, including self-injury.

The Self-Injury Site

Web site: www.palace.net/~llama/psych/injury.html

This excellent site has won several awards. It includes information, personal stories, a support group, and links.

STRESS MANAGEMENT

BOOKS

The Relaxation & Stress Reduction Workbook, 3rd ed. by Martha Davis, Elizabeth Robbins Eshelman, and Matthew McKay (Oakland, CA: New Harbinger, 1988). I was thinking of writing a book about stress management until I saw this book. I doubt it can be done better than this. The book covers every major technique of stress management, including relaxation, meditation, yoga, modifying beliefs, and so on.

SUBSTANCE ABUSE/DEPENDENCE

BOOKS

Alcoholics Anonymous, 3rd ed. (New York: Alcoholics Anonymous World Services, 1976). The basic book for AA recovery groups.

The Handbook of Secular Recovery (LifeRing Secular Recovery, 1999). Describes a secular alternative to 12-step programs. Hard copy (current cost $10) available at www.lifering.com/handbook/hardcopy.htm and Web version for downloading available at www.lifering.com/handbook /onlined.htm.

Rational Recovery: The New Cure for Substance Addiction by Jack Trimpey (New York: Pocket Books, 1996). Jack Trimpey's "Rational Recovery" (RR) approach offers an alternative to 12-step programs for addiction. It is not based on religious principles, although people are welcome to use their spiritual beliefs; it rejects the disease model of drug addiction, and it also discourages joining recovery groups. RR is based on the notion that drug addiction is motivated by cravings for pleasure. These books outline the philosophy and a plan of action.

The Small Book: A Revolutionary Alternative for Overcoming Alcohol and Drug Dependence by Jack Trimpey (New York: Delacorte, 1992).

ORGANIZATIONS/WEB SITES

Alcoholics Anonymous
475 Riverside Drive, 11th Floor
New York, NY 10115
Web site: www.alcoholics-anonymous.org

With approximately 2 million members, AA is an enormous organization. Their informative Web site is geared to helping you to decide if AA is right for you, and how to get started.

Al-Anon Family Group Headquarters, Inc.

1600 Corporate Landing Parkway
Virginia Beach, VA 23454
Phone: (888) 425-2666 or (757) 563-1600
Web site: www.al-anon.org

To quote their Web site, the purpose of Al-Anon and Alateen is "To help families and friends of alcoholics recover from the effects of living with the problem drinking of a relative or friend."

LifeRing Secular Recovery

Web site: www.unhooked.com

Web site provides information about their organization, meeting locations, anecdotes, scientific articles, poetry, forums, and chats.

Narcotics Anonymous World Services (NAWS, Inc.)

P.O. Box 9999
Van Nuys, CA 91409
Phone: (818) 773-9999
Web site: www.na.org

According to their Web site, "Narcotics Anonymous is an international, community-based association of recovering drug addicts with more than 28,000 weekly meetings in 113 countries." Based on the 12-step model of AA.

Rational Recovery

Web site: http://rational.org

The Rational Recovery Web site includes a "crash course" in "AVRT" (addictive voice recognition technique), which is very impressive. The site also includes information about how to obtain materials. There are no "meetings," as there are for AA and other 12-step programs, though Trimpey does teach some courses on the topic, and the schedule/locations are listed on the Web site.

TIME MANAGEMENT

BOOKS

Don't Sweat the Small Stuff, And It's All Small Stuff: Simple Ways to Keep the Little Things from Taking over Your Life by Richard Carlson (Thorndike, ME: G.K. Hall, 1998). This terrific little book is really about living in the moment and getting your priorities in order.

How to Get Control of Your Time and Your Life by Alan Lakein (New York: New American Library, 1973). Helps the reader to be more organized, efficient, and effective.

The 7 Habits of Highly Effective People by S. R. Covey (New York: Simon and Schuster, 1989); and *First Things First* by S. Covey, A.R. Merrill, and R.R. Merrill, (New York: Fireside, 1996). "Wise" is not the word that first comes to mind when I think of most time-management books. Covey's two books are filled with wisdom, which is why they have transcended the genre. They're about putting your priorities in order, and organizing your life so that you have time for the important things.

WOMEN'S ISSUES

BOOKS

The New Our Bodies, Ourselves by The Boston Women's Health Collective (New York: Simon & Schuster, 1992). Contains excellent discussions of many topics, including chapters on body image, food, alcohol/drugs, holistic health, psychotherapy, environmental health, violence against women, and sexuality. Embraces diversity and difference, and highlights aspects of our culture that are destructive, particularly to women.

YOGA

BOOKS

Starting Yoga by D. Hall (London: Ward Lock, 1996). Covers basic postures by genuine-looking people who do not appear to be made entirely of rubber and sinew. A nice place to start.

Light on Yoga by B.K.S. Iyengar (New York: Schocken, 1977). An outstanding and classic guide to yoga, this book is still widely available. Considered by many to be the best book available on yoga.

Yoga for Dummies by Georg Feuerstein and Larry Payne (Foster City, CA: IDG Books Worldwide, 1999). Clearly written and comprehensive, with some very funny cartoons thrown in. Foreword is by Lilias Folan, of the famed PBS yoga TV show, *Lilias*.

AUDIOTAPES/VIDEOS

Companion audiotapes to J. Kabat-Zinn's book, *Full Catastrophe Living* (Delta, 1990). The Yoga-I sequence is easy and can be done by almost anyone; the second yoga sequence is more challenging. Kabat-Zinn's love of yoga is obvious. In addition, Kabat-Zinn gets the balance between self-acceptance and challenging one to grow just right. These are excellent yoga tapes, possibly the best on the market.

Power Yoga for Beginners—Strength (Living Arts, 1999).

Power Yoga for Beginners—Stamina (Living Arts, 1999).

Power Yoga for Beginners—Flexibility (Living Arts, 1999).

To be honest, I'm not entirely happy with any of the yoga videotapes on the market. The best I have seen is the Living Arts series. These gorgeously produced videos often show yoga sequences from magnificent settings such as Big Sur and Yosemite National Park. Several of the videos use props, which allows a greater range of postures but make the sequences more cumbersome. These tapes are somewhat unbalanced toward improvement over self-acceptance. You may want to try checking them out from your library or video store before purchasing them, to see if you like them. The three-tape "Power" series is quite good. Each sequence is only 20 minutes long, which allows them to fit relatively easily into your schedule. Living Arts can be contacted at (800) 2-Living. I have seen these tapes in "alternative" bookstores, and would not be surprised if they are available in large bookstores such as Borders or Barnes & Noble. I would rate them "good," but not outstanding.

ORGANIZATIONS/WEB SITES

AlternativeMedicine.com

Web site: www.alternativemedicine.com

Has an excellent yoga section, including a list of many major yoga organizations.

Himalayan Institute of Yoga, Science, and Philosophy
R.R.I. Box 400
Honesdale, PA 18431
Phone: (800) 822-4547 or (717) 253-5551

Books, tapes, and a network of yoga centers across the country.

Yoga Journal
Web site: www.yogajournal.com

Web site contains articles about yoga and a directory to find a yoga teacher.

Appendix C: Medication Algorithms

An algorithm is a systematic way of pursuing treatment. It suggests an order of medications to try, based on which are most likely to be effective and what their side effects are. Dr. Paul Soloff's algorithms provide a step-by-step approach, based on a thorough review of the scientific literature, to what medications are most likely to be effective in the treatment of symptoms common to borderline personality disorder. Algorithm 1 is for the treatment of cognitive-perceptual symptoms (suspiciousness, paranoid ideation, mild thought disorders, and so on); algorithm 2 is for the treatment of affective dysregulation (depressed, angry, anxious, or labile mood); and algorithm 3 is for the treatment of impulsive-behavioral symptoms (impulsive aggression, bingeing, self-injury).

If patients have suspiciousness, paranoid ideation, or mild thought disorder, for example, the recommendation is that their doctor first try a low-dose neuroleptic (antipsychotic; for example, haloperidol, 1 to 4 milligrams per day; see algorithm 1, step 2). That will be either effective, partially effective, or ineffective (step 3). If it is effective, continue for 4 to 6 weeks (step 4). If it is partially effective or ineffective, then the dose should be increased (step 5). If the result is still insufficient, and the person has affective symptoms (emotional symptoms, such as depression or mood swings), then add an SSRI (for example, Prozac) or MAO inhibitor. If the low-dose neuroleptic is ineffective, then switch to an atypical neuroleptic (steps 6, 7, and 8).

For a complete discussion of the steps for all three algorithms, see P. Soloff, "Algorithms for Pharmacological Treatment of Personality Dimensions: Symptom-Specific Treatments for Cognitive-Perceptual, Affective, and Impulsive-Behavioral Dysregulation," *Bulletin of the Menninger Clinic* 62, no. 2 (1998): 195–214; also available at www.mhsanctuary.com/borderline /soloff1.htm.

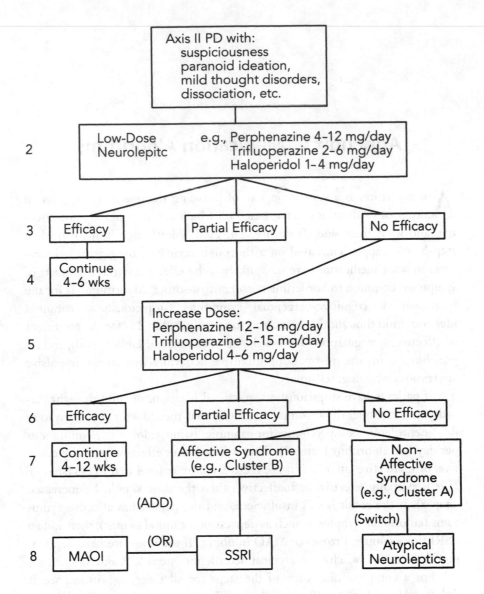

Algorithm 1—*For Treatment of Cognitive-Perceptual Symptoms*

Source: *P.H. Soloff, "Algorithms for Pharmacological Treatment of Personality Dimensions: Symptom-Specific Treatments for Cognitive-Perceptual, Affective, and Impulsive-Behavioral Dysregulation," Bulletin of the Menninger Clinic 62, no. 2 (1998). Reprinted with permission of The Guilford Press.*

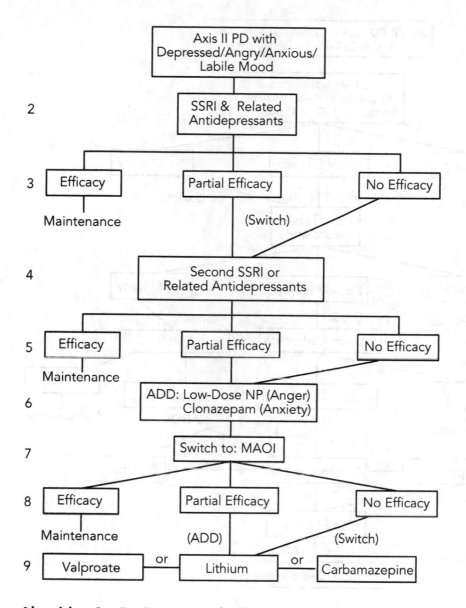

Algorithm 2—*For Treatment of Affective Dysregulation*

Source: *P.H. Soloff, "Algorithms for Pharmacological Treatment of Personality Dimensions: Symptom-Specific Treatments for Cognitive-Perceptual, Affective, and Impulsive-Behavioral Dysregulation," Bulletin of the Menninger Clinic 62, no. 2 (1998). Reprinted with permission of The Guilford Press.*

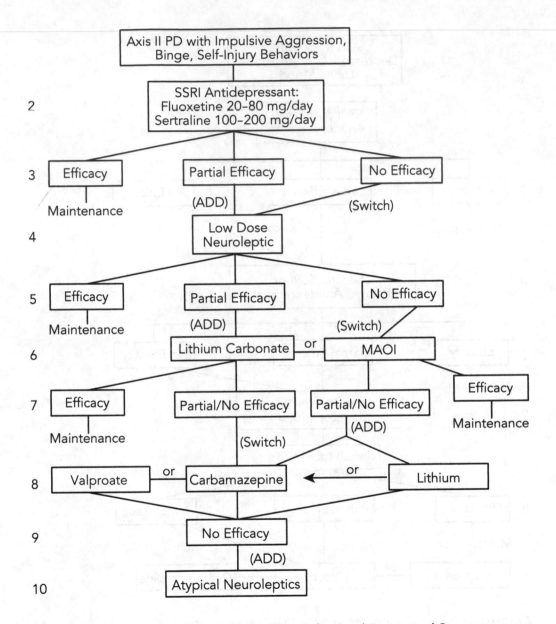

Algorithm 3—*For Treatment of Impulsive-Behavioral Dyscontrol Symptoms*

Source: *P.H. Soloff, "Algorithms for Pharmacological Treatment of Personality Dimensions: Symptom-Specific Treatments for Cognitive-Perceptual, Affective, and Impulsive-Behavioral Dysregulation," Bulletin of the Menninger Clinic 62, no. 2 (1998). Reprinted with permission of The Guilford Press.*

Notes

Introduction

1. P.H. Soloff, "Psychobiology of suicidal behavior in BPD," www.nimh
.nih.gov/research/suiabs.cfm, accessed May 2, 2002; and J. Paris, "Completed suicide in borderline personality disorder," *Psychiatric Annals*, 20
(1990): 19–21.
2. J.G. Gunderson, C. Berkowitz, and A. Ruiz-Sancho, "Families of borderline patients: A psychoeducational approach," *Bulletin of the Menninger
Clinic* 61, no. 4 (1997): 446–457.

Chapter 1

1. P.T. Mason and R. Kreger, *Stop Walking on Eggshells: Taking Your Life
Back When Someone You Care About Has Borderline Personality Disorder*
(Oakland, CA: New Harbinger, 1998): 27.
2. J.J. Kreisman and H. Straus, *I Hate You—Don't Leave Me: Understanding
the Borderline Personality* (New York: Avon, 1989): 36, 40.
3. S.B. Smith, *Diana in Search of Herself: Portrait of a Troubled Princess* (New
York: Times Books, 1999).
4. T. Hayward, "Blood on the Clownsuit," www.media-alliance.org/voices
street/clownsuit.html, accessed July 19, 2001.
5. "Mental illness no laughing matter for one comedian," August 29, 2000,
CNN.com, www.cnn.com/2000/HEALTH/08/29/newsstand.ferrari, accessed July 19, 2001.
6. T. Millon and R. Davis with C. Millon, et al., *Personality Disorders and
Modern Life* (New York: Wiley, 2000): 414.
7. M.M. Linehan, *Cognitive Behavioral Treatment of Borderline Personality
Disorder* (New York: Guilford, 1993): 125.
8. Ibid., 127.

9. "Why Do You SI? How Does It Make You Feel?" Llama central, http ://crystal.palace.net/~llama/psych/qwhy.html, accessed April 24, 2002.

10. Poems by Lori, a 36-year-old woman with BPD, BPD Central, www .bpdcentral.com/nook/nook.htm, accessed March 1, 2001.

11. "Poetry of a woman with borderline personality disorder," Soul's Self-Help Central, www.soulselfhelp.on.ca/dbpd.html, accessed March 1, 2001.

12. N. Bockian, "Systemic-behavioral treatment of a personality disorder and abusive behavior on a spinal cord injury unit: A case illustration," *SCI Psychosocial Process* 7, no. 4 (1994): 153–160.

13. "Poetry of a woman with borderline personality disorder," Soul's Self-Help Central, www.soulselfhelp.on.ca/dbpd.html, accessed March 1, 2001.

14. A. Stern, "Borderline group of neuroses," *Psychoanalytic Quarterly* 7 (1938): 467–489.

15. T. Millon with R. Davis, *Disorders of Personality: DSM-IV and Beyond* (New York: Wiley, 1996): 17.

16. J.B. Watson, *Behaviorism* (New York: Norton, 1925), cited in H. Gleitman, *Psychology* (New York: Norton, 1981): 168.

17. K.R. Silk, "Overview of Biologic Factors," *Psychiatric Clinics of North America* 23, no. 1 (2000): 61–75.

18. P.F. Goyer, P.J. Andreason, W.E. Semple, et al., "Emission Tomography and Personality Disorders," *Neuropsychopharmacology* 10, no. 1 (1994): 21–28.

19. Ibid.

20. P.H. Soloff, C.C. Meltzer, P.J. Greer, et al., "A fenfluramine-activated FD8-PET study of borderline personality disorder," *Biological Psychiatry* 47 (2000): 540.

21. M. Leyton, et al., "Brain regional alpha-[-sup-1-sup-1C]Methyl-l-tryptophan trapping in impulsive subjects with borderline personality disorder," *American Journal of Psychiatry* 158, no. 5 (2001): 775–782.

22. M. Driessen, J. Herrmann, K. Stahl, et al.,"Magnetic resonance imaging volumes of the hippocampus and the amygdala in women with borderline personality disorder and early traumatization," *Archives of General Psychiatry* 57, no. 12 (2000): 1115–1122.

23. M.C. Zanarini, C.R. Kimble, and A.A. Williams, "Neurological dysfunction in borderline patients and Axis II control subjects," in K.R. Silk, ed., *Biological and Neurobehavioral Studies of Borderline Personality Disorder* (Washington, DC: American Psychiatric Press, 1994): 159–175.

24. K. O'Leary and R. Cowdry "Neuropsychological testing results in borderline personality disorder," (1994): 147, in K.R. Silk, ed., *Biological and*

Neurobehavioral Studies of Borderline Personality Disorder (Washington, DC: American Psychiatric Press, 1994): 147.

25. Ibid., 149.
26. Linehan, *Cognitive Behavioral Treatment of Borderline Personality Disorder,* 52–53.
27. Ibid., 53–54.
28. T. Millon, "On the genesis and prevalence of the BPD," *Journal of Personality Disorders* 1, no. 4 (1987): 354–372.
29. P. Cushman, "Why the self is empty," *American Psychologist* 45, no. 5 (1990): 599–611.

Chapter 2

1. *Diagnostic and Statistical Manual of Mental Disorders,* 4th ed., *Text Revision* (Washington, DC: American Psychiatric Association, 2002): 708; and J.G. Gunderson, *Borderline Personality Disorder* (Washington, DC: American Psychiatric Association, 1984).
2. J.G. Johnson, P. Cohen, B.P. Dohrenwend, et al., "A longitudinal investigation of social causation and social selection processes involved in the association between socioeconomic status and psychiatric disorders," *Journal of Abnormal Psychology* 108, no. 3 (1999): 490–499.
3. L. Collins, "Illustrating feminist theory: Power and psychopathology," *Psychology of Women Quarterly* 22 (1998): 97–112.
4. C. Haney, C. Banks, and P. Zimbardo, "Interpersonal dynamics in a simulated prison," *International Journal of Criminology and Penology* 1, no. 1 (1973): 69–97.
5. J.H. Williams, *Psychology of Women: Behavior in a Biosocial Context,* 3rd ed. (New York: Norton, 1987); and B. Skeggs, *Formations of Class and Gender* (London: Sage, 1997).
6. D. Becker and S. Lamb, "Sex bias in the diagnosis of borderline personality disorder and post-traumatic stress disorder," *Professional Psychology: Research and Practice* 25, no. 1 (1994): 55–61.
7. S. Kaysen, *Girl, Interrupted* (New York: Vintage Books, 1993).
8. D. Tannen, *You Just Don't Understand: Women and Men in Conversation* (New York: Ballantine, 1990).
9. D. Dutton, *The Abusive Personality: Violence and Control in Intimate Relationships* (New York: Guilford, 1998).
10. J. Wanklin, *Let Me Make It Good: A Chronicle of My Life with Borderline Personality Disorder* (Buffalo, NY: Mosaic, 1997).

11. Ibid., 283.

12. P.T. Mason and R. Kreger, *Stop Walking on Eggshells: Taking Your Life Back When Someone You Care About Has Borderline Personality Disorder* (Oakland, CA: New Harbinger, 1998): 19.

13. *Diagnostic and Statistical Manual of Mental Disorders, 4th ed.* (Washington, DC: American Psychiatric Press, 2000): 685.

14. *DSM-IV-TR* defines a total of 10 personality disorders.

15. M.B. First, R.L. Spitzer, M. Gibbon, et al., "The structured clinical interview for *DSM-III-R* personality disorders (SCID-II), Part I: Description," *Journal of Personality Disorders* 9, no. 2 (1995): 83–91, 92–104; and B. Pfohl, N. Blum, and M. Zimmerman, *Structured Interview for DSM—IV Personality Disorders* (Iowa City: University of Iowa Hospitals and Clinics, 1994); and A.W. Loranger, V.L. Susman, J.M. Oldham, et al., "The Personality Disorder Examination (PDE): A preliminary report," *Journal of Personality Disorders* 1 (1987): 1–13.

16. J.G. Gunderson, J.E. Kolb, and V. Austin, "The Diagnostic Interview for Borderline Patients," *American Journal of Psychiatry* 138 (1981): 896–903.

17. T. Millon with R. Davis, *Disorders of Personality: DSM-IV and Beyond* (New York: Wiley, 1996): 18.

18. M.T. Shea, T.A. Widiger, and M.H. Klein, "Comorbidity of personality disorders and depression: Implications for treatment," *Journal of Consulting and Clinical Psychology* 60, no. 6 (1992): 857–868.

19. *Diagnostic and Statistical Manual of Mental Disorders*, 4th ed. (Washington, DC: American Psychiatric Press, 1994): 356. Reprinted with permission of the American Psychiatric Association.

20. D.A. Santor, D.C. Zuroff, J.O. Ramsay, et al., "Examining scale discriminability in the BDI and CES-D as a function of depressive severity," *Psychological Assessment* 7, no. 2 (1995): 131–139.

21. M.C. Zanarini, F.R. Frankenburg, E.D. Dubo, et al., "Axis-I comorbidity of borderline personality disorder," *American Journal of Psychiatry* 155, no. 12 (1998): 1733–1739.

Chapter 3

1. J. Gunderson and P. Links, "Borderline personality disorder," in G.O. Gabbard and S.D. Atkinson, *Synopsis of Treatments of Psychiatric Disorders*, 2nd ed. (Washington, DC: American Psychiatric Press, 1996): 969.

2. J.C. Perry, E. Banon, and F. Ianni, "Effectiveness of psychotherapy for personality disorders," *American Journal of Psychiatry* 156 (1999): 1312–1321.

3. K. Koerner and M.M. Linehan, "Research on dialectical behavior therapy for patients with borderline personality disorder," *Psychiatric Clinics of North America* 23, no. 1 (2000): 151–167.

4. M.M. Linehan, H.E. Armstrong, A. Suarez, et al., "Cognitive-behavioral treatment of chronically parasuicidal borderline patients," *Archives of General Psychiatry* 48, no. 12 (1991): 1060–1064.

5. M.M Linehan, K.A. Comtois, K. Koerner, et al., "Dialectical behavior therapy for opiate abusers with borderline personality disorder: Findings to date from two randomized controlled trials," presented at the 32nd Annual Meeting of the Association of the Advancement of Behavior Therapy, Washington, DC, November 1998, cited in Koerner and Linehan, "Research on dialectical behavior therapy for patients with borderline personality disorder," 151–167.

6. M.M. Linehan, H.L. Heard, and H.E. Armstrong, "Naturalistic follow-up of a behavioral treatment for chronically parasuicidal borderline patients," *Archives of General Psychiatry* 50 (1993): 971–974; and Linehan, Armstrong, Suarez, et al., "Cognitive-behavioral treatment of chronically parasuicidal borderline patients."

7. *Diagnostic and Statistical Manual of Mental Disorders, 4th ed.* (Washington, D.C.: American Psychiatric Association, 2000): 34.

8. Ibid.

9. Linehan, Heard, and Armstrong, "Naturalistic follow-up of a behavioral treatment for chronically parasuicidal borderline patients."

10. M.M. Linehan, *Cognitive-Behavioral Treatment of Borderline Personality Disorder,* (New York: Guilford, 1993): 202.

11. Ibid., 109.

12. A. Stern, "Psychoanalytic investigation of and therapy in the borderline group of neuroses," *Psychoanalytic Quarterly* 7 (1938): 467–489, reprinted in M.H. Stone, *Essential Papers on Borderline Disorders* (New York: New York University, 1986): 54–73.

13. J. Eckert and M. Wuchner, "Long-term development of borderline personality disorder," in R. Hutterer, G. Pawlowsky, P.F. Schmid, and R. Stipsits, eds., *Client Centered and Experiential Psychotherapy: A Paradigm in Motion* (New York: Peter Lang, 1996): 213–233.

14. L.S. Benjamin, *Interpersonal Psychotherapy of Personality Disorders* (New York: Guilford, 1996).

15. I.D. Glick, R.A. Dulit, E. Wachter, et al., "The family, family therapy, and borderline personality disorder," *Journal of Psychotherapy Practice and Research* 4 (1995): 244.

16. A. James and M. Vareker, "Family therapy for adolescents diagnosed as having borderline personality disorder," *Journal of Family Therapy* 18, no. 3 (1996): 273.

17. M.M. Linehan and H.L. Heard, "Borderline personality disorder: Costs, course, and treatment outcomes," in N.E. Miller and K.M. Magruder, eds., *The Cost-Effectiveness of Psychotherapy* (New York: Oxford University, 1999): 301–302.

18. E. Marziali and H. Monroe-Blum, "An interpersonal approach to group psychotherapy with borderline personality disorder," *Journal of Personality Disorders* 9, no. 3 (1995): 179–189.

19. H. Monroe-Blum and E. Marziali, "A controlled trial of short-term group treatment for borderline personality disorder," *Journal of Personality Disorders* 9 (1995): 190–198.

20. T. Springer and K.R. Silk, "A review of inpatient group therapy for borderline personality disorder," *Harvard Review of Psychiatry* 3, no. 5 (1996): 268–278.

21. A. Bateman and P. Fonagy, "Effectiveness of partial hospitalization in the treatment of borderline personality disorder: A randomized controlled trial," *American Journal of Psychiatry* 156 (1999): 1563–1569.

22. T. Wilberg, S. Friis, S. Karterud, et al., "Outpatient group psychotherapy: A valuable continuation treatment for patients with borderline personality disorder treated in a day hospital? A 3-year follow-up study," *Nordic Journal of Psychiatry* 52, no. 3 (1998): 213–221.

23. Springer and Silk, "A review of inpatient group therapy for borderline personality disorder."

24. M. Campo-Redondo and J. Andrade, "Group psychotherapy and borderline personality disorder: A psychodynamic approach," *Psychodynamic Counselling* 6, no. 1 (2000): 17–30.

25. Linehan, *Cognitive-Behavioral Treatment of Borderline Personality Disorder*; and Bateman and Fonagy, "Effectiveness of partial hospitalization in the treatment of borderline personality disorder."

Chapter 4

1. L.A. Dimeff, J. McDavid, and M.M. Linehan, "Pharmacotherapy for borderline personality disorder: A review of the literature and recommendations for treatment," *Journal of Clinical Psychology in Medical Settings* 6 (1999): 113–138.

2. J. Brinkley, D. Beitman, and R. Friedel, "Low dose neuroleptic regimens in the treatment of borderline patients," *Archives of General Psychiatry* 36

(1979): 319–326, cited in P. Soloff, "Psychopharmacology of borderline personality disorder," *Psychiatric Clinics of North America* 23, no.1 (2000): 171; and N.F. Leone, "Response of borderline patients to loxapine and chlorpromazine," *Journal of Clinical Psychiatry* 43, no. 4 (1982): 148–150, cited in E.F. Coccaro, "Clinical outcome of psychopharmacologic treatment of borderline and schizotypal personality disordered subjects," *Journal of Clinical Psychiatry* 59, suppl. 1 (1998): 30–35; and G. Serban and S. Siegel, "Response of borderline and schizotypal patients to small doses of thiothixene and haloperidol," *American Journal of Psychiatry* 141, no. 11 (1984): 1455–1458, cited in Coccaro, "Clinical outcome of psychopharmacologic treatment," 32.

3. R.W. Cowdry and D.L. Gardner, "Pharmacotherapy of borderline personality disorder: alprazolam, carbamazepine, trifluoperazine, and tranylcypromine," *Archives of General Psychiatry* 45, no. 2 (1988): 111–119, cited in Soloff, "Psychopharmacology of borderline personality disorder," 172; and S.C. Goldberg, S.C. Schulz, P.M. Schulz, et al., "Borderline and schizotypal personality disorders treated with low-dose thiothixene vs placebo," *Archives of General Psychiatry* 43, no. 7 (1986): 680–686, cited in Soloff, "Psychopharmacology of borderline personality disorder," 172; and P.H. Soloff, A. George, R.S. Nathan, et al., "Amitriptyline versus haloperidol in borderlines: Final outcomes and predictors of response," *Journal of Clinical Psychopharmacology* 9, no. 4 (1989): 238–246, cited in Soloff, "Psychopharmacology of borderline personality disorder,"172.

4. S. Kasper, S. Quiner, C. Barnas, et al., "Zotepine in the treatment of acute hospitalized schizophrenic episodes," *International Clinical Psychopharmacology* 16, no. 3 (2001): 163–168; and S.J. Cooper, A. Butler, J. Tweed, et al., "Zotepine in the prevention of recurrence: A randomised, double-blind, placebo-controlled study for chronic schizophrenia," *Psychopharmacology (Berl)* 150, no. 3 (2000): 237–243; and S.J. Cooper, J. Tweed, J. Raniwalla, et al., "A placebo-controlled comparison of zotepine versus chlorpromazine in patients with acute exacerbation of schizophrenia," *Acta Psychiatry Scandinavica* 101, no. 3 (2000): 218–225.

5. M.C. Zanarini and F.R. Frankenburg, "Olanzapine treatment of female borderline personality disorder patients: A double-blind, placebo-controlled pilot study," *Journal of Clinical Psychiatry* 62, no. 11 (2001): 849–854.

6. J. Geddes, N. Freemantle, P. Harrison, et al., "Atypical antipsychotics in the treatment of schizophrenia: Systematic overview and meta-regression analysis," *British Medical Journal* 321 (2000): 1371–1376.

7. Zanarini and Frankenburg, "Olanzapine treatment of female borderline personality disorder patients," 849–854.

8. S.C. Schulz, K.L. Camlin, S.A. Berry, et al., "Olanzapine safety and efficacy in patients with borderline personality disorder and comorbid dysthymia," *Biological Psychiatry* 46, no. 10 (1999): 1429–1435.

9. K.N. Chengappa, T. Ebeling, J.S. Kang, et al., "Clozapine reduces severe self-mutilation and aggression in psychotic patients with borderline personality disorder," *Journal of Clinical Psychiatry* 60, no. 7 (1999): 477–484.

10. F. Benedetti, L. Sforzini, C. Colombo, et al., "Low-dose clozapine in acute and continuation treatment of severe borderline personality disorder," *Journal of Clinical Psychiatry* 59, no. 3 (1998): 103–107.

11. F.R. Frankenburg and M.C. Zanarini, "Clozapine treatment of borderline patients: A preliminary study," *Comprehensive Psychiatry* 34, no. 6 (1993): 402–405.

12. H.R. Khouzam and N.J. Donnelly, "Remission of self-mutilation in a patient with borderline personality during risperidone therapy," *Journal of Nervous & Mental Disease* 185, no. 5 (1997): 348–349.

13. D.W. Hough, "Low-dose olanzapine for self-mutilation behavior in patients with borderline personality disorder," *Journal of Clinical Psychiatry* 62, no. 4 (2001): 296–297.

14. K.N. Chengappa, R.W. Baker, and C. Sirri, "The successful use of clozapine in ameliorating severe self-mutilation in a patient with borderline personality disorder," *Journal of Personality Disorders* 9 (1995): 76–82.

15. E.M. Szigethy and S.C. Schulz, "Risperidone in comorbid borderline personality disorder and dysthymia," *Journal of Clinical Psychopharmacology* 17, no. 4 (1997): 326–327.

16. T. Steinert, P.O. Schmidt-Michel, and W.P. Kaschka, "Considerable improvement in a case of obsessive-compulsive disorder in an emotionally unstable personality disorder, borderline type under treatment with clozapine," *Pharmacopsychiatry* 29, no. 3 (1996): 111–114.

17. D.M. Taylor and R. McAskill, "Atypical antipsychotics and weight gain: A systematic review," *Acta Psychiatrica Scandinavica* 101, no. 6 (2000): 416–432; and T. Wetterling, "Body weight gain with atypical antipsychotics: A comparative review," *Drug Safety: An International Journal of Medical Toxicology and Drug Experience* 24, no. 1 (2001): 59–73.

18. A.J. Gelenberg and E.L. Bassuk, *The Practitioner's Guide to Psychoactive Drugs*, 4th ed. (New York: Plenum Medical, 1997): 177.

19. D.L. Hedberg, J.H. Hauch, and B.C. Gleuch, "Tranylcypromine-trifluoperazine combination in the treatment of schizophrenia," *American Journal of Psychiatry* 127 (1971): 1141–1146.

20. M.R. Liebowitz and D.G. Klein, "Inter-relationship of hysteroid dysphoria and borderline personality disorder," *Psychiatric Clinics of North America* 4 (1981): 67–87.

21. Soloff, "Psychopharmacology of borderline personality disorder," 180.

22. D.E. Sternberg, "Pharmacotherapy and affective syndromes in borderline personality disorder," paper presented at the 140th meeting of the American Psychiatric Association, Chicago, IL, May 12, 1989, cited in Soloff, 176.

23. P.H. Soloff, A. George, R.S. Nathan, et al., "Paradoxical effects of amitriptyline in borderline patients," *American Journal of Psychiatry* 143 (1986): 1603–1605, cited in Coccaro, "Clinical outcome of psychopharmacologic treatment of borderline and schizotypal personality disordered subjects," 30–35.

24. Coccaro, "Clinical outcome of psychopharmacologic treatment of borderline and schizotypal personality disordered subjects," 33.

25. P.J. Markovitz, "Psychopharmacology of impulsivity, aggression, and related disorders," in E. Hollander and D. Stein, eds., *Impulsivity and Aggression* (Surrey, UK, Wiley, 1995): 263–287, cited in Soloff, 179.

26. Ibid.

27. C. Salzman, A.N. Wolfson, A. Schatberg, et al., "Effect of fluoxetine on anger in symptomatic volunteers with borderline personality disorder," *Journal of Clinical Psychopharmacology* 15 (1995): 23–29, cited in Soloff, "Psychopharmacology of borderline personality disorder," 179; and E.F. Coccaro, J.L. Astill, J.L. Herbert, et al., "Fluoxetine treatment of impulsive aggression in *DSM-III-R* personality disorder patients," *Journal of Clinical Psychopharmacology* 10 (1990): 373–375, cited in Coccaro, "Clinical outcome of psychopharmacologic treatment of borderline and schizotypal personality disordered subjects," 33; and R.J. Kavoussi, J. Liu, and E.F. Coccaro, "An open trial of sertraline in personality disordered patients with impulsive aggression," *Journal of Clinical Psychiatry* 55, no. 4 (1994): 137–141, cited in Coccaro, "Clinical outcome of psychopharmacologic treatment of borderline and schizotypal personality disordered subjects," 33; and J.R. Cornelius, P.H. Soloff, J.M. Perel, et al., "Fluoxetine trial in borderline personality disorder," *Psychopharmacology Bulletin* 26 (1990): 151–154, cited in Soloff, "Psychopharmacology of borderline personality disorder," 178; and P.J. Markovitz, J.R. Calabrese, S.C. Schulz, et al.,

"Fluoxetine in the treatment of borderline and schizotypal personality disorders." *American Journal of Psychiatry* 148 (1991): 1064–1067, cited in Soloff, "Psychopharmacology of borderline personality disorder," 178; and Markovitz, Calabrese, Schulz, et al., "Fluoxetine in the treatment of borderline and schizotypal personality disorders," 1064–1067, cited in Soloff, "Psychopharmacology of borderline personality disorder," cited in E.F. Coccaro, "Clinical outcome of psychopharmacologic treatment of borderline and schizotypal personality disordered subjects," 33.

28. P.S. Links, M. Steiner, I. Boiago, et al., "Lithium therapy for borderline patients: Preliminary findings," *Journal of Personality Disorders* 4, no. 2 (1990): 173–181.

29. D.J. Stein, D. Simeon, M. Frenkel, et al., "An open trial of valproate in borderline personality disorder," *Journal of Clinical Psychiatry* 56, no. 11 (1995): 506–510; and M.H. Townsend, K.M. Cambre, and J.G. Barbee, "Treatment of borderline personality disorder with mood instability with divalproex sodium: Series of ten cases," *Journal of Clinical Psychopharmacology* 21, no. 2 (2001): 249–251.

30. J.M. De La Fuente and F. Lotstra, "A trial of carbamazepine in borderline personality disorder," *European Neuropsychopharmacology* 4 (1994): 479–486.

31. O.C. Pinto and H.S. Akiskal, "Lamotrigine as a promising approach to borderline personality: An open case series without concurrent *DSM-IV* major mood disorder," *Journal of Affective Disorders* 51, no. 3 (1998): 333–343.

32. E. Hollander, A. Allen, R.P. Lopez, et al., "A preliminary double-blind, placebo-controlled trial of divalproex sodium in borderline personality disorder," *Journal of Clinical Psychiatry* 62, no. 3 (2001): 199–203.

33. D.L. Garner and R.W. Cowdry, "Positive effects of carbamazepine on behavioral dyscontrol in borderline personality disorder," *American Journal of Psychiatry* 143, no. 4 (1986): 519–522.

34. De la Fuente and Lotstra, "A trial of carbamazepine in borderline personality disorder," 479–486.

35. Cowdry and Gardner, "Pharmacotherapy of borderline personality disorder," 111–119.

36. Soloff, "Psychopharmacology of borderline personality disorder," 185.

37. G. Stein, "Drug treatment of the personality disorders," *British Journal of Psychiatry* 161 (1992): 174.

38. Soloff, "Psychopharmacology of borderline personality disorder," 185.

39. Ibid., 187.

40. P. Soloff, "Algorithms for pharmacological treatment of personality dimensions: symptom-specific treatments for cognitive-perceptual, affective, and impulsive-behavioral dysregulation," *Bulletin of the Menninger Clinic* 62, no. 2 (1998): 195–214; also in Soloff, "Psychopharmacology of borderline personality disorder," 186–187; available at www.mhsanctuary.com/borderline/soloff.htm.

41. Soloff, "Psychopharmacology of borderline personality disorder," 189.

Chapter 5

1. D. Quigley and C.F.A. Dean, "Yoga," *Clinician's Complete Reference to Complementary and Alternative Medicine*, ed. D.W. Novey (St. Louis, MO: Mosby, 2000): 141–151.

2. Ibid., 143.

3. M. Murphy and S. Donovan, *The Physical and Psychological Effects of Meditation: A Review of Contemporary Research with a Comprehensive Bibliography 1931–1996* (Sausalito, CA: Institute of Noetic Sciences, 1997): 25.

4. N. Janakiramaiah, B.N. Gangadhar, P.J. Naga Venkatesha Murthy, et al., "Antidepressant efficacy of Sudarshan Kriya Yoga: A randomized comparison with electroconvulsive therapy (ECT) and imipramine," *Journal of Affective Disorders* 57 (2000): 255–259.

5. P. Sahajpal and R. Ralte, "Impact of induced yogic relaxation training (IYRT) on stress level, self-concept, and quality of sleep among minority group individuals," *Journal of Indian Psychology* 18 (2000): 66–73.

6. M. Mishra and R.K. Sinha, "Effect of yogic practices on depression and anxiety," *Journal of Projective Psychology and Mental Health* 8 (2001): 23–27.

7. J. Kabat-Zinn, *Full Catastrophe Living* (New York: Delta, 1990); and J.R. Johannson, *Effects of Mindfulness Meditation on the Sense of Coherence*, unpublished doctoral dissertation, Illinois School of Professional Psychology, 1998.

8. K.R. Eppley, A.I. Abrams, and J. Shear, "Differential effects of relaxation techniques on trait anxiety: A meta-analysis," *Journal of Clinical Psychology* 45 (1989): 957–974; and G.A. Clum and R. Surls, "A meta-analysis of treatments for panic disorder," *Journal of Consulting and Clinical Psychology* 61 (1993): 317–326.

9. A. Hossack and R.P. Bentall, "Elimination of posttraumatic symptomatology by relaxation and visual-kinesthetic dissociation," *Journal of Traumatic Stress* 9, no. 1 (1996): 99–110.

10. T.P. Turchiano, "A meta-analysis of behavioral and cognitive therapies for children and adolescents with attention deficit hyperactivity and/or impulsivity disorders," *Dissertation Abstracts International: Section B: Sciences and Engineering* 60, no. 11-B (2000).

11. K.L. Godbey and M.M. Courage, "Stress-management program: Intervention in nursing student performance anxiety," *Archives of Psychiatric Nursing* 8, no. 3 (1994): 190–199; and K.J. Godfrey, A.S. Bonds, M.E. Kraus, et al., "Freedom from stress: A meta-analytic view of treatment and intervention programs," *Applied H.R.M. Research* 1, no. 2 (1990): 67–80.

12. C.M. Morin, J.P. Culbert, and S.M. Schwartz, "Nonpharmacological interventions for insomnia: A meta-analysis of treatment efficacy," *American Journal of Psychiatry* 151 (1994): 1172–1180.

13. E.C. Devine, "Meta-analysis of the effects of psychoeducational care in adults with asthma," *Research in Nursing and Health* 19 (1996): 367–376; and F. Andrasik, "The role of behavioral techniques in the treatment of migraine," *Japanese Journal of Biofeedback Research* 22 (1995): 14–18; and W. Linden and L. Chambers, "Clinical effectiveness of non-drug treatment for hypertension: A meta-analysis," *Annals of Behavioral Medicine* (1994): 35–45; and R.G. Jacob, M.A. Chesney, D.M. Williams, et al., "Relaxation therapy for hypertension: Design effects and treatment effects," *Annals of Behavioral Medicine* 13 (1991): 5–17.

14. N. Rogers, *The Creative Connection: Expressive Arts as Healing* (Palo Alto, CA: Science and Behavior, 1993): 2.

15. Ibid., 4.

16. M. Ritter and K.G. Low, "Effects of dance/movement therapy: A meta-analysis," *Arts in Psychotherapy* 23, no. 3 (1996): 249–260; and R.F. Cruz and D.L. Sabers, "Dance/movement therapy is more effective than previously reported," *Arts in Psychotherapy* 25, no. 2 (1998): 101–104.

17. J. Standley, "Music as a therapeutic intervention in medical and dental treatment: research and clinical applications," in T. Wigram, B. Saperston, and R. West, eds., *The Art and Science of Music Therapy: A Handbook* (Chur, Switzerland: Harwood Academic, 1995): 3–22.

18. Ibid.

19. B.C. Hunter, "Music therapy," in *Clinician's Complete Reference to Complementary and Alternative Medicine*, D.W. Novey, ed. (St. Louis, MO: Mosby, 2000): 86.

20. Ibid., 87.

Chapter 6

1. D.M. Eisenberg, R.C. Kessler, C. Foster, et al., "Unconventional medicine in the United States: Prevalence, costs, and pattern of use," *New England Journal of Medicine* 328, no. 4 (1993): 246–252.

2. C.N. Shealy, ed., *The Complete Family Guide to Alternative Medicine* (Rockport, MA: Element Books, 1996).

3. B.D. Moyers, *Healing and the Mind*, 1st ed. (New York: Doubleday, 1993); and Public Affairs Television, *Healing and the Mind* (New York: D. Grubin Productions, 1993), videotape.

4. J.J.B. Allen, R.N. Schnyer, and S.K. Hitt, "The efficacy of acupuncture in the treatment of major depression in women," *Psychological Science* 9, no. 5 (1998): 397–401.

5. According to Peightel and associates, the work of Romeli (1993), Chen (1992), and Kurland (1976) support the efficacy of acupuncture for depression; see J.A. Peightel, T.L. Hardie, and D.A. Baron, "Complementary/alternative therapies in the treatment of psychiatric illnesses," in J.W. Spencer and J.J. Jacobs, eds., *Complementary/Alternative Medicine: An Evidence-Based Approach* (Chicago: Mosby, 1999): 208–247.

6. Y. Xiujuan, "Clinical observation on needling extrachannel points in treating mental depression," *Journal of Traditional Chinese Medicine* 14 (1994): 14, cited in Peightel, Hardie, and Baron, "Complementary/alternative therapies in the treatment of psychiatric illnesses."

7. L. Hechun, "Clinical and Experimental Studies on Treatment of Depression with Electro-Acupuncture," Joint Meeting of the Amercian Psychiatric Association and the Chinese Medical Association, Advances in Psychiatry: Chinese and American, Beijing, China, 29–31 in V. Brewington, M. Smith, and D. Lipton, "Acupuncture as a detoxification treatment: An analysis of controlled research," *Journal of Substance Abuse Treatment* 11, no. 4 (1994): 306.

8. D.L. Tao, "Research on the reduction of anxiety and depression with acupuncture," *American Journal of Acupuncture* 21, no. 4 (1993): 327, cited in J.A. Peightel, T.L. Hardie, and D.A. Baron, "Complementary/

alternative therapies in the treatment of psychiatric illnesses," in J.W. Spencer and J.J. Jacobs, eds., *Complementary/Alternative Medicine: An Evidence-Based Approach* (Chicago: Mosby, 1999): 246.

9. M.L. Bullock, et al. "Acupuncture treatment of alcoholic recidivism: A pilot study. Alcoholism," *Clinical Experimental Research* 11 (1987): 292–295; and M.L. Bullock, et al., "Controlled trial of acupuncture on severe recidivist alcoholism," *The Lancet* (June 24, 1989): 1435–1438.

10. R.H. Bannerman, "Acupuncture: The WHO view," *World Health* (English edition) (Dec. 24–29, 1979).

11. American Foundation of Medical Acupuncture, "Biomedical research on acupuncture: An agenda for the 1990s," conference summary (Los Angeles, 1993).

12. P.D. Culliton, and T.J. Kiresuk, "Overview of substance abuse acupuncture treatment research," *Journal of Alternative and Complementary Medicine* 2, no. 1 (1996): 149–159.

13. Brewington, Smith, and Lipton, "Acupuncture as a detoxification treatment."

14. J.M. Helms, "Medical acupuncture," in W.B. Jonas and J.S. Levin, eds., *Essentials of Complementary and Alternative Medicine* (Philadelphia: Lippincott, Williams & Wilkins, 1999): 340–354.

15. Peightel, Hardie, and Baron, "Complementary/alternative therapies in the treatment of psychiatric illnesses," 245.

16. Q.H. Ma, Y.L. Ju, and Z.L. Zhang, "Immunological study of inefficiency schizophrenics with deficiency syndrome treated with xin shen ling," *Chung His I Chieh Ho Tsa Chih* 11, no. 4 (1991): 197, 215, cited in Peightel, Hardie, and Baron, "Complementary/alternative therapies in the treatment of psychiatric illnesses," 245.

17. Peightel, Hardie, and Baron, "Complementary/alternative therapies in the treatment of psychiatric illnesses," 239.

18. M. Murphy and S. Donovan, *The Physical and Psychological Effects of Meditation: A Review of Contemporary Research with a Comprehensive Bibliography 1931–1996* (Sausalito, CA: Institute of Noetic Sciences, 1997).

19. D. Goleman, *Emotional Intelligence* (New York: Bantam, 1995).

20. C.N. Alexander, P. Robinson, and M. Rainforth, "Treating and preventing alcohol, nicotine, and drug abuse through transcendental meditation: A review and statistical meta-analysis," *Alcoholism Treatment Quarterly* 11, no. 1–2 (1994): 13–87; and K.R. Eppley, A.I. Abrams, and J. Shear, "Differential effects of relaxation techniques on trait anxiety: A

meta-analysis," *Journal of Clinical Psychology* 45, no. 6 (1989): 957–974; and J.S. Brooks and T. Scarano, "Transcendental meditation in the treatment of post-Vietnam adjustment," *Journal of Counseling and Development* 64 (1985): 212–215; and C.N. Alexander, M.V. Rainforth, and P. Gelderloos, "Transcendental meditation, self-actualization, and psychological health: A conceptual overview and statistical meta-analysis," *Journal of Social Behavior & Personality* 6, no. 5 (1991): 189–248.

21. S.I. Nidich, R.H. Schneider, R.J. Nidich, et al., "Maharishi Vedic vibration technology on chronic disorders and associated quality of life," *Frontiers in Bioscience* 6 (2001): 1–6.

22. D. Ullman, *The Consumer's Guide to Homeopathy* (Los Angeles: Tarcher, 1995): 30.

23. K. Linde, N. Clausius, G. Ramirez, et al., "Are the clinical effects of homeopathy placebo effects? A meta-analysis of placebo-controlled trials," *The Lancet* 350 (1997): 834–843.

24. There are other scientific studies and scientific controversies regarding homeopathy that are beyond the scope of this book. The interested reader is referred to Ullman, *The Consumer's Guide to Homeopathy*, 41–61.

25. Ullman, *The Consumer's Guide to Homeopathy*.

Chapter 7

1. M.R. Werbach, *Textbook of Nutritional Medicine* (Tarzana, CA: Third Line, 1999).

2. Ibid.

3. Ibid., 11.

4. R. Elkins, *Depression and Natural Medicine* (Woodland, 1999).

5. L.L. Rogers and R.B. Pelton, "Glutamine in the treatment of alcoholism: A preliminary report," *Quarterly Journal of Studies on Alcohol* 18, no. 4 (1957): 581–587, cited in Werbach, *Textbook of Nutritional Medicine*, 95, 98.

6. Werbach, *Textbook of Nutritional Medicine*.

7. S. Schoenthaler, S. Amos, W. Doraz, et al., "The effect of randomized vitamin-mineral supplementation on violent and non-violent antisocial behavior among incarcerated juveniles," *Journal of Nutritional and Environmental Medicine* 7 (1997): 343–352, cited in Werbach, *Textbook of Nutritional Medicine*, 84, 88.

8. Werbach, *Textbook of Nutritional Medicine*, 110, 153, 302–303.

9. A. Swain, et al., "Salicylates, oligoantigenic diets, and behaviour," letter, *The Lancet* ii (1985): 41–42, cited in Werbach, *Textbook of Nutritional Medicine*, 85, 88.

10. B.F. Feingold, "Hyperkinesis and learning disabilities linked to the ingestion of artificial food colors and flavors," *Journal of Learning Disabilities* 9, no. 9 (1976): 551–559, cited in Werbach, *Textbook of Nutritional Medicine*, 159, 161.

11. B.F. Feingold, *Why Your Child Is Hyperactive* (New York: Random House, 1985).

12. M.F. Jacobson and D. Schardt, *Diet, ADHD, and Behavior: A Quarter Century Review* (Washington, DC: Center for Science in the Public Interest, 1999), available at www.cspinet.org/diet.html.

13. B.Q. Hafen, K.J. Karren, K.J. Frandsen, et al., *Mind Body Health: The Effects of Attitudes, Emotions, and Relationships* (Boston: Allyn and Bacon, 1996): 2.

14. L.L. Craft and D.M. Landers, "The effect of exercise on clinical depression and depression resulting from mental illness: A meta-analysis," *Journal of Sport and Exercise Psychology* 20, no. 4 (1998): 339–357.

15. B.C. Long and R. van Stavel, "Effects of exercise training on anxiety: A meta-analysis," *Journal of Applied Sport Psychology* 7, no. 2 (1995): 167–189.

Chapter 8

1. T. Nhat Hanh, *The Miracle of Mindfulness* (Boston: Beacon Press, 1975): 37.

2. D. Goleman, *Emotional Intelligence* (New York: Bantam Books, 1995): 46.

3. Hanh, *The Miracle of Mindfulness*, 27.

4. B.J. Stordy and M.J. Nicholl, *The LCP Solution: The Remarkable Nutritional Treatment for ADHD, Dyslexia, and Dyspraxia*, 1st ed. (New York: Ballantine, 2000).

5. M. Smith, *When I Say No I Feel Guilty* (New York: Bantam, 1975): 28.

6. R. Alberti and M. Emmons, *Your Perfect Right* (San Luis Obispo, CA: Impact, 1978): 7.

7. Goleman, *Emotional Intelligence*, 102.

8. J.C. Norcross, J.W. Santrock, L.F. Campbell, et al., *Authoritative Guide to Self-Help Resources in Mental Health* (New York: Guilford, 2000).

9. A.T. Beck and G. Emory, with R.L. Greenberg, *Anxiety Disorders and Phobias: A Cognitive Perspective* (New York: Basic Books, 1985): 201–202.

Note: David Burns uses a method similar to the 3-column technique, called a "Daily Record of Dysfunctional Thoughts"; see D. Burns, *Feeling Good: The New Mood Therapy* (New York: Signet, 1980): 154.

10. J.H. Goldstein, "Therapeutic Effects of Laughter," in W.F. Fry and W.A. Salameh, eds., *Handbook of Humor and Psychotherapy* (Sarasota, FL: Professional Resource Exchange, 1987): 1–20.

11. Hanh, *The Miracle of Mindfulness*, 5.

12. C. Maurice, *Let Me Hear Your Voice* (New York: Ballantine, 1993): 57–58.

13. Ibid., 60

14. Ibid., 59–60.

15. J. Fawcett, B. Golden, and N. Rosenfeld, *New Hope for People with Bipolar Disorder*, (Roseville, CA: Prima Publishing, 2000): 155.

16. S. Mehta and A. Farina, "Is being 'sick' really better? Effect of the disease view of mental disorder on stigma," *Journal of Social & Clinical Psychology* 16, no. 4 (1997): 405–419.

Chapter 10

1. J.C. Perry, E. Banon, and F. Ianni, "Effectiveness of psychotherapy for personality disorders," *American Journal of Psychiatry* 156 (1999): 1312–1321.

2. E. Coccaro, "Impulsive Aggression: Biologic and Treatment Correlates," NIMH Abstracts of Currently Funded Research Grants Pertaining to Suicidal Behavior, www.nimh.nih.gov/research/suiabs.cfm, acessed April 30, 2002.

3. P.H. Soloff, "Psychobiology of suicidal behavior in BPD," NIMH Abstracts of Currently Funded Research Grants Pertaining to Suicidal Behavior, www.nimh.nih.gov/research/suiabs.cfm, accessed April 30, 2002.

4. J.J. Mann, "The neurobiology of suicidal behavior," NIMH Abstracts of Currently Funded Research Grants Pertaining to Suicidal Behavior, www.nimh.nih.gov/research/suiabs.cfm, accessed April 30, 2002.

5. M. Linehan, "Senior Scientist Award: Assessment & treatment of parasuicide patients" and "Assessment & treatment of parasuicide patients," NIMH Abstracts of Currently Funded Research Grants Pertaining to Suicidal Behavior, www.nimh.nih.gov/research/suiabs.cfm, accessed April 30, 2002.

6. B. Stanley, "Treating suicidal behavior & self-mutilation in BPD," NIMH Abstracts of Currently Funded Research Grants Pertaining to Suicidal Behavior, www.nimh.nih.gov/research/suiabs.cfm, accessed April 30, 2002.

7. S. Chisholm-Stockard, "DBT effectiveness for borderline depressed patients," NIMH Abstracts of Currently Funded Research Grants Pertaining to Suicidal Behavior, www.nimh.nih.gov/research/suiabs.cfm, accessed April 30, 2002.

8. O. Kernberg, Weill Medical College, Cornell University [research study], www.borderlineresearch.org/current_projects/index.html, accessed April 30, 2002.

9. M.S. Warner, "A client-centered approach to therapeutic work with dissociated and fragile process," in L.S. Greenberg, J.C. Watson, and G. Lietaer, eds., *Handbook of Experiential Psychotherapy* (New York: Guilford, 1998): 368–387; and M.S. Warner, "Fragile Process," www.focusing resources.com/articles/fragileprocess.html, accessed April 30, 2002.

10. J.G. Gunderson, C. Berkowitz, and A. Ruiz-Sancho, "Families of borderline patients: A psychoeducational approach," *Bulletin of the Menninger Clinic* 61, no. 4 (1997): 446–457.

11. NIMH Abstracts of Currently Funded Research Grants Pertaining to Suicidal Behavior, www.nimh.nih.gov/research/suiabs.cfm, accessed April 30, 2002.

12. M.M. Linehan, *Treating Borderline Personality Disorder: The Dialectical Approach* (New York: Guilford, 1995, video).

13. S. Greenspan and S. Wieder with R. Simons, *The Child with Special Needs: Encouraging Intellectual and Emotional Growth* (Reading, MA: Perseus, 1998): 450–451.

14. E.R. Kandel, "Overview: Borderline Personality Disorder Research Foundation (BPDRF)," www.borderlineresearch.org/about_org, accessed April 30, 2002.

Glossary

aerobic exercise   Exercise that causes an elevated heart rate but the body is still able to supply necessary oxygen to the muscles. When you go for a brisk walk, but can still talk with a friend while walking, you are exercising aerobically.

affective dysregulation   Unstable or unbalanced mood, including inappropriate/intense anger, mood swings, feelings of emptiness, sadness, loneliness, and lack of pleasure in activities.

agranulocytosis   A dangerous medical condition in which one's white-blood-cell count is severely reduced.

akathisia   An uncomfortable state of motor restlessness that makes you feel "all wound up" inside.

akinesia   Difficulty moving.

all-or-none thinking   Conceptualizing people or events in black-and-white, either-or terms, such as a person is either all-good or all-bad. *See* splitting

amygdala   A part the brain that is related to emotional functioning and social behavior.

anaerobic exercise   Exercise of an intensity that the body cannot get enough oxygen to the muscles to complete the chemical reaction used to make energy; the result is lactic acid, which creates a burning feeling in the muscles.

analysis of the transference   When a therapist interprets the meaning of a client's thoughts, feelings, and behaviors towards him/her (the therapist) in terms of the client's previous relationship with another person.

antipsychotics   *See* neuroleptics

anxiety   Feelings of nervousness and worry, often accompanied by somatic sensations such as "butterflies" in the stomach, sweating, and increased heart rate.

behavioral contract   A written contract designed to modify a client's behavior, often involving rewards for new behaviors.

biopsychosocial approach   The theory that biology, psychology, and sociology all play important roles in determining a person's life course.

black-and-white thinking   *See* all-or-none thinking

catastrophizing   Blowing things out of proportion. A typical example of catastrophizing is believing that if you do poorly at a task it means you are a failure and will never do well, or believing that, because you had one bad date, you will never have a good relationship.

chi   The life force, in traditional Chinese medicine; also spelled "qi."

client-centered therapy   A type of psychotherapy built on the premise that the power to heal rests within the person; the therapist's main task is to create an environment within which the client's natural healing emerges.

cognitive-behavioral therapy   A type of psychotherapy that helps you to change your negative feelings by challenging your negative thoughts, and building new and productive skills and behaviors.

constitutional remedy   In homeopathy, a treatment that takes into account the totality of the person, and ameliorates symptoms by strengthening the individual's defenses.

CT (computed tomography)   Scans related to x-ray technology that are able to show the basic structure of the brain.

DBT (dialectical behavior therapy)   A form of psychotherapy that is a combination of Eastern thought and cognitive-behavioral therapy.

delusions   An incorrect belief that is rigidly held; often involves the belief that one is being singled out and persecuted.

depression   Excess feelings of sadness, often accompanied by difficulties with sleep and appetite.

diathesis stress model   The theory that stress and biological vulnerability contribute systematically to developing a disorder.

DIR (developmental, individual-difference, relationship-based)   A comprehensive system of psychotherapy that integrates biological and psychological aspects of development. *See* floor time.

double-blind   In an experiment, neither the person giving the treatment, nor the person receiving the treatment, knows which treatment it is (for example, whether it is a medication or a placebo).

empathy   Sensing another person's feelings.

endorphins   Morphine-like substances that are naturally produced by the brain.

essential job function   An absolute job requirement; for example, a receptionist must be able to answer a telephone.

extrapyramidal symptoms   Parkinson-like symptoms, such as tremors, writhing motions of the wrist and face, and difficulties with voluntary movement.

family systems therapy   Family therapists assume that the best way to help someone heal is to engage the whole family. They generally focus on relationships and interaction patterns.

field dependence   A way of processing information whereby one is influenced by context, rather than one's "internal compass."

field independence   A way of processing information whereby one is influenced by one's "internal compass" rather than by context.

figural memory   Memory for figures, such as the ability to remember that one has seen a triangle, a face, or a complex drawing (such as a group of different shapes).

floor time   Interacting with children in a manner that helps them to regulate their emotions. *See* DIR

frontal lobes   Located near the forehead, a part of the brain involved in consciousness, judgment, planning, emotional responses, voluntary movement, and language.

GAF (Global Assessment of Functioning) scale   A clinician rating of overall functioning.

gender bias   Discriminating against someone because of his or her sex (being a male vs. being a female); for example, limiting a woman from getting a job promotion, or not allowing a man to stay at home and raise children.

gender-stereotyping   Having oversimplified beliefs about a person based on their sex; for example, believing that all women should stay at home and be mothers, or that all men are insensitive to the feelings of others.

group therapy   Skill-building groups tend to be educational in nature and lead to the acquisition of new skills (such as assertiveness or mindfulness). Process groups focus on interactions among the group members and tend to lead to insights about how we impact one another.

hallucinations   Sensory misperceptions, especially perceiving things that are not really there. Can involve any of the senses (hearing, seeing, touching, tasting, smelling).

hierarchical relationship   Affiliation in which one person is superior in status to another.

hippocampus   A part of the brain which is critical for memory.

identity diffusion   Difficulty establishing a coherent sense of self, including vocational pursuits, hobbies, and a consistent style of relating to others; difficulty knowing yourself and your true feelings.

impulsiveness   Acting on a whim.

invalidating environment   Part of dialectical behavior therapy (DBT) theory; involves a person being in a long-term situation (such as being in a family) in which he/she experiences consistent invalidation. Thought to be one of the factors that causes borderline personality disorder.

invalidation   One person telling another that his/her feelings, thoughts, and perceptions are not real or don't count.

journaling   Writing in a journal (a log or diary).

limbic system   Part of the brain, located in the middle of the brain, which is essential in the processing of emotions.

mantra   In transcendental meditation, a word repeated over and over.

mindfulness   Derived from Eastern meditation practices, mindfulness refers to being fully aware of one's moment-to-moment experience.

MRI (magnetic resonance imaging)   Uses adjusted radio waves and powerful magnetic fields, and provides far more detailed images than the CT.

neuroleptics   Medications that impact dopamine and reduce psychosis. Also called *antipsychotics*.

neuron   A nerve cell; the cells in the brain are neurons.

neuropsychology   The study of the relationship between activity in the neurons (especially the brain) and psychological phenomena such as thoughts, feelings, behaviors, and perceptions.

neurotransmitters   Specific chemicals in the nervous system that carry a nerve impulse from one neuron to the next.

occipital lobes   A part of the brain near the brain stem that control vision.

panacea   A cure-all; a remedy for all problems and diseases.

parietal lobes   A part of the brain located immediately behind the frontal lobes that are involved in visual attention, touch perception, and sensory integration.

personality disorder   According to the *DSM-IV*, a personality disorder is defined as "an enduring pattern of inner experience and behavior that deviates markedly from the expectations of the individual's culture, is pervasive and inflexible, has an onset in adolescence or early adulthood, is stable over time, and tends to lead to distress or impairment."

PET (positron emission tomography) scans   Scans that detect the activity of glucose, providing a measure of activity levels in the brain.

placebo   An inactive compound that is used as a control in an experiment.

placebo effect   The observation that inert compounds (placebos) lead to improvements in medical and mental health conditions.

prana   The life force (Vedic medicine), similar to chi in Chinese medicine.

prefrontal cortex   A part of the brain at the front of the cerebrum, which controls concentration, planning, and problem-solving.

prolactin   A hormone that causes women to produce milk.

promiscuous   Excessively sexually active, especially having large numbers of sexual partners.

psychiatrist   A medical doctor specializing in mental health.

psychodynamic psychotherapy   A psychological intervention that focuses on your early relationships, as well as your inner conflicts.

psychoeducational   Education or training regarding a psychological topic; for example, social skills training or smoking cessation are generally psychoeducational interventions.

psychologist   A person who studies the mind and behavior; in this book, refers to a clinical psychologist, which is someone with an advanced degree in psychology who learns how to intervene in order to help individuals with mental and behavioral difficulties.

psychosis   A loss of contact with reality.

radical acceptance   Total acceptance of a person or situation.

randomized   An experiment that uses random assignment, that is, individuals are assigned to group on the basis of chance.

reasonable accommodations   Associated with the Americans with Disabilities Act of 1990, a modification of the environment that allows someone with a disability to perform a task (such as a job or school-related assignment).

reinforcer   Rewards, such as money, food, and praise. When a person or animal is given a reinforcer, the likelihood that the behavior will occur again increases.

reuptake   When neurotransmitters that were released into the synapse are brought back into the neuron.

self-esteem   A person's assessment of his/her own self-worth.

serotonin   A neurotransmitter; among its many roles in the brain, it is believed to be important in impulsivity, depression, and harm avoidance behavior in human beings.

sexual abuse   Unwanted sexual contact from another person; usually involves at least some degree of physical or psychological coercion.

social worker   Master's level social workers have an M.S.W., and are qualified to do psychotherapy.

splitting   The process of idealizing then devaluing others and dividing people into separate "black-and-white" categories. *See* all-or-none thinking

SSRI (selective serotonin reuptake inhibitors)   A class of antidepressant medications.

synapse   The space between two neurons; messages are transferred from neuron to neuron via neurotransmitters in the synapse.

synergistic   In herbalism, when two or more herbs enhance each other's effectiveness and/or decrease side effects.

temperament   The individual's constitutional inborn disposition to activity and emotionality.

temporal lobes   A part of the brain located underneath the frontal lobes and part of the parietal lobes, control hearing, memory, and some aspects of categorization.

thalamus   A part of the brain that is involved in sensory integration and connects to the centers of memory and emotion.

transference   Having beliefs, feelings, and behaviors towards another person based on one's relationship with a different person in the past; for example, acting towards a therapist as if he were your father, or acting towards your wife as if she were your mother.

unconscious   Mental processes that influence thoughts, emotions, and behaviors but which occur outside of one's awareness; emphasized in psychodynamic theory.

visuomotor integration   Putting together visual information and movements in a meaningful way; this ability is required to do many tasks (such as doing puzzles, driving, and so on).

Index

About the Authors

Neil R. Bockian, Ph.D., received his bachelor's degree in psychology from Wesleyan University in Connecticut, and his Ph.D. in clinical psychology from the University of Miami in Florida, where he studied with internationally renowned personality disorders expert, Dr. Theodore Millon. Lead author of *The Personality Disorders Treatment Planner*, as well as over 30 scientific presentations and publications, Dr. Bockian is an associate professor in the Doctoral Clinical Psychology program at the Illinois School of Professional Psychology, a division of Argosy University. Throughout his career he has always maintained a part-time or full-time clinical practice. Dr. Bockian lives in Chicago with his wife and two children.

Valerie Porr, M.A., has a bachelor's degree in psychology and a master's degree in chemistry and education from the College of the City of New York. An artist, designer, and teacher, she ran a successful business designing couture evening clothes for twenty years. Borderline personality disorder in a family member led her to founding the Treatment and Research Advancements Association for Personality Disorder (TARA APD), the largest national nonprofit education and advocacy organization representing consumers, families, and providers affected by BPD. She has published numerous articles on BPD, gives talks around the country to professionals and families, and has developed a course teaching dialectical behavior therapy (DBT) skills to families. She lives in New York City.

Nora Elizabeth Villagran, M.A., has a bachelor's degree in the behavioral sciences from San Jose State University and a master's degree in journalism from the University of Oregon, where she served as a graduate teaching fellow. A reporter for the *San Jose Mercury News*, she is a frequent speaker at colleges and high schools on writing, journalism, and inspirational topics. Born in Mexico City and raised in the Bay Area, she currently shares a Victorian flat in San Francisco's sunny Noe Valley with her daughter, Lisa.